Unseen Scars

Unseen Scars

Vicarious Trauma at Holocaust Museums, Exhibitions & Memorial Sites

By Julie J. Golding

BLOOMSBURY ACADEMIC
NEW YORK • LONDON • OXFORD • NEW DELHI • SYDNEY

BLOOMSBURY ACADEMIC
Bloomsbury Publishing Inc, 1359 Broadway, New York, NY 10018, USA
Bloomsbury Publishing Plc, 50 Bedford Square, London, WC1B 3DP, UK
Bloomsbury Publishing Ireland, 29 Earlsfort Terrace, Dublin 2, D02 AY28, Ireland

BLOOMSBURY, BLOOMSBURY ACADEMIC and the Diana logo are trademarks of Bloomsbury Publishing Plc

First published in the United States of America 2026

Library of Congress Cataloging-in-Publication Data

Library of Congress Control Number: 2025027817

ISBN: HB: 979-8-216-38122-8
PB: 979-8-216-38120-4
ePDF: 979-8-216-38123-5
eBook: 979-8-216-38124-2

Typeset by Deanta Global Publishing Services, Chennai, India

For product safety related questions contact productsafety@bloomsbury.com.

In memory of my mother
Rebecca Hellmann

Contents

Foreword

Permit me a moment of personal pride.

I first met Julie Golding when she joined the educational staff of the Amud Aish Museum, a proposed Haredi project in Borough Park, the heart of the American Haredi community. I was impressed by her drive and her insight. I appreciated that she was never reticent to express her views and challenge other people's views, including mine. She understood the educational issues involved in creating a museum, and she also understood the unique background of those who would visit it.

As we worked together, she was considering graduate school in Jewish education, and I encouraged her at each turn, including her pursuit of a Wexner Fellowship for graduate studies that would take her far beyond the confines of the Haredi community to meet fellow graduate students of diverse Jewish backgrounds and levels of observance, but with deep commitments to the Jewish people and Jewish values. We remained in touch throughout this time. I never had the opportunity to teach her in a classroom, but I was delighted to be one of her mentors (I suspect one of many). She understands the Talmudic dictum: "Who is wise? One who learns from each person." And Julie Golding has learned from many. She also knows what to learn from teachers and mentors, students and colleagues, institutions and organizations. I did have the opportunity to serve on her dissertation committee and to see the progress of her work. I marvelled how the working mother of six—as of this writing—could do so much, so well.

As she concluded her dissertation, a work of considerable distinction, I again encouraged the newly minted Dr. Golding to do what is often most difficult for newly minted PhDs—to take her work apart and then to put it back together as a book for a broader audience, which she promptly did with diligence, competence, and determination. The result is before you.

Readers will see that Golding not only possesses a theoretical understanding of Holocaust education in a museum setting but has vast experience as a curator who has created exhibitions, as a teacher who has brought students of different backgrounds to several different Holocaust museums, as the creator of memorials, as a museum educator who meets with students before and after their visits, and above all a wise soul who trains their teachers on how to maximize the impact of such visits.

Readers will be most impressed by her sensitivity to individual visitors, most especially when the Holocaust triggers something deep within them that may, yet most often may not, be related to the Holocaust. They will learn that the power of the material that is presented in a Holocaust exhibition—that reflects in part the power of the Event itself—requires that museum curators and educators, docents and teachers be trained to deal not only with the historical information but also with the psychological impact of a visit.

Readers will learn terms that should be familiar, but often are not, such as vicarious trauma and vicarious resilience. They will come to understand what John Roth has said that when dealing with the Holocaust, "handle with care." Readers will also benefit from Golding's consideration of other trauma-laden exhibitions such as the 9/11 Museum and the Nova exhibition depicting the traumatic events of October 7th

Golding touches on many subjects—photographs and films, survivor testimony and technology, design and memorialization, artifacts, and even architecture—each a component of Holocaust museum work. She is a critical visitor with acute sensitivity and a keen sense of what makes for a positive educational experience. She has been to so many Holocaust museums and observed what they share in common and where they differ and why.

She is also quite attuned to the nature of the visitors and their learning styles. Some researchers maintain that as a result of these different motivations and learning styles, visitors "get" what they expect of a visit, not necessarily what curators and museum staff hope to achieve.

When I plan an exhibition, I am mindful that a museum must meet the expectations of three different types of visitors: skimmers, swimmers, and deep divers. A good museum must deal with different learning styles, diverse backgrounds and interests, and even—with schools, especially—the amount of time visitors are prepared to give to a museum visit.

She observes how researchers have divided museumgoers into three types of learners: "idea preference visitors" who seek information, facts, and statistics; "people preference visitors" who are primarily interested in emotions, stories, biographies, and photographs; and "object preference visitors" who seek reflective moments while reviewing artifacts.

However you parse the differences in types of visitors, one thing is clear after reading this book—no one will leave it unchanged. There are many gems of wisdom throughout this work. Golding is reflective and critical, insightful, and demanding. This book is significant reading for those planning museums, for teachers bringing students to museums, for docents who shape visits to a museum, for visitors to the museums, and for Holocaust and trauma-related educators.

Be prepared to be challenged and be prepared to be impressed. This reader is simply grateful.

Michael Berenbaum
American Jewish University
Los Angeles, California
Lag B'Omer 5785

Acknowledgments

Eight years ago, I left my position as director of education at a Holocaust museum to begin researching museum visitor experiences. My years in classrooms and museum spaces had left me with pressing questions about how students process information about the Holocaust and, more importantly, how educators like me could teach this difficult history while safeguarding students' psychological well-being. I returned to school to pursue a doctorate and contribute to the growing field of research on vicarious trauma. The already demanding task of writing a dissertation was further complicated by the onset of the Covid-19 pandemic, which shuttered Holocaust museums—my primary research sites—for months. Once the dissertation was complete, I turned my attention to making the knowledge I had gained accessible to others in the field. The book you now hold is the result of those efforts.

With the ideas and research in this book now taking shape in two iterations, I am keenly aware of the many individuals who contributed to this work in meaningful ways and to whom I owe a profound debt of gratitude. Foremost among them are my students—both the thousands of museum visitors I encountered during tours and workshops, and the classroom students who spent a year fully immersed in studying the Holocaust. Although names and identifying details have been changed to protect their privacy, I remain thankful to each one for their questions, vulnerability, courage, and stories of resilience. Their voices have significantly shaped the way I teach and lead.

This work began as a dissertation project at the Azrieli Graduate School of Education at Yeshiva University. I am especially grateful to Dean Rona Novick for opening the door to this journey and for encouraging me to stay focused on the ultimate goal. Dr. David Pelcovitz, chair of my dissertation committee, believed in this project from our very first meeting, and I am indebted to him for his steady mentorship throughout the writing process. Dr. Karen Shawn, a committee member whose own research laid important groundwork for this study, provided thoughtful feedback and invaluable guidance in imagining how to adapt my academic research into this book. Dr. Moshe Sokolow, also a member of the committee, generously dedicated his time and insight to support the success of this work. I'm also appreciative of other Yeshiva University faculty, including Dr. Laya Solomon, Dr. Scott Goldberg, Dr. Christine Vyshedsky, Dr. Moshe Krakowski, Rabbi Dr. Mordechai Schiffman, and Dr. Jenny Isaacs, whose teaching played a formative role in my development as a researcher and educator.

I owe a special debt of gratitude to Dr. Michael Berenbaum for his expert mentorship and enduring support. I've had the privilege of working with him professionally on two museum projects over the past fifteen years, and in that time, he has consistently championed my growth in the field of Holocaust education. While he has always treated me as a colleague, I have learned tremendously from his knowledge and experience. I'm especially thankful for his encouragement to write this book, his generous review of both my dissertation and this manuscript, and for honoring this work with his powerful and moving foreword.

My research has been supported by the generosity of exceptional institutions and individuals. I thank Yeshiva University for awarding me the Rabbi Mordecai E. Zeitz Doctoral Fellowship, which provided valuable opportunities throughout my doctoral studies. I also benefited enormously from a fellowship granted by the Mandel Center for Studies in Jewish Education at Brandeis University under the leadership of Dr. Ilana Horwitz. Most of all, I offer my sincere thanks to the Wexner and Davidson Foundations for their generous support and for creating a vibrant, supportive community. I am especially thankful for the continued encouragement of Or Mars, Stephanie Zelkind, and Dr. Shaul Kelner. Becoming a Wexner Graduate Fellow/Davidson Scholar marked the start of this journey, and their belief in me helped see it through to completion.

The Auschwitz exhibit study would not have been possible without the opportunity to meet and survey museum visitors. I am indebted to Dr. Paul Radensky, who served as an outside reader on my dissertation and helped facilitate my research at the Museum of Jewish Heritage. I also thank Dr. Elizabeth Edelstein, Joanna Arruda, and Phoebe Ellman for their help coordinating the data collection process. Likewise, I'm grateful for the assistance of Andrea Winograd and Abigail Miller at the Holocaust Museum

& Center for Tolerance and Education for their enthusiastic support of this research.

This project has been enriched by the insight, feedback, and encouragement of many scholars, colleagues, and friends: Dr. Suzanne Brooks, Dr. Elana Rand, Dr. Carly Namdar, David Layman, Rabbi Michael Beyo, Clifford Chanin, Erica Napach, Sara Softness, Dr. Andrew Ergas, Dr. Rafa Kern, Sarah Ossey, Hannah Dym, Luis Ferreiro, Nicole Friedman, Shani Lourie-Farhi, Deborah Herzog, Sarri Singer, Esther Almo, Sherry Krupka, Eliane Dreyfuss, Rabbi Shua Brick, Yael Krumbein, Atara Weinstein, Rabbi Aubrey Hersh, Ari Scharf, Rabbi Moshe Yehuda Turner, Dr. Leslie Ginsparg-Klein, and Cynthia Darrison. To the educators and mental health professionals whose names have been changed for privacy and appear as first names only in this book, I am deeply thankful for your willingness to share your experiences and for trusting me with your stories of both successes and failures.

To Dina Mounitz, Shaindy Landerer, and Robin Pantierer—my "village" throughout this journey—thank you, from the bottom of my heart.

I am deeply grateful to two individuals who were instrumental in bringing this book to life. Charles Harmon, my publisher at Bloomsbury Publishing, offered unwavering support and enthusiasm from the very beginning. Dr. Olson Pook, my editor, expertly guided me through every stage of the process—helping me visualize the project, refine my ideas, and express them with clarity. His meticulous attention to every word and detail shaped this book in ways I could never have achieved alone.

I'm blessed with a loving and supportive family who stood by me through every stage of this journey. I am especially grateful to my father, Nathan Hellmann, who consistently offered guidance, help, and unwavering support. He regularly checked in on the progress of my work, giving me the encouragement I needed to keep writing. My heartfelt thanks also go to my mother-in-law, Goldie Golding, whose example as a writer, leader, and educator continues to inspire me. I am grateful to my sister, Esty Silver, for her listening ear and for stepping in when I needed her. My brother, Rabbi Meir Hellmann, made himself available to help with researching our family's history and archives, and I am truly thankful for his assistance. Likewise, I am indebted to Naomi Hellmann, Rabbi Yosef Chaim Golding, and Mordechai Golding for readily sharing their knowledge of the family history in this book and for their unceasing encouragement.

As the granddaughter of Holocaust survivors, this work is not only a professional endeavor but also a deeply personal one. My grandparents, Norbert and Helen Hellmann—whose stories are shared in these pages—were a profound source of inspiration. Their Holocaust experiences left a lasting imprint on my childhood, shaped my path as a Holocaust educator, and sparked my interest in the field of historical trauma. I feel profoundly grateful to have known them so well and to have heard their stories firsthand. May their memory be a blessing.

To my amazing children—Chani, Yehuda, Chava, Talia, Ella, and Riki—thank you for your endless patience and encouragement. Whether I was caught up in writing, preparing for teaching, or away at conferences, you always understood. I especially appreciate your willingness to let every family vacation double as a research trip, helping me find and explore local Holocaust museums and memorials wherever we went.

Most of all, I want to thank my husband, Meir. I don't have the words to express how much his support and dedication have meant to me, or how crucial they were in making this project possible. From urging me to go back to school and supporting me through every stage, to managing life at home during my travels and ensuring I could dedicate myself fully to this work, he has been there through it all. I couldn't have done this without him.

Finally, this book is dedicated to the memory of my mother, Rebecca Hellmann, of blessed memory. She was an incredible woman who believed deeply in my potential and never missed a chance to remind me to "publish or perish." Though she passed away far too young and didn't get to see this work in print, I know she would have been proud. Her pride in my work and her deep belief in me gave me the determination to complete this project. I hope to continue honoring her memory and legacy for many years to come.

Introduction

It was the winter of 1996, just three years after the opening of the United States Holocaust Memorial Museum (USHMM) in Washington, D.C., and the release of Steven Spielberg's *Schindler's List*. Across America, Holocaust education was gaining new prominence in school curricula, and my grandfather had been asked to teach a new Holocaust studies course to eighth-grade boys at his school in New York City.

Few were more qualified for this task. As a young man in 1938, he had ridden his bicycle through the streets of Würzburg during Kristallnacht, watching Torah scrolls burn and seeing the Jewish Teachers' Seminary—founded by his own great-grandfather—engulfed in flames. After fleeing to the Netherlands, he slipped underground when the roundups began, joining the Dutch resistance. Under the alias Jacob Van Weelden, he posed as a Dutch worker for a German engineering company, attempting daring escapes across the Pyrenees mountains and even trying to cross into Spain by clinging to the undercarriage of a train. When caught with counterfeit documents, he was sent to Neuengamme concentration camp, where he survived by never revealing his Jewish identity. In the war's final days, he narrowly escaped death when he was transferred from the ill-fated Cap Arcona—a ship later bombed by Allied forces—just three days before the tragedy. He emerged from the war as the sole survivor of a family murdered in the gas chambers of Sobibor. (See Figure 0.1)

My grandfather did not share much about these experiences. As a child, I would watch him stand outside and gaze into the distance, an ever-present cigar in his hand, and wonder, "What is he thinking about? His family? The war?" It was an unspoken rule to never ask these questions. We just listened when he did choose to speak.

However, given this history and his forty years of teaching experience in the school, it seemed fitting that he would lead this new educational initiative. My grandfather approached teaching the Holocaust with the gravity it deserved. He carried not just knowledge but lived experience—a perspective no textbook could provide.

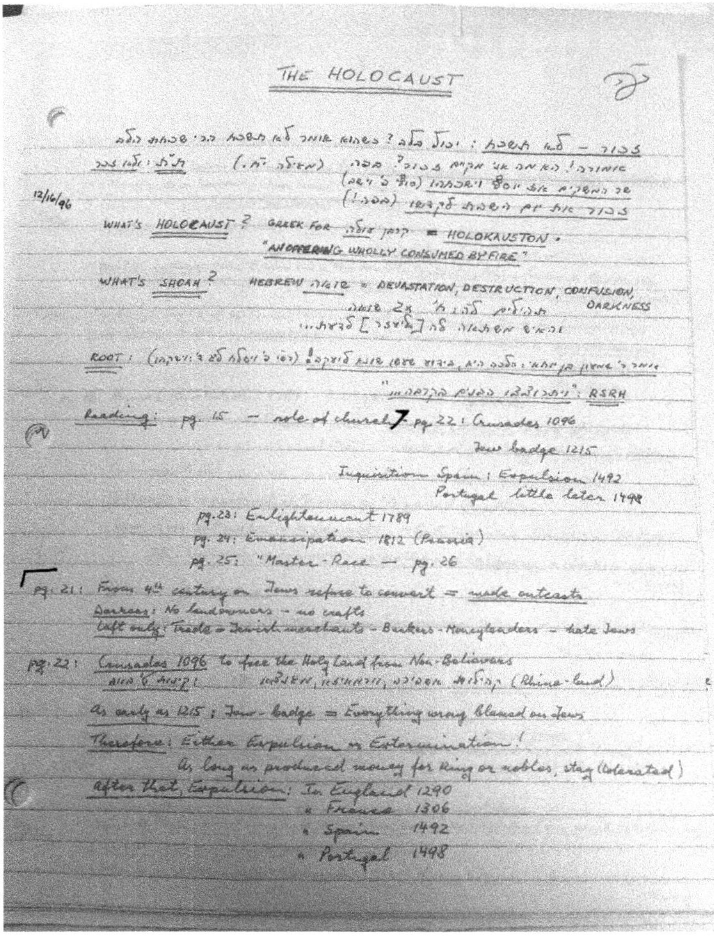
THE HOLOCAUST

12/16/96

WHAT'S HOLOCAUST? GREEK FOR = HOLOKAUSTON.
"AN OFFERING WHOLLY CONSUMED BY FIRE"

WHAT'S SHOAH? HEBREW = DEVASTATION, DESTRUCTION, CONFUSION, DARKNESS

ROOT:

RSRH

Reading: pg. 15 — role of church, pg. 22: Crusades 1096
Jew badge 1215
Inquisition Spain: Expulsion 1492
Portugal little later 1498
pg. 23: Enlightenment 1789
pg. 24: Emancipation 1812 (Prussia)
pg. 25: "Master-Race — pg. 26

pg. 21: From 4th century on Jews refuse to convert = made outcasts
Barred: No landowners - no crafts
Left only: Trade = Jewish merchants - Bankers - Moneylenders - hate Jews

pg. 22: Crusades 1096 to free the Holy Land from Non-Believers (Rhine-land)

As early as 1215; Jew-badge = Everything wrong blamed on Jews
Therefore: Either Expulsion or Extermination!
As long as produced money for King or nobles, stay (tolerated)
After that, Expulsion: In England 1290
" France 1306
" Spain 1492
" Portugal 1498

Figure 0.1 My grandfather's handwritten lesson plan from 1996.

But on a relatively warm December day, just ten days and six classes into the new course, everything changed. As he made his way up the stairs to his classroom that morning, he heard one wisecracking student say to another: "Here comes Mr. Hellmann . . . off we go to the gas chambers again."

Without a word, my grandfather turned around and walked out. Though he continued teaching French, Dikduk (Hebrew grammar), and other religious subjects at the school for another decade, never again did he attempt to teach school-age children about the Holocaust. The chasm between his lived experience and their casual remarks was simply too great to bridge.

What happened in that stairwell was not simply a teacher walking away from a class. It was a man who had survived the unimaginable, who had witnessed the destruction of his world and lost his entire family, confronting the impossible task of translating that experience to children who could turn it into a joke. But was this young boy truly being disrespectful? Perhaps. Or perhaps he was deeply uncomfortable learning about the Holocaust and channeled his difficult emotions through inappropriate humor. We will never know because, on that day, the conversation ended before it could begin.

The difficulty of learning about the Holocaust is not limited to that boy's time and place, nor was it unique to him. Across generations, students continue to struggle with this traumatic history, though their responses manifest in different ways. Years later, I became a Holocaust educator myself, following a path my grandfather ultimately couldn't continue. Only last week, I received this note from a student:

> *Hi Dr. Golding,*
>
> *I had a very difficult time with the reading [you assigned] and I had to put the book down multiple times. I didn't even get 100 pages in. I'm really not in a strong enough emotional state for this kind of material, and I'm struggling to get through the first part. I wrote my response on what I got through so far but I can't see myself getting through much more. I'll try my best, but I trembled and cried through a lot of what I was reading—so much so that my father "forced" (for lack of a better word) me to put the book down. This topic is very difficult for me to read about or listen to, and if you noticed I usually have something else on my desk during your class. I mean it not to be disrespectful, but because I genuinely cannot be fully present in your classroom. I'll try my best with the reading, but I might just have to flip through each part and find a couple of sentences that stick out at me. I just wanted to let you know in advance as I do not want to seem as if I am not taking the assignment seriously and just flipping through the book. I genuinely have a very difficult time reading it.*

These two moments—separated by decades yet strikingly similar in their emotional core—capture the fundamental tension at the heart of this book. On one side stands my grandfather, a Holocaust survivor who walked away from teaching when faced with a student's inappropriate humor; on the other, my own student who cannot bear to look directly at the history I'm teaching, yet struggles with guilt about her avoidance.

How do we bridge the distance between those who lived through history and those who must learn from it? As the generation of survivors dwindles, how do we preserve not just the facts, but the human dimension of their experiences? The question I want to look at in these pages is how we teach about traumatic historical events in ways that honor both the experiences of those who lived through them and the emotional well-being of today's students. How do we navigate the complex interplay between historical trauma and contemporary psychology? And what happens when the educational imperative to remember collides with the very human impulse—whether expressed through deflective humor or tearful avoidance—to turn away from suffering?

Interpreting a Historical Tragedy

The Holocaust, also known as the Shoah or Churban Europe, was the systematic murder and destruction of European Jews and their communities between 1933 and 1945. During the Holocaust, some six million Jews were murdered by the Nazi German regime and their collaborators. It was a unique historical event that took place in recent memory, bringing death to millions of individuals across Europe and destruction to thousands of years of Jewish life and culture. The Holocaust is distinguished from other atrocities and genocides because of the extent to which the perpetrators sought to systematically annihilate every member of the Jewish people for ideological purposes.[1] As a result, the Holocaust has become a "cornerstone of contemporary Western culture: ubiquitously memorialized in stone, film, and print,"[2] and learning about it is considered a fundamental component of education around the world.[3]

However, the very fundamentals of Holocaust education, including its definition, purpose, and structure, remain subjects of debate. These ongoing discussions mirror the general discourse concerning Holocaust memory and restitution.[4] Conflicts are "waged around the globe," as Plessow notes, "to determine the Shoah's discursive position in memory and history."[5] Even the date of Holocaust commemoration has become a controversial subject.[6] While January 27, the date of the liberation of Auschwitz, has been marked by the United Nations General Assembly, the European Union, and many other European countries as International Holocaust Remembrance Day, the Israeli government chose a different approach. They selected the twenty-seventh of the Hebrew month of Nissan for remembrance, calling it "Yom HaZikaron laShoah ve-laG'vurah" (Yom HaShoah). This date was chosen to commemorate the Warsaw Ghetto Uprising, and many Jewish communities around the world observe Yom HaShoah. At the same time, some Orthodox Jewish groups reject the date and commemorate the Holocaust on either the Tenth of Tevet or the Ninth of Av. These controversies have far-reaching consequences and contribute to the highly debated topics of the causes, definitions, and political repercussions of antisemitism—and even how it is taught.[7]

The meaning and interpretation of the Holocaust and thus how it is taught vary dramatically by country and context. Along with other major historical events, the Holocaust occupies space in the national identities and historical foundations of Germany, Poland, and other major European countries, as well as Israel.[8] Although the Holocaust is a shared legacy throughout Europe, the impact of the event differs in each country, resulting in different discourses in each locale.[9] These variations reflect not just historical relationships to the events, but ongoing political and cultural tensions around responsibility, victimhood, and the lessons to be drawn from this history.

In Germany, for example, there are strong demands for history education about National Socialism and the historical responsibility of the country, though studies show that the actual quality of education has historically been very poor.[10] After the establishment of the Memorial for the Murdered Jews of Europe in Berlin in 2005, there was a stronger focus on teaching responsibility and on active remembrance. However, recent waves of immigration and the arrival of record-high numbers of refugees (many of whom come from Arab countries that have contentious histories with the Jewish people and Israel) are creating new challenges and opportunities for teaching about antisemitism and xenophobia.[11] These demographic changes have also contributed to the rise of far-right movements, where antisemitism plays a "central role" in their xenophobic, nationalistic, and racist ideologies.[12] While both the far-right and Islamist movements in Germany are deeply rooted in antisemitism, they influence society differently, often expressing antisemitic and hate messages through music and social media.[13]

In Israel, Holocaust memory and commemorations occupy a large part of national identity; they are a cornerstone of holidays, school curricula, civil dialogue, and part of the creation and justification of state and government policies.[14] This widespread institutional presence reflects how deeply the

Holocaust is embedded in both formal and informal Israeli culture, from descriptions of October 7th hostages looking as if they are "Holocaust survivors"[15] to "to the point where the vast majority of Israelis [. . .] occasionally ponder what they would have done had they been in the Holocaust."[16] The subject is not without controversy; polarized messaging about the Holocaust vacillates between victimhood and heroism, weakness and power, and memory of the dead combined with an imperative to build a new nation so that such destruction will never happen again. At Yad Vashem, the World Holocaust Remembrance Center, these divergent messages are communicated with emphasis on the Jews as a group or collective, while resistance fighters are lauded for their individuality, which in turn is key to the "collective resurrection."[17]

Approaches and Challenges to Holocaust Education

With competing opinions on the importance and consequences of the Holocaust today, it is no wonder that the approaches to teaching it will significantly differ depending on where it is taught. Researchers note that while there is a National Curriculum in England that requires the teaching of the Holocaust, schools are free to decide how the curriculum will be structured and what information will be taught.[18] Similarly, there is also a largely autonomous educational framework for teaching about the Holocaust in the United States that grants classroom educators the opportunity to develop their own curricula and select the resources that they deem most appropriate for their students.[19] Furthermore, competing educational organizations ascribe to countless models and pedagogical approaches, with little agreement about what exactly needs to be taught, leading to a situation where the teaching of the Holocaust in America and elsewhere lacks uniformity, clear objectives, and well-developed assessments.[20]

The results are as one might expect. In the United States, a 2018 report commissioned by The Conference on Jewish Material Claims Against Germany[21] found a significant lack of Holocaust knowledge, including the statistic that 45 percent of Americans could not name any of the 40,000 concentration camps and ghettos in German-occupied Europe. Shortly thereafter, the 116th Congress of the United States passed the "Never Again Education Act," which provides ten million dollars for the USHMM to increase online and in-person educational programs that teach about intolerance, bigotry, and antisemitism through the context of the Holocaust. The Act was based on the premise that "learning how and why the Holocaust happened is an important component of the education of citizens of the United States."[22] The bill to support increased Holocaust education passed unanimously in the Senate and received an impressively bipartisan House vote of 395–5.[23]

This legislative support parallels a dramatic increase in Holocaust museums and informal education programs throughout the United States in recent years. Older institutions, including the USHMM, Holocaust Museum Houston, St. Louis Kaplan Feldman Holocaust Museum, Dallas Holocaust and Human Rights Museum, and the Museum of Jewish Heritage, have undergone or are currently updating their original core exhibitions. This growth has been attributed to the "shifting social and cultural circumstances"[24] of American Jewry and a new ethnic definition of Jewishness that utilizes the Holocaust as part of its identity. It is a cultural shift occurring simultaneously with the passing of the Holocaust survivor generation, leaving Holocaust museums to assume an outsized role in preserving Holocaust memory in their place.

Holocaust and genocide education has also increased as a response to the rise in antisemitism in the United States. According to the Anti-Defamation League (ADL), there have been over 10,000 antisemitic incidents in the United States since the October 7 Hamas attack in Israel, the highest number of incidents for a one-year period ever since the ADL began tracking them.[25] Museums' responses to antisemitism are evident in the many press releases, stakeholder reports, and revised mission statements of Holocaust museums across America. These institutions often serve as immediate educational resources following antisemitic incidents in their communities. For example, after a local incident involving students drawing swastikas at a party, the Los Angeles Museum of the Holocaust noted in its Annual Report that the students received a tour of the museum. "Once the students came face to face with artifacts and heard testimonies firsthand from survivors, they understood what their actions represented. Our board made a strategic decision to expand our focus to become a statewide resource for Holocaust education."[26]

Museums, Memorials, and Public Memory

Museums occupy a unique space in the field of Holocaust studies, serving as both independent institutions dedicated to preserving history and memory and as educational resource centers utilized by classroom educators.[27] Adults choose to visit Holocaust museums and memorial sites of their own volition. They have various motivations for their visits, including curiosity about death, educational goals, cultural interests, and interest in genealogy.[28] In contrast, nearly all student visits are involuntary; they come during scheduled times because of educational requirements. While nearly every high school throughout the country touches on the Holocaust in literature or history classes, the depth of coverage varies significantly. In over twenty states, schools include specialized units or full semester courses to fulfill varying levels of Holocaust education requirements—ranging from suggestions to formal mandates.[29] Many schools take their students to visit local or national Holocaust museums, with more than eleven million students visiting the USHMM in Washington, D.C., since its opening. Before the Covid-19 pandemic, the Illinois Holocaust Museum (the second-largest Holocaust museum in the United States) and the Museum of Jewish Heritage in New York City both educated more than 60,000 student visitors every year.[30]

During a visit to a Holocaust museum, students typically encounter text, photographs, historical footage, and recorded survivor testimony that have been curated to create an exhibition that connects them to the past.[31] Sometimes they meet a survivor and hear firsthand testimony. A common belief is that by teaching about atrocities during the Holocaust and integrating knowledge about man's inhumanity to man into the foundations of the educational experience, teachers can cultivate empathy in their students and train them to be morally responsible adults and citizens.[32]

However, the psychological impact of these encounters is both complex and understudied. Despite claims that exhibiting images of atrocities objectifies victims and violates their privacy, graphic images continue to be used to jar viewers and raise awareness about genocides and human rights.[33] Some museums aim to affect the emotions of their visitors by creating exhibitions that shock or horrify them.[34] For many visitors, it is an emotionally intense experience, and some become distressed because the horrific knowledge is too much for them to process cognitively or psychologically.

Most of what has been studied or written about Holocaust education in public spaces and museums has focused on the educational and historical information within the exhibit, not the emotional or psychological experience and welfare of the museum visitor. Surprisingly, there is a dearth of knowledge about the effectiveness of such educational programming and its effects on the beliefs or attitudes of the viewers. While Holocaust museums are dark tourist sites that link millions of people to death and tragedy each year,[35] an extensive review of the literature uncovered very few empirical studies investigating student coping styles during museum tours and how Holocaust education may result in vicarious trauma for visitors.[36] At the same time, many Holocaust educators anecdotally report a wide range of student responses. These range from an inability to process traumatic information and negative emotional reactions to a form of productive obsession—where students feel compelled to learn more, discuss, and write about the Holocaust as they attempt to integrate its meaning into their lives.

As educators seek to create connections and meaningful lessons for students of Holocaust studies, they often ask students to make personal connections to the resources by reflecting upon similarities that can be drawn between their own lives and those who endured the Holocaust. Students are encouraged to "explore the facts against a backdrop informed by their own experiences and ideals."[37] For example, the Holocaust is often used as a case study in teaching about the dangers of racism because racism in Nazi Germany was a contributing factor that led to genocide.[38] Researchers note that this phenomenon can occur at the expense of teaching accurate historical contexts, risking the danger that "students might acquire simplistic moral and universal lessons which, though well-intentioned, typically will be ill-informed and fuel the prevalence of troubling myths and misconceptions."[39] However, a well-developed lesson or exhibition about the Holocaust will tell the truth about what happened while walking a fine line between addressing specific audiences and not tainting the narrative with ideological beliefs or biases.

The balance between teaching about Holocaust atrocities and considering the unique psychological and emotional needs of each student can be challenging, especially for museum docents who generally do not know much about their visitors and may lack training in trauma-informed pedagogy. This challenge is further complicated when visitors bring their own traumatic histories to these spaces, creating complex resonances between historical traumas and personal ones. Without proper attention to these psychological dimensions, Holocaust education risks either overwhelming students emotionally or reducing complex historical events to simplistic moral lessons.

Given the complex psychological and educational challenges involved in Holocaust education, this book seeks to provide an in-depth examination of how we engage with these difficult histories. By exploring the multifaceted approaches to understanding and teaching about the Holocaust in the chapters that follow, I attempt to address the critical question of how we can meaningfully confront historical trauma while protecting the psychological well-being of those who learn about it.

Outline of the Book

Chapter 1 investigates the terrain of "difficult histories," particularly focusing on Holocaust memorialization and dark tourism. The chapter delves into the psychological dynamics of confronting tragic histories, examining the tension between the human impulse to both witness and turn away from atrocity. This analysis unpacks how museums, educators, and visitors negotiate the intricate interplay of remembrance, education, and emotional preservation when encountering sites of profound human suffering.

Chapter 2 scrutinizes the multifaceted dimensions of trauma, dissecting its psychological, neurological, and educational implications. Drawing from diverse experiences—including Holocaust education, school shooting responses, and individual traumatic memories—the chapter illuminates how trauma echoes through individual lives, educational institutions, and collective memory. The exploration maps trauma's impact from its neurological origins to its generational transmission, revealing the challenge of teaching difficult histories while protecting vulnerable learners.

Chapter 3 critically examines the pedagogical challenges of Holocaust education, investigating the concept of historical empathy and its implications for teaching traumatic histories. Through an in-depth analysis of various educational approaches, the chapter probes how educators create meaningful connections between students and Holocaust experiences while carefully balancing historical understanding, emotional engagement, and psychological safety. It evaluates the methods used to generate empathy, questioning whether current pedagogical strategies enable deep historical comprehension or risk oversimplifying profound human suffering.

Chapter 4 examines the critical role of Holocaust survivor testimony, investigating how personal narratives shape our understanding of historical trauma. The chapter analyzes the evolving landscape of survivor storytelling, from live testimonies to technological innovations like holographic recordings, while scrutinizing the pedagogical and emotional complexities of bearing witness. It explores how survivor stories create empathetic connections, preserve historical memory, and challenge listeners to engage with the deeply personal experiences of those who survived one of history's darkest periods.

Chapter 5 investigates the critical function of museums in presenting traumatic histories, analyzing how institutions mediate between historical documentation and emotional engagement. Through an analysis of exhibition design, artifacts, photographs, and architectural spaces, the chapter examines how museums create meaningful connections between visitors and difficult historical narratives. It looks at the challenges of representing trauma, the power of objects and images, and the evolving approaches museums use to help visitors comprehend and emotionally process deeply significant historical experiences.

Chapter 6 navigates the intricate psychological terrain of encountering traumatic histories, investigating how individuals cope with and process difficult knowledge. Through the lens of the Awareness, Balance, and Connection (ABC) framework, the chapter unpacks the challenges of teaching and experiencing Holocaust narratives while protecting psychological well-being. It examines the delicate balance between historical education and emotional safety, offering insights into how museums, educators, and individuals can meaningfully engage with traumatic histories without causing further psychological harm.

Chapter 7 pivots to consider the question of vicarious resilience as a counterbalance to vicarious trauma when engaging with Holocaust history. The chapter frames resilience not as merely overcoming hardship, but as transformation—allowing oneself to be fundamentally changed by traumatic experiences while finding meaning and purpose. It investigates how witnesses to Holocaust testimony can experience positive transformation through engagement with survivors' stories, mirroring the concept of vicarious resilience first identified in therapists working with trauma survivors. This final chapter brings together the book's themes of trauma, memory, education, and empathy, offering insights into how we might honor difficult histories while cultivating our own capacity for resilience.

The Appendix presents a case study conducted at the "Auschwitz: Not Long Ago, Not Far Away" exhibit, investigating how students experience vicarious trauma during Holocaust museum visits. Through survey data analysis of museum experiences, coping mechanisms, and adverse childhood experiences, the research provides empirical evidence for educators seeking to maximize educational impact while safeguarding students' emotional well-being when confronting difficult historical knowledge.

Who the Book Is For

My grandparents met as refugees just days after the Second World War and the Holocaust came to an end. In Sweden, my grandfather first arrived under his resistance alias, Jacob Van Weelden, with nothing but the clothes he wore. When my grandmother Helen Bamberger, who had fled to Sweden during the 1943 rescue of Danish Jews, came searching for survivors from Würzburg on behalf of her father, my grandfather finally revealed his true identity. They discovered they were second cousins, connected by a shared past and homeland that no longer existed. Their marriage lasted sixty-nine years, ending only when they died just thirty-three days apart. In America, they built a simple, happy life, raising a family and creating a new beginning far from the ashes of their past. This rebuilding was itself an act of resistance, a declaration that life would continue despite all they had lost.

When I would ask my grandfather for advice, he would thoughtfully answer my questions, but rarely offered more than what I explicitly asked about. My grandmother, on the other hand, took a keen interest in my teaching career. She would constantly inquire about my work, peppering me with questions like "Are your students really interested in what happened?" and "What do you teach them about?" I would describe my classes and experiences in detail, and she would grow quiet, her expression impossible to read. For years, this pattern continued—her curiosity followed by silence—until I finally mustered the courage to ask what hearing about my work stirred in her thoughts. The story she shared in response has stayed with me ever since. (See Figure 0.2)

Figure 0.2 Holocaust Memorial Miami Beach, designed by architect Kenneth Treister and completed in 1990 in South Florida. Library of Congress, Prints & Photographs Division, photograph by Carol M. Highsmith [reproduction number, e.g., LC-USZ62-12345].

As they grew older, my grandparents would spend a few weeks each winter in Florida, escaping the cold New York City winters. One year, they decided to visit the Holocaust Memorial in Miami Beach. They took a taxi from their hotel to the memorial and instructed the driver to wait for them. But as they approached the memorial, they stopped in their tracks. Before them loomed an imposing 40-foot-tall "outstretched arm, reaching for the skies as hundreds of small human figures cling to it and to each other." My grandparents froze at the sight, and as my grandmother described it, "we started to cry. So we turned around and went right back to the taxi to take us home."

She paused then, her large blue eyes distant with memory, before turning to me with an insight that would fundamentally reshape my perspective on Holocaust education: "Those memorials are not for us, those who went through the Holocaust. They are for you and the people who weren't there to learn about what happened to us."

Her words crystallized a central challenge facing Holocaust education today. How do we create learning experiences that honor survivors' memories while remaining accessible to those who never experienced these events firsthand? How do we bridge the gap between the visceral memories of those who lived through history and the educational needs of those who must learn about it secondhand? And most critically, how do we ensure that difficult histories are taught in ways that create understanding rather than trauma? These questions have guided my work as both a Holocaust educator and museum curator, shaping how I approach the delicate balance between historical truth and psychological well-being.

This book explores the memorials and museums built for us—those who were not there and did not experience the Holocaust firsthand. It examines how visitors process learning about the Holocaust in these spaces that are designed to invoke empathy and strong emotional reactions. While many excellent works address how to design and curate these spaces, this book focuses instead on how to thoughtfully engage with what has already been created. The museums, exhibitions, and memorial sites described here were developed by designers, curators, and specialists who dedicated themselves to telling difficult histories with sophistication and sensitivity. Yet once the artifacts have been installed behind glass and the construction crews have departed, it falls to museum staff, docents, and educators to guide visitors through these spaces. How we do this matters a great deal.

Drawing on research in trauma studies, museum design, and educational psychology, this book examines the challenge of teaching difficult histories—the psychological impact of visiting Holocaust museums, exhibits, and memorial sites. It investigates the effects of vicarious trauma on visitors and how encounters with difficult histories may affect individuals with traumatic pasts. Through this lens, I explore questions central to the museum experience: How do different visitors process traumatic historical content? What happens when a visitor's personal trauma history intersects with historical narratives? How can educators prepare visitors for potentially traumatic encounters with history and support them afterward? What responsibility do museums and educators have to protect visitors from psychological harm while still conveying historical truth?

My goal is to equip those who teach about the Holocaust and other difficult histories with the knowledge and tools they need to better support their students before, during, and after visits to Holocaust museums—ensuring that these powerful educational experiences create understanding rather than trauma, and that they honor both the historical truth and the psychological well-being of those who encounter it. Whether you are an educator, museum professional, or simply someone interested in how we confront challenging histories, the pages that follow offer insights into how we can learn from the past without being overwhelmed by it.

Notes

1 Bauer, as cited in Ruth-Anne Lenga, "Seeing Things Differently: The Use of Atrocity Images in Teaching about the Holocaust," in *Holocaust Education: Contemporary Challenges and Controversies*, ed. Stuart Foster, Andy Pearce, and Alice Pettigrew (London: UCL Press, 2020), 195–220, https://doi.org/10.2307/j.ctv15d7zpf.16.

2 Rebecca Jinks, *Representing Genocide: The Holocaust as Paradigm?* (London: Bloomsbury Academic, 2016), 1.

3 Monique Eckmann, Stevick Doyle, and Ambrosewicz Jolanta Jacobs, *Research in Teaching and Learning About the Holocaust: A Dialogue Beyond Borders* (Berlin: Metropol, 2017).

4 Andy Pearce, "Challenges, Issues, and Controversies: The Shapes of 'Holocaust Education' in the Early Twenty-First Century," in *Holocaust Education: Contemporary Challenges and Controversies*, ed. Andy Pearce, Stuart Foster, and Alice Pettigrew (London: UCL Press, 2020), 1–27, https://doi.org/10.2307/j.ctv15d7zpf.7.

5 Oliver Plessow, "Agents of Transnational Memory? Holocaust Museums in Australia and Germany," *Memory Studies* 13, no. 6 (2020): 1232–45, https://doi.org/10.1177/1750698020908494, 317.

6 Leon Weissberg and Caren Schnur Neile, "Never Forget: March of the Living and Place-Based Holocaust Storytelling," *Storytelling, Self, Society* 11, no. 1 (2015): 121–36, https://doi.org/10.13110/storselfsoci.11.1.0121.

7 Rebecca Ruth Gould, "The IHRA Definition of Antisemitism: Defining Antisemitism by Erasing Palestinians," *The Political Quarterly* 91, no. 4 (2020): 825–31, https://onlinelibrary.wiley.com/doi/pdfdirect/10.1111/1467-923X.12883.

8 Dan Michman, "Historiography on the Holocaust in Poland: An Outsider's View of Its Place within Recent General Developments in Holocaust Historiography," in *New Directions in the History of the Jews in the Polish Lands*, ed. Antony Polonsky, Hanna Węgrzynek, and Andrzej Żbikowski, (Boston: Academic Studies Press, 2018), 386–401, https://doi.org/10.2307/j.ctv7xbrh4.38.

9 Eckmann et al., *Research in Teaching and Learning.*

10 Wolfgang Meseth and Matthias Proske, "Mind the Gap: Holocaust Education in Germany Between Pedagogical Intentions and Classroom Interactions," in *As the Witnesses Fall Silent: 21st Century Holocaust Education in Curriculum, Policy, and Practice*, ed. Zehavit Gross and E. Doyle Stevick (Berlin: Springer International Publishing, 2015), 159–82, https://doi.org/10.1007/978-3-319-15419-010.

11 Monica Vitale and Rebecca Clothey, "Holocaust Education in Germany: Ensuring Relevance and Meaning in an Increasingly Diverse Community," *FIRE: Forum for International Research in Education* 5, no. 1 (2019): 44–62, https://doi.org/10.32865/fire201951139.

12 Bundesamt für Verfassungsschutz, "Right-Wing Extremism," Bundesamt für Verfassungsschutz, https://www.verfassungsschutz.de/EN/topics/right-wing-extremism/right-wing-extremism_node.html (March 4, 2025).

13 Günther Jikeli, "Anti-Semitism within the Extreme Right and Islamists' Circles," in *Being Jewish in 21st-Century Germany*, ed. Haim Fireberg and Olaf Glöckner, 1st ed. (Berlin: De Gruyter, 2015), 188–207.

14 Olga Gershenson, "Meta-Memory: About the Holocaust in New Israeli Video Art," *Jewish Film & New Media: An International Journal* 6, no. 1 (2018): 67–90, https://doi.org/10.13110/jewifilmnewmedi.6.1.0067.

15 Gideon Sa'ar (@gidonsaar), "Hamas has Committed Crimes Against Humanity Against Civilian Hostages. This Hamas-Nazi Evil Must be Eradicated!," X (formerly Twitter), February 11, 2025, https://x.com/gidonsaar/status/1888194414964781493.

16 Lia Friesem, "Holocaust Tweets as an Act of Resistance," *Israel Studies Review* 33, no. 2 (2018): 85–104, https://www.jstor.org/stable/48563790.

17 Irit Keynan, "The Memory of the Holocaust and Israel's Attitude Toward War Trauma, 1948–1973: The Collective vs. the Individual," *Israel Studies* 23, no. 2 (2018): 110, https://doi.org/10.2979/israelstudies.23.2.05.

18 Andy Pearce and Arthur Chapman, "Holocaust Education 25 Years On: Challenges, Issues, Opportunities," *Holocaust Studies* 23, no. 3 (2017): 223–30, https://doi.org/10.1080/17504902.2017.1296082.

19 Plessow, "Agents of Transnational Memory."

20 Thomas D. Fallace, *The Emergence of Holocaust Education in American Schools* (New York: Palgrave Macmillan, 2014); Susanne Hillman, "Grim Expectations: Video Testimony in the College Classroom," *The History Teacher* 48, no. 2 (2015): 295–320, http://www.jstor.org/stable/43264406.

21 Conference on Jewish Material Claims Against Germany, "New Survey by Claims Conference Finds Significant Lack of Holocaust Knowledge in the United

States," Claims Conference, https://www.claimscon.org/study/ (January 15, 2022).

22 Never Again Education Act of 2020, H.R. 943, 116th Cong., https://www.congress.gov/bill/116th-congress/house-bill/943/text.

23 Carolyn B. Maloney, "Maloney's Never Again Education Act Signed into Law," *Press Release*, May 29, 2020, https://maloney.house.gov/media-center/press-releases/maloney-s-never-again-education-act-signed-into-law.

24 Shaul Magid, "The Holocaust and Jewish Identity in America: Memory, the Unique, and the Universal," *Jewish Social Studies* 18, no. 2 (2012): 101, https://doi.org/10.2979/jewisocistud.18.2.100.

25 Anti-Defamation League, "Over 10,000 Antisemitic Incidents Recorded in the U.S. since Oct. 7, 2023, According to ADL Preliminary Data," *Anti-Defamation League*, October 6, 2024, https://www.adl.org/resources/press-release/over-10000-antisemitic-incidents-recorded-us-oct-7-2023-according-adl.

26 Los Angeles Holocaust Museum, "2019 Annual Report," Los Angeles Holocaust Museum, https://www.holocaustmuseumla.org/financials (January 23, 2022).

27 Michael Bernard-Donals, "Synecdochic Memory at the United States Holocaust Memorial Museum," *College English* 74, no. 5 (2012): 417–36, http://www.jstor.org/stable/23212923; Robert M. Ehrenreich and Jane Klinger, "War in Context: Let the Artifacts Speak," in *Does War Belong in Museums?: The Representation of Violence in Exhibitions*, ed. Wolfgang Muchitsch (Wetzlar, Germany: Transcript Verlag, 2013), 145–54, http://www.jstor.org/stable/j.ctv1wxr1z.14; Marea Piotrowska, Kamila Ferenc, Radecka-Mikulicz, and Justyna Majewska, "Curatorial and Educational Challenges in Creating the Holocaust Gallery," in *New Directions in the History of the Jews in the Polish Lands*, ed. Antony Polonsky, Hanna Węgrzynek, and Andrzej Żbikowski, (Boston: Academic Studies Press, 2018), 29–39, https://doi.org/10.2307/j.ctv7xbrh4.10.

28 Barbara Buntman, "Tourism and Tragedy: The Memorial at Belzec, Poland," *International Journal of Heritage Studies* 14, no. 5 (2008): 422–48, https://doi.org/10.1080/13527250802284867; Erik H. Cohen, "Educational Dark Tourism at an In Populo Site: The Holocaust Museum in Jerusalem," *Annals of Tourism Research* 38 (2011): 193–209; Anna Farmaki and Katerina Antoniou, "Politicising Dark Tourism Sites: Evidence from Cyprus," *Worldwide Hospitality and Tourism Themes* 9, no. 2 (2017): 175–86, https://doi.org/10.1108/WHATT-08-2016-0041.

29 United States Holocaust Memorial Museum, "Where Holocaust Education is Required in the US," United States Holocaust Memorial Museum, https://www.ushmm.org/teach/fundamentals/where-holocaust-education-is-required-in-the-us (February 15, 2022).

30 Illinois Holocaust Museum & Education Center, "History," Illinois Holocaust Museum & Education Center, https://www.ilholocaustmuseum.org/about/history/ (January 15, 2022); Museum of Jewish Heritage—A Living Memorial to the Holocaust, "Mission," Museum of Jewish Heritage, https://www.mjhnyc.org/mission (January 3, 2022). By contrast, there are approximately one million visitors to the Yad Vashem museum every year: Yad Vashem, The World Holocaust Remembrance Center, "What is Yad Vashem," Yad Vashem, https://www.yadvashem.org/about/yad-vashem.html (February 9, 2022).

31 Victoria Aarons and Alan L. Berger, *Third-Generation Holocaust Representation: Trauma, History, and Memory* (Evanston, IL: Northwestern University Press, 2017), http://www.jstor.org/stable/j.ctt22727kb; Steffi de Jong, *The Witness as Object: Video Testimonies in Holocaust Museums* (New York: Berghahn Books, 2018), https://doi.org/10.2307/j.ctv3znzsd.

32 Elaine A. Culbertson, "A Reflection on the Use of Iconic Holocaust Resources," in *Essentials of Holocaust Education: Fundamental Issues and Approaches*, ed. Samuel Totten and Stephen Feinberg (New York: Routledge, 2016), 131–46.

33 Carolyn J. Dean, "Atrocity Photographs, Dignity, and Human Vulnerability," *Humanity: An International Journal of Human Rights, Humanitarianism, and Development* 6, no. 2 (2015): 239–64, https://doi.org/10.1353/hum.2015.0020.

34 Linda Norris, Danny Cohen, and Stacey Mann, "When Histories Horrify: Supporting Visitors' Responses through Responsible Interpretation," *History News* 67, no. 4 (2012): 16–20, https://www.jstor.org/stable/26453343.

35 Dan Johnson and Rhiannon Pickin, "Suffering on Display: An Argument for Historical Nuance in British Prison Museums," *Crime, Histoire & Sociétés* 23, no. 1 (2019): 5–26, http://www.jstor.org/stable/45215848.

36 Julie J. Golding, *Vicarious Trauma Experienced by Visitors to a Central Holocaust Museum* (PhD diss., Yeshiva University, 2023), https://repository.yu.edu/items/2b5e4d06-4b25-46b7-8a22-d1fa3001e85c.

37 Alexander Karn, "Toward a Philosophy of Holocaust Education: Teaching Values without Imposing Agendas," *The History Teacher* 45, no. 2 (2012): 229, http://www.jstor.org/stable/23265920.

38 Zehavit Gross, "The Process of the Universalization of Holocaust Education: Problems and Challenges," *Contemporary Jewry* 38, no. 1 (2018): 5–20, http://www.jstor.org/stable/45209113.

39 Stuart Foster, Andy Pearce, and Alice Pettigrew, eds., *Holocaust Education: Contemporary Challenges and Controversies* (London: UCL Press, 2020), 29, https://doi.org/10.2307/j.ctv15d7zpf.

1 Difficult Exhibitions

Exploring the Complexities of Challenging Histories

It was an ordinary Thursday afternoon when I found the box that would change everything. Tucked away beneath stacks of archival materials in my local Holocaust museum, the small plexiglass container seemed unremarkable at first glance. But as I lifted it from its resting place, a yellow sticky note caught my eye. In neat cursive handwriting were three words that made my heart stop: "Ashes from Chelmno?"

As the museum's new collections specialist, I was tasked with inventorying artifacts during our move to a new location. But nothing in my training had prepared me for this moment. Most Holocaust museums have strict policies against accepting human remains into their collections. Even without formal guidelines, curators typically discourage such donations, instead directing donors to more appropriate venues for burial. Yet somehow, this box had found its way into our collection.

What I held in my hands wasn't just another artifact—it was potentially the remains of human beings murdered in the first Nazi death camp. The dust and bone fragments inside the box looked innocuous enough—like dirt or debris one might sweep up from the floor. But their possible origin told a far darker story.

Chelmno, located thirty miles from Łódź, Poland, was where the Nazis first perfected their methods of mass murder. Opening in December 1941, the camp became the site where at least 172,000 people would meet their deaths—not in gas chambers, but in vans converted into mobile execution chambers. Jews who arrived were forced to undress and enter these ordinary-looking vehicles, unaware that a tube had been attached to the exhaust pipe, ready to pump lethal carbon monoxide into the sealed cargo area. The vans would drive to burial sites while their human cargo suffocated inside. By 1942, following complaints from neighboring residents about the smell of decomposition, the Nazis began cremating bodies in open-air ovens, even exhuming and burning those previously buried in mass graves. Though the camp ceased operations in March 1943, it would reopen during June and July 1944 for one final, grim purpose: the liquidation of the Łódź ghetto.

Our research revealed that the box had come to us through the Znamirowski family nearly two decades earlier. Teddy Znamirowski, a Holocaust survivor from Łódź, had taken his family on what they called a "heritage trip" to Poland. At Chelmno, where Teddy's family members had been killed, his wife Rita collected these ashes. An old newspaper article quoted her matter-of-factly: "In Chelmno we picked up ashes and bones from where my husband's family was murdered."[1] (See Figure 1.1)

As a practicing Jew, I knew what needed to be done. Jewish law requires human remains to be buried, and these ashes—confirmed by experts to be human cremains—had waited over seventy years for a proper burial. What followed were months of navigating legal, religious, and financial challenges to ensure these victims would receive the dignity they had been denied in death. From the legal point of view, since the remains had been taken without permission from the site of a concentration camp in Poland, they were essentially stolen property that had been brought to the United States. In recent years, there have been several incidents where visitors took artifacts from Nazi concentration camp sites and had charges pressed against them. For example, in 2015, two British teenagers stole buttons and glass from Auschwitz and faced prison time,[2] and in 2017, an Israeli student was arrested at the airport for taking items from Auschwitz for an art project.[3] To get permission and avoid an international scandal when the story of the ashes would go public, the museum sought permission from Polish authorities to bury the remains in New York. The Consulate General of the Republic of Poland in New York wrote that they were "highly appreciative of your intention to prepare a funeral and burial of the remains" and that the government was "supportive of your intention" to move forward with the memorial.[4]

Then there was the question of Jewish law, which dictates that if a person chooses to be cremated, their remains cannot be buried in a Jewish cemetery. Could the remains then be buried? Tragically, this was not the first time this question had been posed. During Kristallnacht, the November Pogrom of 1938, 30,000 Jewish men and boys were arrested and taken to concentration camps like Buchenwald and Dachau. Many prisoners died, and for a fee, the German authorities cremated their remains and sent them back in an urn

Figure 1.1 Lid of an urn from the Buchenwald concentration camp on exhibit at Yad Vashem. The urn contained the cremains of Stefan Kande, a Jewish dentist from Vienna. Photograph by author, June 30, 2024.

to their relatives. In January 1939, Rabbi Menachem Mendel Kirschbaum wrote a responsa guiding those in his community on the issue of what to do. He stated that since these victims had been cremated against their will, they could be buried in a Jewish cemetery, and all the customs of a standard Jewish burial should be observed. We therefore followed the guidelines that he set forth in his responsa, placing burial shrouds, a prayer shawl, and dirt from the Land of Israel in the coffin and arranged a Chevra Kadisha (Jewish Burial Society) to bury them.

I never expected what happened next. On September 28, 2019, more than 500 people gathered at the Monsey Jewish Cemetery to attend the burial. The crowd included museum supporters and community members, but also people whose own relatives had vanished at Chelmno. As I watched them weep openly by the graveside, I understood that for them, this wasn't just a burial of anonymous ashes. This was perhaps their only chance to say goodbye to grandparents, aunts, uncles, and cousins who had disappeared into the machinery of genocide. (See Figure 1.2)

Today, the Memorial to the Victims of the Chelmno Death Camp stands at the site, its inscription in English, Hebrew, and Yiddish telling the story of these remains and the lives they represent. The paved walkway that encircles it has become one of many places that draw visitors to confront death, tragedy, and human suffering. Yet the crowds who gather here aren't merely motivated by morbid curiosity. They come for countless personal reasons: to educate themselves about the past, to seek connection with lost family members, to make sense of incomprehensible tragedy, or simply because they feel compelled to bear witness.

That small plexiglass box led me to understand something essential about human nature. We are simultaneously drawn to and repelled by sites of tragedy—a paradox that reveals our deep need to confront the darkest periods of the past, even as we struggle to comprehend them. Whether we visit such places as pilgrims, historians, mourners, or simply curious observers, these encounters with tragic chapters of human history serve a vital purpose: they transform abstract statistics into tangible reality and help ensure that what happened at places like Chelmno will never be forgotten.

The Attraction of Darkness: Understanding Dark Tourism

This growing interest in mortality-themed exhibitions[5] reflects a broader cultural phenomenon known as "thanatourism" or "dark tourism"—places that are linked to death, violence, disaster, or suffering.[6] These destinations, which include Holocaust museums and memorial sites, operate with the goal of creating visitor-friendly, accessible educational experiences that connect visitors with atrocities and tragic moments in history. The scope of dark tourism encompasses memorial sites for terror attacks, concentration

Figure 1.2 Memorial to victims of the Chelmno Death Camp. Photograph by author, September 22, 2024.

camps, cemetery tours, and prison museums. While some dark tourist sites, such as the remains of Pompeii in Italy, are created by natural disasters, others arise from human actions. Perhaps most striking is how potential dangers to visitors' safety and health fail to deter interest in certain locations. For example, while the remains of a nuclear reactor in Chernobyl, Ukraine, still contain risks of radiation poisoning, it remains a tourist hot spot, with visitors arriving at the site regularly.[7]

While many individuals find dark tourist sites too morbid to visit, others feel inexplicably drawn to these spaces. Dark tourism is popular because it thrives on the fundamental aspects of human nature involved in "attraction and revulsion"—the desire to see something that fascinates while simultaneously trying to look away.[8] This same impulse drives people to tune into news outlets to learn about death and tragedies and explains the snarling traffic jams caused by rubbernecking when there is an accident on the side of the road.

Understanding this psychological dynamic helps explain why dark tourism encompasses such diverse sites and experiences. Death is often a main component of a dark tourist site, but visitors' motivations extend far beyond interest in death or the macabre. They may visit for a variety of reasons, including (but not limited to) pilgrimages, historical interest, adventure, or just novelty.[9] While educational goals remain the primary motivation for many individuals who visit Holocaust museums and memorial sites, others are drawn by commemorative events.[10] (See Figure 1.3)

This diversity of visitor motivations shapes how dark tourism sites are designed and integrated into the landscape. Some memorials are established in parks or other quiet spaces that encourage reflection and introspection. Others are placed in city centers or along major thoroughfares, forcing pedestrians to confront difficult histories during everyday activities.

This tension between accessibility and reverence is exemplified by the New England Holocaust Memorial in Boston, Massachusetts. The memorial consists of six large glass towers, each named after one of the Nazi death camps established in German-occupied Poland. Visitors walk along a path lined with steam vents that create a smoke effect reminiscent of the gas chambers where millions of Jews were murdered and pass through shadows that appear to "tattoo" numbers on their bodies.[11]

When I visited, I was surprised to find the large Holocaust memorial alongside a bustling pedestrian walkway lined with shops and cafes. The urban setting created practical challenges—like finding parking in the area—and philosophical ones as well, like trying to experience the memorial purely as a memorial. Yet this location served a clear purpose: I recognized that placing the memorial here maximized the number of passersby who would see and engage with the knowledge and history that the site had to offer. At the same time, I was distracted by the honking of cars and the buzz of activity around me. It was only after I returned home that I could fully read about and absorb information about the different elements of the memorial and learn more about the significance of its architecture and design.

Figure 1.3 New England Holocaust Memorial. Photograph by author, August 25, 2022.

The boundaries of dark tourism extend beyond explicitly memorial spaces. Many well-visited tourist sites have histories associated with death, unexpectedly linking them in the category of dark tourism. Ghost tours in various cities, the Eiffel Tower with its history of suicides, and the many tombs and pyramids of Egypt fall into this category.[12]

I encountered this unexpected intersection of leisure tourism and dark history during a fun family vacation to "America's Mountain"—Pike's Peak in Colorado. Pike's Peak, a mountain so tall that visitors often experience altitude sickness because of low oxygen, stands at an elevation of 14,115 feet. As our bright red cog railway car ascended to the top, I enjoyed listening to the conductor's talk about the various sites that we passed along the way. For more than an hour, he pointed out all sorts of fascinating rock formations, waterfalls, trees, and animals. Then, amid this cheerful commentary, the conductor unexpectedly pointed out two memorial sites: one for a donkey that was blown up carrying dynamite up the mountain to help build the railroad, and the other for two hikers who died on the mountain.

The story of these hikers proved particularly haunting. As legend has it, Mr. and Mrs. William A. Skinner, a newlywed couple from Texas on their honeymoon, were determined to climb Pike's Peak despite several warnings that a storm was approaching and it was dangerous to ascend the mountain. When the storm hit, they could not reach shelter, and they died from exhaustion and exposure to the elements. Their bodies were found in the snow a few days later. Ironically, a letter found in Mr. Skinner's pocket read, "I hope you are having the time of your life in Colorado . . . do not freeze to death on Pike's Peak."

What struck me most was how this morbid tale has become commercialized—not only is the story remembered on every train ride up the mountain, but a postcard with a picture of their dead bodies is available for purchase in the gift shop. According to the gift shop employees, this postcard is the most popular item they sell.

Digital Darkness: Virtual Experiences and Social Media

While physical sites remain central to dark tourism, digital technology is expanding both access and engagement. Dark tourism creates an intentional intersection between modern visitors and horrific pasts, and the internet has amplified these connections. Virtual dark tourism includes, but is not limited to, virtual reality tours, live video conferencing, and on-demand 3D tours of the sites. A quick online search will bring up a host of such activities, including tours of slave plantations, the Alcatraz Island Virtual Citadel Tour, and Nazi concentration camp sites. These tours have broad appeal, providing visitors the opportunity to learn about the spaces without traveling to the physical site and offering unique perspectives through drone footage that reveals views not seen from the ground. In my own experience, attending virtual tours of the Auschwitz and Sobibor concentration camps, I appreciated the opportunity to ask questions directly to the curators and guides who work at the site.

The quality and authenticity of these virtual experiences vary by source. Some tours are offered by the official organizations or staff who work at the site, maintaining the educational standards of physical visits. However, it frequently happens that as the guides walk through the site with live video conferencing, the wind in the background or an unstable internet connection creates challenges in maintaining a high-quality interactive tour. Other tours are created by private individuals or organizations dedicated to teaching about the subject, often with different educational goals or perspectives. One notable example is Six Million Voices, a nonprofit based in Phoenix, Arizona, that offers virtual tours of Auschwitz. Their tours offer crisp video and photographic imagery, drone footage, and 3D visualizations, allowing the viewers to see the site from many different angles. The organization has an ambitious goal of reaching six million tour participants, commemorating the six million Jews who were murdered during the Holocaust, who will then become a "voice for moral clarity" after taking the tour.[13]

Museums have also embraced virtual platforms. Holocaust Museum LA offers one-hour virtual tours that "tak[e] students on an immersive, virtual journey through the Museum's exhibits from the convenience of their classrooms or homes."[14] Similarly, the Illinois Holocaust Museum offers both synchronous and asynchronous virtual field trips. These digital options have proven particularly valuable for schools that are located too far away or lack the funding for a physical field trip to the museum.

The intersection of dark tourism with digital culture has created both opportunities and ethical complexities. While social media has increased awareness and knowledge about dark tourism, it has also fundamentally altered the visitor experience. The impulse to document through photographs and selfies at these sites can sometimes overshadow the sacredness of the place upon which visitors are standing.[15]

This tension came to a head in 2017 when Shahak Shapira, an Israeli artist, author, and comedian living in Berlin, noticed a disturbing trend: visitors to Berlin's Holocaust Memorial to the Murdered Jews of Europe were regularly posing and taking selfies at the site. They would smile, jump, and perform yoga poses on the concrete slabs meant to honor victims of the Holocaust. These antics and their subsequent celebration on social media revealed the visitors' disregard for the very atrocities that the memorial was meant to commemorate. Though the original design of the memorial was controversial, with some suggesting that it was too abstract and did not address the issue of guilt expected at a Holocaust memorial in the heart of Germany, this new phenomenon of performative selfies reflected a whole new level of disrespect.[16]

Disturbed by this trend, Shapira took creative action. He created a project called YOLOCAUST, where he combined selfies that people posted on social media with footage from Nazi extermination camps. The resulting images proved shocking, and YOLOCAUST went viral, reaching more than 2.5 million viewers within one week—including the twelve selfie-takers featured in the original photographs, many of whom apologized and removed the photographs from their social media accounts.[17] Far more than just a witty photographic endeavor, YOLOCAUST became a project that forced people to grapple with the horrific history commemorated by the space.

Confronting the Challenge of Difficult Histories

The profound discomfort that dark tourism sites evoke reflects their role in presenting what scholars call "difficult" history. This term is deliberately chosen over "controversial" histories to reflect the affective component and discomfort that is felt when teaching or learning "histories rooted in the traumas, suffering and violent oppression of groups of people—such as racism, apartheid, genocides and the like."[18] The concept of "difficult" history gained prominence in reference to the diary of Anne Frank, where the reader's confrontation with victimization and hatred offers a powerful demonstration of the intersection of pedagogy and historical atrocities.[19]

What makes these histories so challenging to confront? Researchers note that "some history can be difficult because it is traumatic; because it is difficult for most people in the present to fathom; or because it raises issues of identity, marginalization, and oppression that are more easily ignored than addressed for many students and teachers."[20] Learning about such events creates a "dynamic interplay between being told too much and knowing too little that occurs when one attempts to engage in learning about the unimaginable but terrifyingly real situations of genocide."[21] This overwhelming sensation has led some to use the phrase "terrible knowledge," suggesting that this understanding is "so appalling it seems to damage, rather than empower us."[22]

The anxiety these encounters provoke stems from multiple sources. On a personal level, it forces us to confront our vulnerability and that of those we know and love.[23] Even more disturbing is the realization that atrocities and genocide like the Holocaust are not mistakes of the human experience; they emerge from calculated, intentional, and legal actions. Perhaps most unsettling is the recognition that "not only was the Holocaust consciously enacted" but it was executed "with the very tools of modernity that were supposed to, and continue to be supposed to, provide everyone access to progress and the good life. So what can a lesson hope to accomplish?"[24] These layers of discomfort—personal vulnerability, human intentionality, and the betrayal of progress itself—make encountering difficult histories a profound challenge for both educators and learners.

While difficult history is difficult for anyone at any age, it poses unique challenges for children to grasp, raising questions about both the right age for students learning about the Holocaust and the many factors that influence how they process and learn about it. One particularly poignant example comes from Esther Almo, a young professional living in New York City today, who shared how childhood misunderstandings of the Holocaust can leave lasting impressions.

Esther is the granddaughter of Greek Jews who were taken to Auschwitz during the Holocaust, and she grew up in a community of Greek and Sephardic immigrants steeped in Ladino language and culture. When Esther was five years old, her older seven-year-old cousin made a well-meaning attempt to explain their family history: "Did you know that Grandma and Grandpa were in this thing where the bad people put all the Jews? And if you escaped, you escaped, but everybody else died." From these words, Esther constructed an image that would stay with her for decades: She pictured the Holocaust as a huge white tent where they put all the Jews. In what she imagined to be a black and white scene from long ago, younger versions of her grandparents were inside the tent with many other people. "I picture it to be frantic, packed in there, kind of hazy in the air. . . . Tons of people were kind of running, kind of trying to find their way out, with gas coming out." In her child's mind, anyone who managed to get out of the tent "escaped the Holocaust," while anyone who remained inside was someone who died.[25]

Though Esther can't remember when she formally learned about the Holocaust or the real details about her grandparents' experiences in Auschwitz, the emotional impact of that early understanding persisted. As a child, she experienced a considerable amount of anxiety about the Holocaust, worrying that it would happen again and that she would be taken away from her family. Later, as a teenager she attended Holocaust commemoration events at her school but found it difficult to watch documentaries or movies about the Shoah. Even now, as an adult she finds it difficult to read any literature about the subject. The trauma echoes in unexpected ways: "I hate the sounds of trains on the tracks. Sometimes if I'm in a packed subway car or hear the tracks of the train, I think about how it must have been when they were going to Auschwitz." Perhaps most strikingly, when someone makes mention of the Holocaust, the image of a white tent still appears in her mind.

In the Classroom: Teaching Trauma and Historical Atrocity

While personal family histories like Esther's provide one path to Holocaust knowledge, many students first encounter these difficult histories in the classroom. This institutional setting presents its own challenges: while all states have codes and standards that regulate ethical conduct within the classroom, it is often left to the teacher to interpret what is considered emotionally safe and age-appropriate for their students.[26] Some educators take a cautious approach, carefully limiting students' exposure to traumatic content and emphasizing distance from difficult material. Others take a bold approach, insisting that teaching must address or include a crisis because of the human nature to connect through emotions of vulnerability and unpredictability that are felt when hearing about a crisis.[27] They argue that teaching about crises will deepen student engagement and knowledge in the same way that featuring crises in news reports increases viewership and interest in the media. As one educator provocatively put it, "My job as a teacher, paradoxical as it may sound, was that of creating in the class the highest state of crisis that it could withstand, without 'driving the students crazy,' without compromising the students' bounds."[28]

Beyond the question of approach lies the challenge of timing and content. Debates persist about how, what, and when to teach children and adolescents about the Holocaust. While discussions frequently revolve around introducing difficult subjects in early grade levels, it is important to recognize developmental differences found even among freshmen, sophomores, juniors, and seniors in high schools. Moreover, teachers must determine a uniform standard for student exposure in the classroom, balancing the needs of students who are overexposed to violence and graphic content with those who are not.

Perhaps surprisingly, it is often teachers themselves who resist teaching or engaging pedagogically with certain aspects of history. This reluctance stems from a range of reasons, including feeling disturbed about traumatic content, fear of students' emotionally charged responses in the classroom, conflicting political views of the subject, and opposition or discomfort toward their values.[29] In a study of Estonian and Latvian teachers tasked with teaching sensitive and controversial issues in history, researchers found that teachers would try to hide or avoid teaching topics they disagreed with. Notably, in these societies divided over issues of historical representation in a post-Soviet era, teachers were more likely to teach sensitive topics if their convictions matched those of the nationally sanctioned perspective.[30] Beyond personal beliefs, teachers may also be hesitant to teach difficult histories because of the complexities of presenting multiple perspectives or their lack of knowledge. Some may even assume it is too controversial or politically charged to be considered in an official curriculum.[31]

The challenges of teaching difficult history become particularly acute during moments of contemporary crisis. I recall when my colleague and fellow history teacher approached me a week after Hamas' October 7th attack on Israel, looking very agitated. "We need to talk. I need to understand how you teach about the Holocaust," she said. "My students are asking me questions about the attack and it's just too much for me to discuss and think about. I don't understand how you can teach about something like the Holocaust every single day." Her distress particularly struck me because this educator, a medievalist with expertise in teaching about the Crusades at the high school and undergraduate level, teaches about tragic and violent histories regularly. "That's different," she explained to me. "The Crusades happened so long ago, I don't relate to the events and neither do my students. But your work is teaching something much more recent. Holocaust survivors are still alive and retelling their personal stories."

Research offers several strategies to help educators navigate these challenges, beginning with the essential work of self-reflection. Educators must concentrate on working through their own emotional and political perspectives while teaching sensitive and controversial topics, a process that can be supported through targeted professional development workshops.[32] This internal preparation allows teachers to better embrace the inherent complexity of difficult histories. Yet even with thorough preparation, teachers must learn to embrace uncertainty. Research examining how teachers address the 1945 nuclear bombing of Hiroshima and Nagasaki demonstrates that educators must become comfortable with leaving certain questions unanswered, acknowledging that some historical issues remain open not just in their classrooms but potentially for generations.[33] Beyond this philosophical approach, practical tools can also help teachers engage with challenging content. An action research study focused on representations of the Vietnam War found that using documentaries and outtakes significantly increased teachers' willingness to explore multiple perspectives of difficult histories, suggesting that multimedia resources can provide both structure and distance for addressing sensitive topics.[34]

Sacred Ground: Memorials as Educational Spaces

While classroom education provides one gateway to difficult histories, the physical act of visiting sites of tragedy represents a fundamentally different kind of encounter—one that lies at the heart of this book. Museums and memorials bear a unique institutional responsibility in creating these encounters—experiences that vary dramatically by visitor. Some actively choose to visit museums and memorials, not recognizing how emotionally challenging the encounter will be, while others approach these spaces less enthusiastically (or even reticently) as part of larger group tours or school trips. From this diversity of visitor engagement emerges a central tension: how to balance exhibiting horrific atrocities with protecting visitors' emotional safety.

This challenge played out explicitly in 1984, when the Museum Planning Committee of the USHMM in Washington, D.C., sought to create points of connection between visitors and Holocaust victims. In discussions about the Hall of Witness, Anna Cohn, the director of museum development (who left the project before the plans were created), argued for using museum design to invoke a memory that is "so strong—so traumatic—as to refuse integration into the historical narrative that leads from the Shoah to the historical present."[35] As documented in the Museum Planning Committee records, she believed that viewing gruesome photographs would transform visitors into witnesses. Cohn was adamant: she didn't "want to give the visitor an easy out [. . .]. If the message you want to convey is sharper than quiet solemnity, then you need to deliver it immediately."[36]

Yet research suggests that such intense emotional manipulation may be counterproductive. Strong affective experiences can prevent visitors from thinking critically about the exhibition's information, potentially undermining important historical perspectives and lessons. Both psychologists and sociologists have shown that "overexposure to empathy-arousing representations of suffering can have a paralyzing effect, acting as a barrier to rather as a motivator of action."[37] In the words of one researcher,

> *Too often, I've seen Holocaust museums appear to be designed in a way that intentionally encourages shock or sadness: the use of sentimental music within a survivor's testimony video, larger-than-life-sized photographs of open mass graves, and museum elevators that resemble gas chambers. I've also observed museum guides using emotionally loaded statements and language (such as, "What you're about to see is quite shocking") that forces onto visitors' particular expectations. Yet, when visitors reach particular sections within exhibitions that use unnecessary and crude treatments, or when guides provide loaded commentary, I've seen visitors shut down. Silence replaces questions and ideas.*[38]

However, completely avoiding difficult content creates its own risks, given the "human tendency to fill in the blanks and personalize material which can sometimes be more traumatizing than even the most graphic documentary evidence of an atrocity."[39] This delicate balance is evident at the National September 11 Memorial & Museum in Manhattan, where curators have observed that visitors' emotions may overwhelm their rational thinking. Their solution involves presenting the most challenging moments in the narrative with a "safe buffer for visitors" where they are "allowed to grieve, to shake their heads in dismay, to be angry, to cry, and even to be numb."[40]

Museums have increasingly turned to multimedia presentations to navigate this balance between impact and avoidance. Researchers have noted that "the moving image has become ubiquitous in museums that deal with traumatic, violent, and difficult histories and could be described as 'memorial museums.'"[41] But like in the classroom, museums' use of film and video installations poses its own challenges. The combination of visual and audial techniques creates a visceral experience that disturbs and provokes visitors' emotions. Many individuals are concerned about their emotional responses to trauma being shown on screen and may be hesitant to engage with these presentations. This hesitation can be especially profound when visitors have personal connections to the history being depicted. For example, Stoddard and colleagues found that in viewing historical representations of plantations and enslaved communities, African Americans were particularly apprehensive because they descend from enslaved people and still experience racism and discrimination today.[42]

The challenge of encountering difficult history took on new meaning for me during the pandemic, when my connection to the Memorial for the Victims of the Chelmno Death Camp unexpectedly deepened. Just a few months after we buried the ashes, the Covid-19 pandemic hit, and museums shuttered their doors for months on end. Then something curious happened: I began to get requests from individuals and groups to take them to the memorial in lieu of a visit to a Holocaust museum. What began as one small school field trip to an outdoor space where people could social distance while learning about the Holocaust turned into a full-fledged tour and educational program that thousands of people have now attended.

With many Holocaust survivors buried near the Holocaust memorial, my tour slowly expanded to include visiting many of these sites and learning about their Holocaust history. Individuals include Mala Orner, a young woman who was a doctor in the Łódź ghetto, William (Bill) Zeck, who prosecuted war crimes at the Nuremberg Trials, and Rabbi Chaim Zanvil Abrahamowitz, or the Ribnitzer Rebbe, a Hasidic leader who is known as a mystic and whose grave attracts 30,000 visitors seeking to pray on the anniversary of the date of his death. Throughout my tours, I weave a story of danger and despair, of survival and hope, and the rebirth of a community built on the ashes of the Holocaust.

Through this unexpected turn of events, I founded Yesodeinu (Our Foundation), an organization dedicated to "teaching about Jewish resilience in the face of adversity through powerful experiences at local cemeteries and historical sites."[43] Program participants have come from across the United States, Canada, and even as far as Europe. While at first many question what a cemetery in the suburbs of New York has to offer on the history of the Holocaust, they quickly come to recognize how this space is linked to other Holocaust-related dark tourist sites.

Through my work at Yesodeinu and the Memorial to the Victims of the Chelmno Death Camp, I've come to understand that encountering difficult histories creates ripple effects that extend far beyond the initial moment of discovery. That small box of ashes sparked not just a burial project, but a broader journey into understanding how we process and present tragic histories. While some visitors to these sites seek connection with lost family members, others come to learn, to remember, or simply to bear witness. Yet regardless of their motivation, each person who encounters these difficult histories must navigate their own emotional response to tragedy.

As I continued to guide visitors through these spaces of memory, I found myself increasingly drawn to a fundamental question: How do we create meaningful encounters with difficult histories while protecting the emotional well-being of those who experience them? The answer, I discovered, requires understanding not just the histories themselves, but how trauma shapes our ability to engage with challenging historical narratives. As museums and memorial sites wrestle with displaying difficult histories, a parallel challenge has emerged that I take up in the next chapter: how to teach about historical trauma in an era of increasing student trauma.

Notes

1 Suzan Clarke, "Holocaust Museum Adds New Exhibits," *The Journal News*, July 25, 2006.

2 Jacob Koffler, "2 Teenagers Arrested for Theft of Auschwitz Artifacts," *TIME*, June 23, 2015, https://time.com/3931830/teenagers-arrested-auschwitz-artifacts/.

3 "Israeli Steals Auschwitz Items for Student Art Project," *BBC*, July 19, 2017, https://www.bbc.com/news/world-middle-east-40656748.

4 Personal communication with Consulate General, August 5, 2019.

5 Lisa Graves, "Death & The Modern Visitor Experience," *Journal of Museum Ethnography* 30 (2017): 49–58, http://www.jstor.org/stable/44841226.

6 Dan Johnson and Rhiannon Pickin, "Suffering on Display: An Argument for Historical Nuance in British Prison Museums," *Crime, Histoire & Sociétés* 23, no. 1 (2019): 6, http://www.jstor.org/stable/45215848.

7 Tony Johnston, "The Geographies of Thanatourism," *Geography* 100, no. 1 (2015): 20–7. http://www.jstor.org/stable/43825410.

8 Annalisa Bolin, "On the Side of Light: Performing Morality at Rwanda's Genocide Memorials," *Journal of Conflict Archaeology* 7, no. 3 (2012): 201, https://www.jstor.org/stable/48601744.

9 José Magano, José António Fraiz-Brea, and Ângela Leite, "Dark Tourism, the Holocaust, and Well-being: A Systematic Review," *Heliyon* 9, no. 1 (2023), https://doi.org/10.1016/j.heliyon.2023.e13064.

10 Amanda Dawson, Sinéad O'Leary, and Noelle O'Connor, "Holocaust Tourism: Education or Exploitation?" *Tourism and Heritage Journal* 4 (2022): 37–52, https://doi.org/10.1344/THJ.2022.4.3.

11 New England Holocaust Memorial, "Design of the Memorial," *New England Holocaust Memorial | A Beacon of Memory and Hope*, March 11, 2013, https://www.nehm.org/the-memorial/design-of-the-memorial/.

12 José Magano, José A. Fraiz-Brea, and Ângela Leite, "Dark Tourists: Profile, Practices, Motivations and Wellbeing," *International Journal of Environmental Research and Public Health* 19, no. 19 (2022): 12100. https://doi.org/10.3390/ijerph191912100.

13 "Why Six Million Voices," *Six Million Voices*, https://sixmillionvoices.org/about-us/ (January 14, 2024).

14 Los Angeles Holocaust Museum, "Student Tours," *Holocaust Museum LA*, 2020, https://www.holocaustmuseumla.org/student-tours.

15 Rebecca Price and Mark Shores, "Dark Tourism: A Guide to Resources," *Reference & User Services Quarterly* 57, no. 2 (2017): 97–101, https://www.jstor.org/stable/90017127.

16 Anthony Faiola, "Berlin's Holocaust Memorial Is 'Not a Place for Fun Selfies,'" *The Washington Post*, January 28, 2017, https://www.washingtonpost.com/world/europe/berlins-holocaust-memorial-is-not-a-place-for-fun-selfies/2017/01/27/2e5b6324-e1ac-11e6-a419-eefe8eff0835_story.html.

17 Shahak Shapira, "YOLOCAUST—The Aftermath," *Yolocaust.de*, 2014, https://yolocaust.de.

18 Britzman, as cited in Michalinos Zembylas, "Teacher Resistance to Engage with 'Alternative' Perspectives of Difficult Histories: The Limits and Prospects of Affective Disruption," *Discourse: Studies in the Cultural Politics of Education* 38, no. 5 (2017): 660, https://doi.org/10.1080/01596306.2015.1132680.

19 Michalinos Zembylas, "Theorizing 'Difficult Knowledge' in the Aftermath of the 'Affective Turn': Implications for Curriculum and Pedagogy in Handling Traumatic Representations," *Curriculum Inquiry* 44, no. 3 (2014): 390–412, http://www.jstor.org/stable/43941648.

20 Michalinos Zembylas, Loizos Loukaides, and Petroula Antoniou, "Teachers' Understandings of Empathy in Teaching about the Holocaust in Cyprus: The Emotional Risks of Identification and the Disruptive Potential of 'Empathic Unsettlement,'" *Teaching and Teacher Education* 89 (2020): 103007, https://doi.org/10.1016/j.tate.2019.103007.

21 Britzman, as cited in H. James Garrett, "Difficult Knowledge: Encounters with Social Trauma in Pedagogy," *Counterpoints* 506 (2017): 22, http://www.jstor.org/stable/45136321.

22 Mara Miller, "Terrible Knowledge and Tertiary Trauma Part I: Japanese Nuclear Trauma and Resistance to the Atomic Bomb in the Classroom," *The Clearing House* 86, no. 5 (2013): 159, http://www.jstor.org/stable/43999342.

23 Garrett, "Difficult Knowledge."

24 Garrett, "Difficult Knowledge," 26–7.

25 Personal communication with Esther Almo, March 12, 2024.

26 Rachel Pawlowicz and Walter E. Grunden, "Teaching Atrocities: The Holocaust and Unit 731 in the Secondary School Curriculum," *The History Teacher* 48, no. 2 (2015): 271–94, http://www.jstor.org/stable/43264405.

27 Felman, as cited in Deborah P. Britzman, "Between Psychoanalysis and Pedagogy: Scenes of Rapprochement and Alienation," *Curriculum Inquiry* 43, no. 1 (2013): 95–117, http://www.jstor.org/stable/23524359; Garrett, "Difficult Knowledge."

28 Felman, as cited in Michalinos Zembylas, "'Pedagogy of Discomfort' and Its Ethical Implications: The Tensions of Ethical Violence in Social Justice Education," *Ethics and Education* 10, no. 2 (2015): 164, https://doi.org/10.1080/17449642.2015.1039274.

29 Zembylas, "Teacher Resistance."

30 Katrin Kello, "Sensitive and Controversial Issues in the Classroom: Teaching History in a Divided Society," *Teachers and Teaching* 22, no. 1 (2015): 35–53, https://doi.org/10.1080/13540602.2015.1023027.

31 Jeremy D. Stoddard, Alan S. Marcus, and David Hicks, *Teaching Difficult History Through Film* (New York: Routledge, 2017), https://doi.org/10.4324/9781315640877.

32 Kello, "Sensitive and Controversial Issues."

33 Miller, "Terrible Knowledge."

34 William Gaudelli, Margaret Crocco, and Alexandra Hawkins, "Documentaries Outtakes and Digital Archives in Teaching Difficult Knowledge and the Vietnam War," *Education and Society* 30, no. 2 (2012): 5–25, https://doi.org/10.7459/es/30.2.02.

35 Michael Bernard-Donals, "Synecdochic Memory at the United States Holocaust Memorial Museum," *College English* 74, no. 5 (2012): 425, http://www.jstor.org/stable/23212923.

36 Cohn, as cited in Bernard-Donals, "Synecdochic Memory," 425.

37 Michalinos Zembylas, Loizos Loukaides, and Petroula Antoniou, "Teachers' Understandings of Empathy in Teaching about the Holocaust in Cyprus: The Emotional Risks of Identification and the Disruptive Potential of 'Empathic Unsettlement'," *Teaching and Teacher Education* 89 (2020): 103007, https://doi.org/10.1016/j.tate.2019.103007.

38 Cohen, in Linda Norris, Danny Cohen, and Stacey Mann, "When Histories Horrify: Supporting Visitors' Responses through Responsible Interpretation," *History News* 67, no. 4 (2012): 19, https://www.jstor.org/stable/26453343.

39 Norris et al., "When Histories Horrify," 19.

40 Mann, in Norris et al., "When Histories Horrify," 19.

41 Silke Arnold-de Simine, "The 'Moving' Image: Empathy and Projection in the International Slavery Museum, Liverpool," *Journal of Educational Media, Memory & Society* 4, no. 2 (2012): 23, http://www.jstor.org/stable/43049390.

42 Jeremy D. Stoddard, Alan S. Marcus, and David Hicks, *Teaching Difficult History Through Film* (New York: Routledge, 2017), https://doi.org/10.4324/9781315640877.

43 "Yesodeinu—Building the Future on the Foundation of the Past," *Yesodeinu.org*, 2021, https://yesodeinu.org.

2 Through Their Eyes

Understanding Vicarious Trauma and Secondary Traumatic Stress

The 2012 Sandy Hook Elementary School shooting in Newtown, Connecticut—where a lone gunman killed twenty students and six staff members—remains the deadliest elementary school shooting in US history. In the years that followed this tragedy, there was barely a month without another school shooting somewhere in the United States. The nation remained on edge: parents worried about their children's safety at school, embracing them tightly before each day, while political debates about gun control raged across the country. Meanwhile, educators, who bore the responsibility of keeping students safe in their school buildings, grappled with what to do next.

Several years after the Sandy Hook shooting, I joined educational leaders at Torah Umesorah's Annual Mid-Winter Principals Conference in Ft. Lauderdale, Florida, where we explored the topic "The Highly Reliable School." While the program featured numerous sessions on educational leadership, supervision, and work-life balance, one presentation left an indelible impression. Dr. Norman Goldwasser, a psychologist from Miami Beach, delivered a compelling session titled "Managing Critical and Traumatic Events." His talk addressed the complex security challenges weighing heavily on school leaders' minds: safe rooms, lockdowns, emergency supplies, and the mounting costs of school security. The session sparked an intense discussion among the more than 200 educators present, all grappling with how to protect students and maintain school safety in the face of ongoing threats to their communities.

The conversation took an unexpected turn when Dr. Goldwasser raised the issue of student mental health during lockdowns, sharing accounts of students traumatized by practice drills and protocol reviews. The mood in the room shifted as educators, one after another, voiced similar concerns about student mental health—a challenge they increasingly faced amid the recent wave of school shootings. The discussion evolved to address how to help students process their feelings and support those triggered by alarms and loud noises. It was here that I first encountered the phrase "trauma-safe schools" and heard growing recognition of the need to address student mental health during lockdowns. Yet despite this emerging awareness, few resources or solutions were available to address these concerns.

I had an epiphany as I listened to these conversations. While the educators around me were striving to minimize their students' exposure to traumatic events, my role as a Holocaust educator required something fundamentally different. I deliberately introduced students to historical mass murder through carefully prepared curricula and lesson plans—complete with videos, slides, readings, and images that addressed hate, starvation, and death. Even when teaching about pre-war Jewish life or stories of survival against overwhelming odds, these lessons were inevitably shadowed by the knowledge of the horrors that preceded or followed. I realized that no matter how sensitively I presented the Holocaust's history or how carefully I chose my language, the core of my subject matter remained inherently frightening. This revelation led me to a crucial question: How was this affecting my students?

An unexpected blizzard in New York, dumping nearly three feet of snow and canceling my flight, gave me an extra day in sunny Florida to reflect. I pondered the stark contrast between typical educators and Holocaust teachers. While most teachers strive to create classrooms filled with excitement and joy, those of us teaching difficult histories navigate darker waters. My thoughts turned to former students who had struggled in ways that had previously puzzled me when learning about the Holocaust. As I sat with these thoughts, I kept coming back to the same idea: Could the emerging insights about supporting students traumatized by school shootings inform how we teach about historical trauma in the Holocaust classroom?

The Ripple Effect: Secondary Trauma and Vicarious Experiences

The American Psychological Association defines trauma as "an emotional response to a terrible event like an accident, rape, or natural disaster."[1] At its core, trauma is described as "a shattering of self and the world," with impacts that extend far beyond the initial event.[2] This definition helps distinguish between tragic events and trauma itself. While an unexpected death is inherently tragic, trauma encompasses the complex psychological and emotional responses that follow such events.[3] Dr. Bessel van der Kolk, noted researcher and author of the bestselling book *The Body Keeps the Score*, explains that an event becomes traumatic when a person is powerless to prevent the inevitable, and the body automatically responds in one of three ways: fight, flight, or freeze.[4]

Modern research frames trauma as "a barrier of sensation and knowledge that protects the organism by placing stimulation within an ordered system of time," suggesting that trauma fundamentally represents "a break in the mind's experience of time."[5] Neuroscience explains this sensation, showing how specific brain regions malfunction during stressful or traumatic events.[6] In the event of danger, the thalamus—which processes external stimuli like images, sounds, and physical sensations—begins to break down, sending only fragmented messages to the amygdala. Sensing a threat, the amygdala triggers one of three bodily responses: fight, flight, or freeze. Meanwhile, the prefrontal cortex, responsible for processing time, decision-making, and empathic understanding, effectively shuts down, preventing normal emotional regulation and event processing. This neural disruption explains why trauma victims often struggle to remember or synthesize the sequence and details of their experience. The psychological impact manifests through various short-term and long-term symptoms, including shock, denial, dissociation, hyperarousal, tics, or defensive mechanisms like inappropriate humor.[7]

Notably, the traditional association between trauma and silence has evolved in the digital age, with social media platforms providing new outlets for talking about trauma that many find more accessible than face-to-face conversations.[8] However, the term "trauma" has become increasingly commonplace, often used synonymously with horror, atrocity, and genocide. This broad application diminishes both its uniqueness and its connections to other terrible human experiences. As one scholar notes, this generalization is "equivalent to using 'Auschwitz' as a synonym for Holocaust history as a whole. It works rhetorically, as many examples show, but is severely limited empirically."[9]

A pivotal moment in trauma studies occurred in 1980 when the American Psychiatric Association officially classified post-traumatic stress disorder

(PTSD) as a disease. This breakthrough emerged from clinicians' work with Vietnam War veterans who struggled to reintegrate into civilian life. Psychologists had initially attempted to treat these veterans for schizophrenia, depression, mood disorders, alcoholism, and substance abuse, but found these diagnoses and their corresponding treatments inadequate. The formal recognition of PTSD not only gave a name to the veterans' suffering but also opened new avenues for understanding, research, and innovative treatment approaches.[10]

In the decades following PTSD's classification, cultural trauma studies examined re-traumatization and post-memory concepts, particularly in relation to Holocaust survivor testimonies and archives.[11] As a mental illness that can develop after actual or potential traumatic or life-threatening events, PTSD manifests as involuntary memory of unresolved events.[12] It "permits the past (memory) to relive itself in the present, in the form of intrusive images and thoughts and in the patient's compulsion to replay old events."[13] Although the traumatic event may be long past, a person will continue to exhibit heightened fear responses and react to other experiences as if the danger is still present. Individuals with PTSD may be triggered by various sensory experiences—specific sights, sounds, tastes, or smells—with triggers being deeply personal and capable of provoking responses ranging from avoidance to angry or violent outbursts.[14]

Trauma's effects can persist across generations, creating patterns that are transmitted both intergenerationally within families and transgenerationally within social systems.[15] This generational transmission provides crucial context for understanding both childhood trauma and broader societal patterns. Within families, traumatic experiences can shape parenting styles and attachment patterns, while at a societal level, historical traumas can affect entire communities across multiple generations. Children of Holocaust survivors, for instance, often exhibit heightened stress responses and anxiety patterns similar to their parents, demonstrating how trauma can echo through generations.[16] Their behavioral and clinical challenges contributed significantly to early epigenetic research, advancing our understanding of how trauma can influence DNA transmission and gene sequencing for survivors' offspring.

Understanding generational patterns sheds light on the need to address childhood trauma in trauma studies. While PTSD affects people of all ages, its impact on children is particularly significant. Childhood trauma is alarmingly common in the United States, affecting two-thirds of all children, with about 30 percent of students with emotional and behavioral disorders showing signs of PTSD.[17]

Trauma manifests in various forms, ranging from isolated incidents to ongoing patterns that affect individuals over time. Children typically encounter three types of traumas: acute, chronic, and complex.[18] Acute trauma arises from a single distressing event such as a natural disaster, car accident, or assault. Chronic trauma, on the other hand, results from prolonged or repetitive experiences like homelessness, ongoing abuse, or chronic illness. Complex trauma involves multiple traumatic events but is categorized differently from chronic trauma because it usually involves a caregiver and is interpersonal in nature. This type of trauma results from persistent and severe neglect, abuse, or violence, and can fundamentally alter a child's developmental trajectory and their ability to form secure attachments.[19]

The Adverse Childhood Experiences (ACE) study established a pivotal framework for measuring childhood trauma.[20] Kaiser Permanente conducted the original ACE research between 1995 and 1997, which remains the most comprehensive investigative tool for studying trauma in individuals under the age of eighteen. The questionnaire is comprised of ten questions, categorized into three main areas: abuse, neglect, and household dysfunction. According to the 2016 National Survey of Children's Health, approximately 45 percent of American children have experienced at least one type of ACE, with 10 percent having endured all three.[21] The effects of these experiences can be severe and long-lasting. Children often experience immediate effects such as feelings of terror, fear, and helplessness, alongside physical and mental developmental challenges and stress reactions that affect daily functioning. The long-term correlation between a higher ACE score and adult behaviors can be equally devastating, including increased risk of drug abuse and alcoholism, higher rates of suicide and depression, and greater likelihood of obesity and other health issues.[22]

Childhood trauma significantly affects educational experiences and outcomes in multiple ways. These challenges often manifest through physical and emotional distress, with researchers finding that increased ACEs and traumatic stress affect growth and development and lead to chronic health conditions.[23] Research also demonstrates that trauma-exposed students show disruptive classroom behaviors,[24] including lower classroom engagement, increased attendance issues, and higher suspension rates.[25]

Unsurprisingly, childhood trauma leads to over 50 percent higher dropout rates.[26]

Research by McLaughlin and Sheridan provides important context for these outcomes, highlighting how exposure to environmental threats conditions children to specific fear responses.[27] Their work demonstrates that these patterns of externalization appear specifically in students with threat exposure, distinguishing them from those experiencing deprivation alone. This understanding is further supported by case studies of trauma, such as research conducted after a tornado in Alabama, which documented both immediate and lasting behavioral changes in the classroom setting.[28]

Bearing Witness: Memory, Testimony, and Educational Spaces

While understanding direct trauma is crucial, equally important is recognizing how trauma creates ripple effects that extend beyond immediate victims. Teachers working with traumatized students, spouses, and children of soldiers returning from war, mental health professionals treating PTSD patients, and first responders at disaster sites all engage regularly with others' trauma narratives. This exposure creates its own form of psychological impact, known as secondary traumatic stress (STS) or vicarious trauma.[29] While the phrases "secondary traumatic stress" and "vicarious trauma" are often used interchangeably in reference to indirect trauma, there are some differences. STS, similar to PTSD, has a quick onset and refers to trauma effects resulting from looking at the trauma of someone else. Vicarious trauma is similar to burnout and is used in reference to a negative worldview developed as a result of frequent trauma exposure.[30]

To explain vicarious trauma, I find it helpful to refer to the analogy comparing it to the effects of breathing in secondhand smoke. This comparison stems from the research proposing that vicarious traumatization results when empathy and interpersonal relationships create a gateway for deeply feeling the pain of others.[31] Hearing or learning about atrocities and crises is a powerful experience in which "the listener to trauma comes to be a participant and a co-owner of the traumatic event: through his very listening, he comes to partially experience trauma in himself."[32]

The deeply personal nature of PTSD and STS triggers can manifest in unexpected ways, particularly when historical trauma intersects with personal experiences. One day, while overseeing a school group visiting the museum, I heard noises that sounded like someone was crying. I ran to a classroom to find Claire, a teacher chaperone for the school group, weeping in a corner. I asked her what had happened, and she responded, "I can't believe they are watching that video!" The film in question was comprised of original footage and survivor testimonies about children being deported from various ghettos to concentration camps during the Holocaust. Parents described coming home to find their children missing, and children spoke of the experience of being forced into cattle cars and traveling for days without food or water. The content of the film was genuinely horrific, but I couldn't understand why this film—of all the exhibits and films at the museum—reduced her to tears. As she caught her breath, she explained what caused her reaction. "I recently went through a very difficult divorce, and I struggled to keep custody of my children. Some have been taken from me, and watching this film is so scary."

Claire's reaction demonstrates how trauma responses can be triggered by seemingly unrelated historical events when they touch upon personal wounds. Contemporary trauma can reshape one's interaction with historical narratives, creating unexpected emotional resonance between past and present experiences. In Claire's case, her role as an educator—a profession already vulnerable to secondary trauma through regular exposure to students' difficulties—heightened her susceptibility to this historical-personal resonance. Such interactions between personal and historical trauma are particularly relevant when considering how trauma extends through professional and educational spaces.

Vicarious trauma is particularly common among professionals who regularly engage with traumatic content. While Claire's emotional response emerged in a museum setting, similar patterns of trauma resonance and reactivation appear frequently among professionals whose work regularly exposes them to others' traumatic experiences. Vicarious trauma commonly occurs among professionals in mental health care and relief workers at disaster sites.[33] People who frequently view graphic images, such as human rights investigators, may experience negative cognitive and behavioral effects because of their indirect exposure to violence.[34] Mental health practitioners with anxiety disorders or personal trauma histories are at increased risk of emotional exhaustion and burnout.[35] For some, trauma history is associated with negative changes in self-perception and worse mental health.[36] Teachers who work with students affected by trauma commonly experience emotional distancing and difficulty feeling academically or emotionally present with their students because of STS.[37] It is recommended that trauma researchers, who regularly listen to interviews of trauma victims, receive psychological support for the vicarious traumatization they experience.[38]

The case of United Hatzalah, an Israeli volunteer-based emergency medical service, illustrates both the severity of this issue and potential solutions. With more than 7,000 volunteers responding to approximately 750,000 emergency calls annually, the organization recognized the need to address vicarious trauma among its first responders. My cousin, Rabbi Yehuda Levi, is a volunteer paramedic for United Hatzalah and invited me on a tour of their headquarters to learn more about their psychotrauma unit and how they respond to national tragedies that deeply affect the first responders. Established in 2017 after a terror attack when a truck ran over a group of soldiers on a day tour, the psychotrauma unit consists of 120 therapists who respond to emergency calls alongside medical responders. These therapists treat both the "silent victims"—witnesses to traumatic events—and the first responders themselves. Dr. Sharon Slater, a volunteer for the unit, describes the work of the psychotrauma therapist as "treating the people who treat."[39]

Studies show high rates of suicide ideation and completion among first responders in the United States.[40] Internationally, approximately 10–15 percent of first responders leave the field because of trauma. However, United Hatzalah's psychotrauma unit has proven extremely effective in mitigating trauma and preventing volunteer attrition. After a crowd crush in 2021 that killed forty-five people during a religious pilgrimage to Mount Meron, of the more than 300 first responders treated by the psychotrauma unit, only two United Hatzalah members left the field.[41]

The ripple effects of trauma extend even further into cultural and national dimensions. Trauma manifests in a nation similarly to how it manifests in an individual: through changed memory patterns that lead to "an insatiable craving for security."[42] This craving is directed both outwardly toward other nations as it asserts its national identity and inwardly among its citizens and soldiers, demanding resilience and strength from its people. Israel's approach to Holocaust education exemplifies this national dimension of trauma. The memory of the Holocaust is ingrained in the very fabric of Israeli education and culture, with streets, synagogues, and neighborhoods named for Holocaust victims and fighters. (See Figure 2.1)

In 1985, Holocaust education became mandatory in all Israeli high schools, and organized education trips to Poland became popular shortly after.[43] Israeli students and members of the Israeli Defense Forces (IDF) visit Yad Vashem, and each year, on Holocaust Remembrance Day, a siren sounds to remember the victims. All those who hear the siren are expected to stop their activities and remain still for its duration. The limited literature about secondary trauma in Holocaust education was found mainly in Israeli studies related to Holocaust Remembrance Day. The siren serves as a "metonymic representation of the Holocaust, symbolizing trauma and, in turn, evoking other traumas," with students experiencing secondary trauma while participating in memorial ceremonies.[44] As trauma therapist Atara Weinstein poignantly observed when meeting with me just a few months after the October 7th terror attack by Hamas, "when the sirens went off, I wasn't surprised. It's almost like I was expecting it to happen at some point, waiting for a Holocaust to happen again."

The complex relationship between trauma and memory extends beyond national remembrance into more intimate spaces of personal testimony and witness. Understanding how trauma affects memory processing helps explain both the challenges and importance of survivor testimony in educational settings.

Trauma has become associated with distinct memory dynamics and occurs when an event is not fully processed at the time of occurrence. This means that survivor testimonies "do not so much retrieve experiences from memory but enable even the person who lived through the traumatic event to experience it for the first time."[45] The listeners play an important part in this experience because the act of witnessing or hearing a narrated past is what creates the testimony itself, making the listener a witness to the trauma.[46]

This witnessing dynamic creates particular challenges in educational settings, where students may experience what researchers call "trauma envy"—the propensity to seek to appropriate a piece of the suffering for themselves.[47] This phenomenon invites the listener to confront tragedy as a first-person victim rather than learning about it second-hand. Such vicarious trauma "invites members of a society to confront, rather than conceal, catastrophes,

Figure 2.1 Members of the Israel Defense Forces tour Yad Vashem. Photograph by author, June 30, 2024.

and in that way might be useful. On the other hand, it might arouse anxiety and trigger defense against further exposure."[48]

The process of memory work itself presents both challenges and opportunities. While it forces people to confront and engage with troubling pasts, it can also serve a therapeutic function, where it "unsettles empathy" and can liberate individuals from traumatic pasts.[49] For survivors providing testimony, there can be a cathartic component, which is "sometimes seen as a way to liberate oneself from trauma."[50] However, the role of listeners as firsthand witnesses during testimony creates its own complications. Listeners have a responsibility to validate the experience of survivors during these interactions, and the narrated past becomes meaningful only through the current emotional engagement between the listeners and the narrator.[51]

Past and Present: When Historical Trauma Meets Current Experience

To better understand these dynamics in educational contexts, researchers recommend separating vicarious trauma into secondary and tertiary categories. Secondary trauma refers to hearing about traumatic experiences directly from the primary victims of the event, such as testimony given by a Holocaust survivor. Tertiary trauma refers to the experience of "someone exposed to the traumatizing events through the mediation of witnesses' accounts, texts, photographs, and so on."[52] This can occur through reading books, watching films, or visiting exhibits about events like the Holocaust.

While both secondary and tertiary trauma can occur in various settings, "nowhere are the stakes in the mediation of traumatic memory higher than in discussion about Holocaust remembrance."[53] This is particularly evident in the plethora of Holocaust museums and memorials around the world that serve as spaces where students, survivors, dignitaries, and visitors of all backgrounds and cultures willingly engage in difficult history for the sake of remembrance. Unsurprisingly, there are ethical concerns about engaging students in narratives about violence and suffering even with tertiary vicarious trauma.[54] Educators need to be aware of the challenges and dangers of teaching these difficult histories at both formal and informal learning sites, especially when students have traumatic backgrounds themselves. According to researchers, "bringing traumatic knowledge front and center into the classroom presents ethical challenges . . . especially if empathetic understanding is employed as a primary pedagogical strategy."[55]

During my first year of teaching Holocaust studies, I encountered firsthand the profound impact that people's life experiences have on the way they learn about and react to knowledge about the Holocaust. Initially excited when offered a position teaching about the Holocaust to twelfth-grade students, I soon discovered that my extensive academic preparation—the research, knowledge, and formal training about the Holocaust's history and controversies—had not adequately prepared me for the psychological complexities of guiding students through this traumatic historical material.

Most students in my Holocaust studies class were deeply engaged, excited at the opportunity to learn about the Holocaust. Many were grandchildren of survivors and enriched our classes by sharing personal family stories. But Rachel was different. She sat in the back of the room in complete silence throughout the entire year. Despite my attempts to encourage her participation, she consistently rebuffed me and maintained her silence. When I consulted the principal about Rachel's behavior, I was simply told she was a very quiet student and to respect her preference for sitting quietly in class.

The significance of Rachel's silence only became clear to me on the last day of the school year. She handed in a completely blank final exam, with just these words written at the top: "Thank you for teaching me this year. Your class wasn't as bad as I expected. I didn't see any dead bodies."

Stunned, I went to the dean demanding an explanation for Rachel's behavior, certain there was more to understand about the quiet student in the back of the room. The dean finally shared a heartbreaking story: when Rachel was seven, she and her younger sister heard an ice cream truck's music coming down their street. They eagerly got money from their parents and ran to the truck. As the sisters crossed the street, a car speeding past the ice cream truck struck and killed Rachel's younger sister instantly. "The truth is," the dean told me, "we should have informed you earlier. When Rachel was in eighth grade, we took her class to the Holocaust Museum in Washington. She had a very hard time on that trip."

This revelation transformed my understanding of my role as a Holocaust educator. I saw that the responsibility extends far beyond teaching just the history and philosophy of the Holocaust—it demands careful consideration of the psychological and emotional impact this difficult knowledge has on each student. While not every class or museum group includes a deeply traumatized student like Rachel, I've come to recognize that each student's individual history and capacity for processing this information remain largely unknown to us as educators. Every student encounters and processes this challenging material through the unique lens of their own lived experience.

These challenges become particularly acute at historic sites of trauma. In 2019, 2,320,000 people visited Auschwitz and Auschwitz-Birkenau, the site of the former German concentration camp in Poland and the largest Holocaust-related dark tourist site in the world. With 340 guides conducting tours of the camp in 21 languages,[56] the site is both a cemetery and an exhibition space. Rather than highlighting the centuries of Jewish life and culture that were destroyed, most Jewish tour groups to Poland focus mainly on the death camps.[57] Research by Bilewicz and Wojcik highlights potential risks to the psychological well-being of emotionally vulnerable visitors during confrontations with Holocaust history sites, demonstrating that trips to sites of past atrocities can elicit secondary trauma among visitors.[58] (See Figure 2.2)

Many individuals who visit Holocaust memorial sites exhibit signs of discomfort. Reactions usually include silence, questioning, or crying. One incident that stands out in my mind occurred in Łódź when leading a group of young professionals on a heritage trip to Poland and Hungary. Before the Holocaust, Łódź, a city in central Poland, had a population of approximately 250,000 Jews. It was the second-largest Jewish community in Poland after Warsaw. As we arrived in Łódź, we immediately headed to Radogoszcz (Radegast in German), the train station from which nearly the entire population of the city was deported to Chelmno, Auschwitz, or other concentration camps. I stood back to observe as our group entered the Holocaust-era cattle car that was used to deport Jews from the ghetto. Most of the group filed silently into the car where they began to sing songs known to have been sung by Jewish prisoners as they were deported to the death camps. But then, as one woman reached the large sliding door, she broke down. She appeared to be having a panic attack and was gasping for breath. Together with other staff members, I went to respond and see how I could help. Although she was well enough to continue with the tour later in the day, no matter what we said or asked, she never shared why she had such a visceral reaction in that exact space. I've always wondered if there was something specific that triggered that reaction.

At the same time, I've also heard many trip attendees recognize and express how their psychological and somatic responses at Holocaust history sites relate to places that they are visiting and the knowledge they are learning. For example, people often share with me how hungry they feel during such trips and question the relationship between their hunger and the stories of starvation told at the sites. It is not uncommon for returning students and adults to say to me, "I don't know why I was so hungry and ate so much while I was in Poland. We were sitting on a bus most of the day—it makes no sense!" As someone recently shared, "Why did I feel the urgency to eat three protein bars and a soda after we made a short stop at a mass grave? Could it have been in response to where we went?"

Figure 2.2 Radegast Station in Łódź, Poland. Photograph by author, July 22, 2014.

Beyond the immediate risk of secondary trauma, this issue is further complicated by the idea that encounters with traumatic history require a "dialogical exchange with the past"—specifically, cognitive self-awareness of one's history or identity and how it relates to the historical subject matter.[59] Rather than "declaring an amorphous 'we are all humans' approach, intercultural memory work depends on the willingness and ability of participants to clarify their agency (or 'subject position') vis-à-vis the historical trauma that defines contentious social relations."[60]

This complex intersection of personal history, trauma, and site management manifested dramatically during a visit to the Auschwitz concentration camp complex with a group of educators. Though it was my second visit to Auschwitz, the scene remained jarringly mundane: a parking lot full of tour buses, thousands of visitors of all different nationalities, and signs to watch for pickpockets. As our Polish tour guide delivered standard instructions about what parts of the camp we would be seeing, how to maintain decorum in the space, and where photography is forbidden, the tension between personal trauma and institutional protocol suddenly erupted when one member of our group became belligerent. "How dare you tell me where I can and cannot take pictures," he shouted. "My grandparents were murdered in Auschwitz, and I can do whatever I want and take whatever pictures I want in this place.

I'm not going to allow anybody to tell me, or my family members, what to do here anymore."

The tour guide responded by explaining the reasoning for the no-photography policy: out of respect for the victims, at specific places throughout the camp where hair or other human remains are on exhibit, pictures and videos are prohibited. "How would you like every tourist here taking home pictures of your grandmother's hair for their photo albums?" the guide asked the teacher, gesturing to the crowds of people walking through Auschwitz.

While the teacher calmed down enough to allow the guide to continue the tour, his visible agitation persisted throughout the day. This incident powerfully illustrated how, regardless of the logic behind the policy and the professionalism of the guide, the teacher's family history defined his experience at the site—a stark example of how personal trauma history shapes one's "subject position" in relation to these spaces of memory.

While individual responses to trauma sites create one set of challenges, Holocaust museums face their own institutional struggle with this tension. The evolution of these spaces reflects the changing understanding of trauma and memory. When the original museum at Yad Vashem in Israel opened in 1957, it was criticized for the lack of connection between exhibit developers and the education department, leaving exhibit conceptualization and design based solely on historical perspectives. This disconnect prompted concern among researchers, who noted that "given the symbolic importance and centrality of these settings in the education of the public, the lack of knowledge about the effects of these museums is remarkable."[61]

In response to such critiques, more contemporary Holocaust museums aim to focus on both cognitive and emotional visitor responses, though this balance can be precarious. They often emphasize the emotional elements of the narrative while focusing on promoting empathetic identification among visitors.[62] This shift has been so dramatic that some Holocaust museums now have a primary goal of evoking emotional responses among visitors at the expense of intellectual engagement. One researcher has even suggested that curators at the Museum of Tolerance in Los Angeles had physical spaces designed in a way that "prevented opportunities to engage intellectually" and instead "sought to appeal to an emotional response."[63]

This privileging of emotional impact over intellectual engagement is powerfully illustrated in the museum's famous "Prejudiced" and "Unprejudiced"

Figure 2.3 *Prejudiced/Unprejudiced* exhibit, Museum of Tolerance. Photo credit: Josh McNair, CaliforniaThroughMyLens.com.

doors. Positioned next to each other, these doors are designed to give the appearance of offering visitors the choice to move through the exhibition by identifying as someone who is prejudiced (red door) or unprejudiced (green door). However, the green door is locked, forcing visitors to confront the idea that everyone is inherently prejudiced. (See Figure 2.3)

The powerful impact of this design became clear to me when visiting as a teenager as part of a camp program. Most of our group assumed our own goodwill and gravitated toward the green door. However, the camp leader headed straight for the red door and loudly pronounced, "You are all denial. I'm honest with myself and know that I am prejudiced." While I don't recall any of the details of the exhibits about the Holocaust, the Warsaw Ghetto, or the concentration camps, the doors stand out in my memory of that day, demonstrating how emotional provocations can overshadow historical content in these spaces.

Teaching in Parallel Times: Holocaust Education amid Contemporary Antisemitism

One day I walked into school and the principal asked if she could speak with me. "I've had a number of students in my office recently saying that something in Holocaust studies class was very frightening. Something about a film. Can you share with me what they might be talking about?" I had to stop and think. It was only November, and we had barely scratched the surface of the curriculum that I expected to cover that year. I had just finished units on the inter-war period and Hitler's rise to power, units that do not usually evoke intense emotional responses in the way that classes about ghettos and death camps do. "The only film that I showed recently was *A Night at the Garden*," I told her. "The film has some vivid imagery of a pro-Nazi rally, but I've never received such a response about the film before." (See Figure 2.4)

A Night At the Garden consists of six minutes of archival footage from a 1939 pro-Nazi rally held in Madison Square Garden. The "Pro American Rally" was an event organized by the German American Bund and its leader Fritz Kuhn. The footage shows 20,000 people packed into a rally in the heart of New York City, with American flags draped across the stage, raising their hands in a Heil Hitler salute. In previous years, the rather bizarre scene elicited incredulous reactions that the event actually occurred on the eve of the Second World War.

During the program, as Kuhn is speaking about the evils of the "Jewish controlled press"[64] and governments, a young man named Isadore Greenbaum jumps up on stage to disrupt the rally. He is quickly apprehended and dragged off the stage with his pants pulled off in the process. Not shown in the film is the fact that Greenbaum was arrested and fined $25 for disorderly conduct. According to a New York Times article at the time, the judge asked Greenbaum, "Don't you realize that innocent people might have been killed?" Greenbaum replied, "Do you realize that plenty of Jewish people might be killed with their persecution up there?"[65]

This short film is a valuable teaching tool that sparks critical thinking about the American response to the Nazi rise to power, the banality of evil, and the courage to resist. But I realized that wasn't what bothered my students that day. It was November 2024, and anti-Israel protests had erupted on college campuses over the last few weeks. The media was flooded with images of large antisemitic rallies protesting Jews and Zionism. Vandalism and antisemitic activities had occurred in their communities and to people they knew. They were being advised to hide their Jewish identity in malls and other public places that they had always assumed to be safe. This year, a film showing an anti-Jewish rally at Madison Square Garden took on new significance in light

Figure 2.4 Screenshot taken from *A Night at the Garden*, directed by Marshall Curry © First Look Media 2017.

of current events. My students were drawing real-life connections between historical footage and their own current lived experiences.

This incident unexpectedly highlighted the tension between emotional impact and intellectual engagement, reflecting a broader challenge in Holocaust education. While emotional connections can make historical events feel immediate and relevant, they also risk oversimplifying complex historical realities or inadvertently triggering trauma responses in vulnerable visitors. Moreover, as demonstrated by both Claire's experience at the museum and Rachel's response in the classroom, we cannot predict how personal trauma histories might intersect with Holocaust education—even seemingly unrelated personal experiences can resonate powerfully with historical narratives.

Museums and educators thus face a delicate balancing act. On one side, they must fulfill their mission of Holocaust remembrance and education, ensuring that historical knowledge is transmitted accurately and meaningfully to new generations. On the other, they must recognize and account for the varied trauma histories their visitors bring to these spaces. The issue is even more complex for museum docents compared to classroom teachers. The former do not have a long-term relationship with the visitor or the ability to follow-up with them in the next class. The challenge isn't simply about choosing between emotional or intellectual approaches, but rather about developing frameworks that can accommodate both while remaining sensitive to the psychological vulnerabilities of different audiences.

These dynamics between trauma and historical empathy took on new urgency when I began examining how we teach about the Holocaust in classrooms and museums. While educators in other historical subjects aim to cultivate a "historical consciousness"—helping students understand events in their original context—Holocaust education faces a fundamentally different challenge. The goal isn't simply to teach what happened "then and not now," but to make sure the memory endures in the present. As we'll explore in the next chapter, this tension between historical distance and present-day resonance creates unique pedagogical challenges, especially for students carrying their own traumatic histories. How do we balance the imperative to remember with the need to protect vulnerable learners, and what happens when the educational goal of generating empathy collides with a student's lived experience of trauma?

Notes

1 American Psychological Association, "Trauma," *APA*, January 23, 2022, https://www.apa.org/topics/trauma.

2 Björn Krondorfer, "Unsettling Empathy: Intercultural Dialogue in the Aftermath of Historical and Cultural Trauma," in *Breaking Intergenerational Cycles of Repetition: A Global Dialogue on Historical Trauma and Memory*, ed. Pumla Gobodo-Madikizela, 1st ed. (Berlin: Barbara Budrich, 2016), 91, https://doi.org/10.2307/j.ctvdf03jc.11.

3 H. James Garrett, "Difficult Knowledge: Encounters with Social Trauma in Pedagogy," *Counterpoints* 506 (2017): 17–48, http://www.jstor.org/stable/45136321.

4 B. A. van der Kolk, *The Body Keeps the Score: Brain, Mind, and Body in the Healing of Trauma* (New York: Viking, 2014).

5 Caruth, as cited in Kate Lawless, "Memory, Trauma, and the Matter of Historical Violence: The Controversial Case of Four Photographs from Auschwitz," *American Imago* 71, no. 4 (2014): 399, https://www.jstor.org/stable/26305100.

6 van der Kolk, *The Body Keeps the Score*; Kredlow, Alexandra M., Richard J. Fenster, Erika S. Laurent, Ewgeni Jakubovski, David A. Pisner, Matthew J. Friedman, Ann M. Rasmusson, Danielle S. Bassett, and Kerry J. Ressler, "Prefrontal Cortex, Amygdala, and Threat Processing: Implications for PTSD,"

Neuropsychopharmacology 47 (2022): 247–59, https://doi.org/10.1038/s41386-021-01155-7.

7 Lawless, "Memory, Trauma, and the Matter of Historical Violence"; American Psychological Association, "Trauma."

8 Anna Menyhért, "Digital Trauma Processing in Social Media Groups: Transgenerational Holocaust Trauma on Facebook," *The Hungarian Historical Review* 6, no. 2 (2017): 355–76, http://www.jstor.org/stable/26374322.

9 Henry Greenspan, Sara R. Horowitz, Éva Kovács, Berel Lang, Dori Laub, Kenneth Waltzer, and Annette Wieviorka, "Engaging Survivors: Assessing 'Testimony' and 'Trauma' as Foundational Concepts," *Dapim: Studies on the Holocaust* 28, no. 3 (2014): 215, https://doi.org/10.1080/23256249.2014.951909.

10 van der Kolk, *The Body Keeps the Score.*

11 Menyhért, "Digital Trauma Processing."

12 Francesca Laguardia, Venezia Michalsen, and Holly Rider-Milkovich, "Trigger Warnings: From Panic to Data," *Journal of Legal Education* 66, no. 4 (2017): 882–903, https://www.jstor.org/stable/26453524; US Department of Veterans Affairs, "Understanding PTSD," *National Center for PTSD*, https://www.ptsd.va.gov (February 1, 2022).

13 Young, as cited in Amit Pinchevski, *Transmitted Wounds: Media and the Mediation of Trauma* (Oxford: Oxford University Press, 2019), 18.

14 Laguardia et al., "Trigger Warnings."

15 Krondorfer, "Unsettling Empathy," 91.

16 Rachel Yehuda and Amy Lehrner, "Intergenerational Transmission of Trauma Effects: Putative Role of Epigenetic Mechanisms," *World Psychiatry* 17 (2018): 243–57.

17 Brian Cavanaugh, "Trauma-Informed Classrooms and Schools," *Beyond Behavior* 25, no. 2 (2016): 41–6, http://www.jstor.org/stable/26381827.

18 Missouri's Early Care & Education Connections, "Trauma-Informed Care | Early Connections," *Earlyconnections.mo.gov*, 2022, https://earlyconnections.mo.gov/professionals/trauma-informed-care.

19 Amanda D. Rumsey and Amy Milsom, "Supporting School Engagement and High School Completion Through Trauma-Informed School Counseling," *Professional School Counseling* 22, no. 1 (2018): 1–10, https://www.jstor.org/stable/26784475.

20 Centers for Disease Control and Prevention, "About the CDC-Kaiser ACE Study," *CDC.gov*, April 6, 2021, https://www.cdc.gov/violenceprevention/aces/about.html.

21 Child and Adolescent Health Measurement Initiative (CAHMI), "2016 National Survey of Children's Health: Child and Family Health Measures and Subgroups," *Data Resource Center for Child and Adolescent Health*, accessed January 15, 2022, www.childhealthdata.org.

22 Vanessa Sacks and David Murphey, "The Prevalence of Adverse Childhood Experiences, Nationally, by State, and by Race or Ethnicity," *Child Trends*, last modified February 12, 2018, www.childtrends.org/publications/prevalence-adverse-childhood-experiencesnationally-state-race-ethnicity.

23 Beverly Ray and Martha Hocutt, "Learning From and Teaching About Disaster: The Case of the April 2011 Tornado Outbreak," *American Secondary Education* 44, no. 2 (2016): 66–84, http://www.jstor.org/stable/45147975.

24 National Child Traumatic Stress Network, "Trauma Informed Care," *NCTSN*, https://www.nctsn.org (January 13, 2022).

25 Sheryl H. Kataoka, Pamela Vona, Alejandra Acuña, Lisa Jaycox, Pia Escudero, Claudia Rojas, Erica Ramirez, Audra Langley, and Bradley D. Stein, "Applying a Trauma Informed School Systems Approach: Examples from School Community-Academic Partnerships," *Ethnicity & Disease* 28 (2018): 417–26, https://www.jstor.org/stable/48667763; Katie A. McLaughlin and Margaret A. Sheridan, "Beyond Cumulative Risk: A Dimensional Approach to Childhood Adversity," *Current Directions in Psychological Science* 25, no. 4 (2016): 239–45, http://www.jstor.org/stable/44318964.

26 Rumsey and Milsom, "Supporting School Engagement."

27 McLaughlin and Sheridan, "Beyond Cumulative Risk."

28 Ray and Hocutt, "Learning From and Teaching About Disaster."

29 Mark R. Evces, "What is Vicarious Trauma?" in *Vicarious Trauma and Disaster Mental Health: Understanding Risks and Promoting Resilience*, ed. Gertie Quitangon and Marc R. Evces (New York: Routledge, 2015), 9–23, https://doi.org/10.4324/9781315761343.

30 Grant J., Devilly, Renee Wright, and Tracey Varker, "Vicarious Trauma, Secondary Traumatic Stress or Simply Burnout? Effect of Trauma Therapy on Mental Health Professionals," *Australian & New Zealand Journal of Psychiatry* 43 (2009): 373–85; Sharon Rae Jenkins and Stephanie Baird, "Secondary Traumatic Stress and Vicarious Trauma: A Validational Study," *Journal of Traumatic Stress: Official Publication of The International Society for Traumatic Stress Studies* 15 (2002): 423–32.

31 Charles R. Figley and Marné Ludick, "Secondary Traumatization and Compassion Fatigue," *Handbook of Trauma Psychology* 1, no. 1 (2017): 573–93, https://doi.org/10.1037/0000019-029.

32 Laub, as cited in Colin Davis, *Traces of War: Interpreting Ethics and Trauma in Twentieth-Century French Writing* (Liverpool: Liverpool University Press, 2018), 12, https://doi.org/10.2307/j.ctt1ps33bb.

33 Tiffany Leung, Fred Schmidt, and Christopher Mushquash, "A Personal History of Trauma and Experience of Secondary Traumatic Stress, Vicarious Trauma, and Burnout in Mental Health Workers: A Systematic Literature Review," *Psychological Trauma: Theory, Research, Practice, and Policy* 15, no. Suppl 2 (2023), https://doi.org/10.1037/tra0001277; Orit Nuttman-Shwartz, "Shared Resilience in a Traumatic Reality: A New Concept for Trauma Workers Exposed Personally and Professionally to Collective Disaster," *Trauma, Violence, & Abuse* 16, no. 4 (2015): 466–75, https://www.jstor.org/stable/26638374.

34 Elise Baker, Eric Stover, Rohini Haar, Andrea Lampros, and Alexa Koenig, "Safer Viewing: A Study of Secondary Trauma Mitigation Techniques in Open Source Investigations," *Health and Human Rights* 22, no. 1 (2020): 293–304, https://www.hhrjournal.org/2020/05/safer-viewing-a-study-of-secondary-trauma-mitigation-techniques-in-open-source-investigations/.

35 M. Alex Wagaman, Jennifer M. Geiger, Clara Shockley, and Elizabeth A. Segal, "The Role of Empathy in Burnout, Compassion Satisfaction, and Secondary Traumatic Stress among Social Workers," *Social Work* 60, no. 3 (2015): 201–9, http://www.jstor.org/stable/24881483.

36 Leung et al., "A Personal History of Trauma."

37 Beth A. Rankin, "Secondary Traumatic Stress: One Teacher's Experience," *The Phi Delta Kappan* 102, no. 4 (2020): 58–9, https://www.jstor.org/stable/26977217.

38 Amelia van der Merwe and Xanthe Hunt, "Secondary Trauma Among Trauma Researchers: Lessons from the Field," *Psychological Trauma: Theory, Research, Practice, and Policy* 11, no. 1 (2019): 10–18, https://doi.org/10.1037/tra0000414.

39 United Hatzalah, "Psychotrauma Trailblazers | Masters of Emergency," *YouTube*, September 24, 2024, https://www.youtube.com/watch?v=Ip7AixA3TBw&list=PLY8odRz2guQxayKUnnqKKjfBZIj4SXqRw&index=9.

40 "Study Examines Higher Suicide Rates among First Responders," *U.S. Fire Administration*, June 16, 2023, https://www.usfa.fema.gov/blog/study-examines-higher-suicide-rates-among-first-responders/.

41 Personal communication with Sharon Slater, June 30, 2024.

42 Irit Keynan, "The Memory of the Holocaust and Israel's Attitude Toward War Trauma, 1948–1973: The Collective vs. the Individual," *Israel Studies* 23, no. 2 (2018): 99, https://doi.org/10.2979/israelstudies.23.2.05.

43 Dalia Ofer, "We Israelis Remember But How?: The Memory of the Holocaust and the Israeli Experience," *Israel Studies* 18, no. 2 (2013): 70–85, https://doi.org/10.2979/israelstudies.18.2.70.

44 Lilach Naishtat Bornstein and Eyal Naveh, "From Empathy to Critical Reflection: The Use of Testimonies in the Training of Holocaust Educators," *Journal of International Social Studies* 8, no. 1 (2017): 14, https://eric.ed.gov/?id=EJ1173482.

45 Caruth, as cited in Silke Arnold-de Simine, "The 'Moving' Image: Empathy and Projection in the International Slavery Museum, Liverpool," *Journal of Educational Media, Memory & Society* 4, no. 2 (2012): 33, http://www.jstor.org/stable/43049390.

46 Arnold-de Simine, "The 'Moving' Image."

47 Davis, *Traces of War*, 27.

48 E. Ann Kaplan, *Trauma Culture: The Politics of Terror and Loss in Media and Literature* (New Brunswick, NJ: Rutgers University Press, 2005), 87.

49 Krondorfer, "Unsettling Empathy."

50 Wierviorka as cited in Greenspan et al., "Engaging Survivors," 219.

51 Arnold-de Simine, "The 'Moving' Image."

52 Mara Miller, "Terrible Knowledge and Tertiary Trauma Part I: Japanese Nuclear Trauma and Resistance to the Atomic Bomb in the Classroom," *The Clearing House* 86, no. 5 (2013): 159, http://www.jstor.org/stable/43999342.

53 Pinchevski, *Transmitted Wounds*, 10.

54 Michalinos Zembylas, "'Pedagogy of Discomfort' and Its Ethical Implications: The Tensions of Ethical Violence in Social Justice Education," *Ethics and Education* 10, no. 2 (2015): 163–74, https://doi.org/10.1080/17449642.2015.1039274.

55 Liora Gubkin, "From Empathetic Understanding to Engaged Witnessing: Encountering Trauma in the Holocaust Classroom," *Teaching Theology and Religion* 18, no. 2 (2015): 108, https://doi.org/10.1111/teth.12273.

56 Auschwitz-Birkenau Memorial and Museum, "2 Million 320 Thousand Visitors at the Auschwitz Memorial in 2019," Auschwitz-Birkenau Memorial and Museum, https://www.auschwitz.org/en/museum/news/2-million-320-thousand-visitors-at-the-auschwitz-memorial-in-2019,1400.html (January 20, 2022).

57 Jonathan Webber, "Jewish Tourism to Poland: The Opportunities for New Museum Narratives to Recontextualize Jewish Histories," in *New Directions in the History of the Jews in the Polish Lands*, ed. Antony Polonsky, Hanna Węgrzynek, and Andrzej Żbikowski, (Boston: Academic Studies Press, 2018), 139–49, https://doi.org/10.2307/j.ctv7xbrh4.21.

58 Michał Bilewicz and Adrian Dominik Wojcik, "Visiting Auschwitz: Evidence of Secondary Traumatization among High School Students," *American Journal of Orthopsychiatry* 88, no. 3 (2018): 328–34, https://doi.org/10.1037/ort0000302.

59 LaCapra, as cited in Krondorfer, "Unsettling Empathy," 98.

60 Krondorfer, "Unsettling Empathy," 98.

61 Leonard Bickman and Karl M. Hamner, "An Evaluation of the Yad Vashem Holocaust Museum," *Evaluation Review* 22, no. 4 (1998): 436, https://doi.org/10.1177/0193841x9802200401.

62 Brenda Trofanenko, "Affective Emotions: The Pedagogical Challenges of Knowing War," *Review of Education, Pedagogy, and Cultural Studies* 36, no. 1 (2014): 22–39, https://doi.org/10.1080/10714413.2014.866820.

63 Witcomb, as cited in Trofanenko, "Affective Emotions," 26.

64 "A Night at the Garden," *A Night at the Garden*, 2017, https://anightatthegarden.com.

65 Paul Sorene, "A Night at the Garden: Incredible Footage of the American Nazi Rally in New York—February 20, 1939," *Flashbak*, October 19, 2017, https://flashbak.com/night-garden-incredible-footage-american-nazi-rally-new-york-february-20-1939-388675/.

3 Teaching in Tension

Holocaust Pedagogy and Memory Education

While Chapter 2 explored how trauma shapes our ability to engage with difficult histories, the question remains: How do we teach about historical trauma in a way that acknowledges these psychological complexities? The challenge for educators is to find approaches that honor both the imperative to remember and the need to protect vulnerable learners. This tension plays out daily in Holocaust education, where teachers must navigate between historical accuracy, emotional engagement, and psychological safety.

This pedagogical balancing act came into sharp focus for me during a visit to a Holocaust memorial site that has long been on my bucket list: Whitwell Middle School. Located in a small rural town in southeastern Tennessee, Whitwell, despite having no Jewish population, has become home to one of the most famous Holocaust memorial sites in the United States.

The project began in 1998 when students raised a question in an after-school Holocaust studies class that focused on "the importance of respecting different cultures while understanding the effects of intolerance."[1] As they learned about the Jews who were murdered during the Holocaust, they struggled to comprehend the enormity of the number six million. The students decided to collect six million paper clips—symbols worn by Norwegians protesting German occupation during the Second World War—and soon discovered just how vast six million truly is.

The project's completion required several years, the dedication of a middle school principal, and international media coverage, but the students ultimately reached their goal and created the Children's Holocaust Memorial outside the school. The memorial now houses the paper clips inside a German Holocaust-era rail car. Inside their school library, students developed a Holocaust exhibit featuring an archive of received letters (including both supportive messages and hate mail), a Torah scroll from Lithuania, and Holocaust artifacts donated by survivors and American soldiers. Today, thousands of visitors from around the world travel to Whitwell to see the memorial, where current middle school students serve as tour guides.

I visited on a beautiful fall day during the holiday of Sukkot and met Taylor McDaniel Kilgore, who oversees the Holocaust memorial. Taylor, originally a student in one of the classes that collected paper clips, now teaches Holocaust studies at the school. She shared memories of counting paper clips by hand and sorting them into bags for the memorial display. These experiences, along with witnessing the rail car's arrival in town, influenced her decision to pursue a master's degree in Holocaust and Genocide studies. Her dedication to the project, more than two decades later, deeply moved me.

Taylor's childhood participation in the paper clips project profoundly shaped her life and career choices. The visceral approach she and her fellow students took raised persistent questions: How did creating the memorial affect the other original students? What impact does serving as a tour guide have on current students? How are children affected when they learn about and discuss the Holocaust? What is it like for students to pass a Holocaust-era rail car each day on their way to class? I wondered how different students respond when encountering both the powerful memorial and a room filled with Holocaust-era artifacts. (See Figure 3.1)

Forging Connection: Historical Empathy and Holocaust Education

The teaching of the Holocaust stands apart from how history is typically taught. The latter aims to cultivate a "historical consciousness," fostering an outlook regarding "the historicity of events"—that they took place "then and not now" and occurred under different circumstances than what presently exists.[2] This approach is in part to help students avoid anachronism—interpreting past events through a modern lens and projecting current values onto historical figures. Anachronistic thinking can lead to flawed analyses and misunderstandings of the past. As a result, the goal of most history teaching today is to inculcate a "historical mindset"—to understand past events and people within their own context rather than judging them by today's standards.

Figure 3.1 The Children's Memorial and Holocaust-era rail car (containing the paper clips) pictured outside the entrance of Whitwell Middle School. Photograph by author, October 3, 2023.

Why do Holocaust educators want to keep the memory present? Many would argue that the key educational achievement is creating a connection between the learners of today and the past by forging an emotional attachment to the six million Jews who were murdered during the Holocaust.[3] As they see it, the urgent goal of Holocaust education is not to "understand" it from a historical mindset but to generate "historical empathy" for its victims.

Holocaust educators typically approach the task of teaching about the systematic, state-sponsored persecution and murder of six million Jews by Nazi Germany during the Second World War with a different primary goal. Instead of simply attempting to put the Shoah in its historical context, their overarching goal is to make sure its memory endures in the *present*. They want to create a modern-day "collective memory" to keep it alive and "insist on [its] continuing presence" in the world today.[4] This emphasis on teaching and perpetuating memory is a unique aspect of teaching the Holocaust and mirrors the efforts of other Jewish communal leaders who "desire to keep the story alive by the most effective means possible."[5] This approach is evident quite clearly through the many commemorative events and other memory projects offered by museums, synagogues, and Jewish cultural spaces.

Yet empathy is an ambiguous term, with scholars frequently noting that it is often confused with its emotional cousins compassion and sympathy, and clarifying the difference is not just important semantically but also pedagogically.[6] While sympathy is trying to "walk in the shoes of another" and feel what they may have felt, historical empathy is the more sophisticated skill of "re-enact[ing] the thought of a historical agent in one's mind."[7] Historical empathy is connected with avoiding anachronism in that it hinges on "the ability to view the world as it was seen by the people in the past without imposing today's values on the past."[8] But it challenges students to differentiate between the cognitive act of trying to *understand* past events through logic and reasoning and the *emotional* act of connecting with the motivations of historical figures and emotions experienced in the past.[9]

Researchers have long suggested that sympathy, specifically simply feeling sorry for Holocaust victims, does not produce real change in the learner. Instead, meaningful learning about the Holocaust requires a deep emotional connection with the victims by empathizing with them.[10] Empathy provides the learner an imaginative entry point into the lives of others because they think about how *they* would have reacted under similar circumstances. Historical empathy is therefore a synthesis of historical contextualization, affective connection to historical figures, and perspective-taking. Used pedagogically, it helps students "contextualize their lived experiences, decisions, or actions" by "understanding how people from the past thought, felt, made decisions, acted, and faced consequences within a specific historical and social context."[11]

The distinction between sympathy and empathy in Holocaust education became starkly clear to me through observing two different groups of students who went through a Holocaust exhibit just weeks apart. Their reactions reinforced the fundamental difference between sympathy and empathy. The first was a group of eighth-grade Hasidic students, many of whom came from homes and communities where they had been exposed to family stories of survival during the Holocaust and had lived among Holocaust survivors. The second group was tenth graders from a Sephardic school, a community less affected by the Holocaust, and one that I assumed would need more encouragement to create deep and meaningful connections to Holocaust history. (See Figure 3.2)

My expectations could not have been more off the mark. The Hasidic students arrived at the museum in high spirits, chatting with their friends.

Figure 3.2 Oodles candy packet. Photograph by author, July 5, 2017.

Most of the students nodded knowingly throughout the tour but did not offer any indication that they truly connected with the exhibit. After they left, I found a packet of Oodles candy left behind by one of the students. It had been distributed by student organizers of the trip, and the message printed on a sticker on the candy (complete with barbed wire motifs) read: "Remember the OODLES of yidden [Jews] that perished in the Holocaust!" This reduction of the memory of millions of people who were murdered less than a century ago to a bag of candy underscored the emotional disconnect they had displayed during their visit. While they clearly sympathized with the stories they heard, they hadn't empathized with the victims of the Holocaust.

In contrast, when the group of students from the Sephardic school arrived at the museum, they filed quietly into the space, studying photographs on the wall and listening intently to the tour. Many students asked deep, probing questions about the artifacts on exhibit. When they reached a display with a yellow star that Jews were forced to wear during the Holocaust, one student turned and announced, "Look, even though our families didn't go through the Holocaust, it is *our* collective Jewish story being told here. We are all connected and must feel the pain that they went through." These students didn't merely have pity for the victims of the Holocaust; they emotionally identified with their pain, embodying what historical empathy looks like.

These contrasting responses reveal a fundamental tension in Holocaust education. While empathy can create powerful learning experiences, as demonstrated by the Sephardic students who felt personally connected to this history, it also raises complex psychological questions. Did the age of the visiting students affect their ability to empathize with the pain of others? Had the worldviews of the Hasidic students, who were raised in homes with Holocaust survivors or their descendants, shifted as a result of vicarious trauma? Most importantly, how can Holocaust educators foster emotional connections to historical trauma without either trivializing the past or overwhelming students in the present? The challenge becomes particularly acute when we consider what we learned in Chapter 2 about how trauma operates—how it can be triggered unexpectedly, how it shapes our ability to process new information, and how it influences our capacity to engage with difficult material. When educators ask students to empathize with Holocaust victims, they are not just asking them to understand historical facts; they are inviting them to forge emotional connections with profound human suffering. This invitation carries both possibilities and risks, especially for students carrying their own trauma histories.

Bringing the Past to Life: Museum Narratives and Personal Stories

For Holocaust educators, a crucial challenge lies in bridging the gap between the lives of students today and individuals and events in the past. Because many people visit historical museums to have an emotional experience, museums often intentionally curate their exhibits to encourage such responses. The term "a pedagogy of feeling" was coined to explain the techniques used in contemporary exhibitions to "stage affective encounters between viewer and viewed through their use of a range of devices to promote sensorial experiences that encourage introspective reflection on the part of visitors."[12] The narratives are told through a combination of textual techniques and spatial arrangements; when combined, these pedagogical tools have a unique power to elicit empathetic emotional responses from viewers.[13] Encounters with historical objects also encourage historical empathy by challenging students' preexisting ideas and conceptions of difficult or traumatic events.[14] This approach's effectiveness was seen in a study of eight exhibitions about the British enslavement of African peoples, where researchers found that museum visitors actively and passively used emotion to frame their responses about engagement during their visit.[15]

Research shows that students find it easier to comprehend historical events when they discover reminders of their own lives. A useful pedagogical technique to create such connections is to focus on the stories of individuals, rather than the larger history of an event, allowing students to create associations with an individual's narrative. These stories offer an easy point of access within the larger historical narrative. As one researcher explained, "It is via the individual that empathy comes to the fore,"[16] resulting in students viewing historical figures as real human beings with real-life experiences. Historical empathy thus "leads to a richer understanding than perspective-taking alone."[17]

One excellent example of telling a larger history through an individual's story is the *Stitching History From the Holocaust*[18] exhibit created by the Jewish Museum Milwaukee. This traveling exhibit brings to life sketches of dress designs by Hedwig Strnad that were found in the attic of a Milwaukee home. The sketches were sent in 1939 by Paul Strnad, Hedwig's husband, to a cousin in America in a desperate attempt to secure visas that would allow them to escape Nazi persecution in Czechoslovakia. Paul hoped that Hedwig's talent in fashion design would help them receive the coveted visas: "By separate mail I have sent you some dress designs my wife made. I hope the dress manufacturer you mentioned in your letter will like them."[19] Tragically, the Strnads never received the paperwork to allow them to leave Europe, and Hedwig was subsequently murdered at Auschwitz. (See Figures 3.3 and 3.4)

When the dress designs were discovered and given to the museum in 1993, curators decided to bring them to life by manufacturing the designs, creating

Figure 3.3 *Stitching History From the Holocaust* exhibit, Museum of Jewish Heritage. Photographs by author, July 7, 2016.

eight dresses from Hedwig's sketches. The beautiful creations were sewn by the costume department of the Milwaukee Repertory Theater, with attention to every detail, from the hats and buttons to the shoes and even the linings of the dresses. The dresses illuminate the hopes and dreams of one individual, giving viewers a glimpse into the incredible loss of life and talent that Hedwig possessed, while simultaneously creating an opportunity for envisioning the millions of others who were unable to find an escape route out of German-occupied Europe.

Beyond Memory: The Universalization of Holocaust Education

In many ways, the widespread presence of Holocaust studies has led to a universalization of the information in museums, classrooms, and other learning spaces, resulting in a shift in the way that the Holocaust is taught in both formal and informal settings. This shift is "characterized by the fact that major urban centers in the United States, and many outside it as well, constructed vastly expensive, and vastly expansive, museums to make

Figure 3.4 *Stitching History From the Holocaust* exhibit, Museum of Jewish Heritage. Photographs by author, July 7, 2016.

permanent its moral lessons."[20] This approach was perfectly summarized in a statement by Rabbi Marvin Hier, one of the driving forces behind the creation of the Simon Wiesenthal Center's Museum of Tolerance in Los Angeles, shortly after the museum's opening. He said: "We didn't want to present the Holocaust unaccompanied by other lessons. . . . This museum says: 'You may not be Jewish and you may not be a Nazi, but you have a stake in this.' Because hatred was not banished (with) Adolf Hitler—it outlived him."[21]

As a result, historical empathy is often promoted by Holocaust museums and educational centers as their central pedagogical approach. For example, IWitness, the online educational program created by the USC Shoah Foundation that grants access to interviews and testimonies, notes in its mission statement that "through powerful, thought-provoking engagement with first-person stories from survivors and witnesses of genocide, students worldwide develop empathy, understanding, and respect."[22] In a similar fashion, Facing History and Ourselves, an organization that uses historical lessons to combat hatred and bigotry, provides many lesson plans to teach empathy through storytelling and other techniques. Their mini-course *Teaching Holocaust and Human Behavior*, for example, describes its goal as allowing "students to wrestle with profound moral questions raised by this history while fostering their skills in ethical and moral reasoning, critical analysis, empathy, and civic engagement."[23]

A common activity in Holocaust studies classrooms and workshops, particularly for young learners, is to present students with a real dilemma faced by an individual during the Holocaust (such as a rescuer who chose to hide Jews at the risk of his own life and the lives of his family members) and ask them "what would you have done under these circumstances?" These lessons aim to (1) encourage student engagement through empathy with Holocaust victims and rescuers and (2) foster character development and moral courage among students so that they, too, will make courageous choices during similar contemporary challenges.

The pedagogical approach of promoting empathy for victims of the Holocaust is utilized not only in classrooms and museums but also during trips to Holocaust memorial sites. These trips to memorial sites in Eastern Europe have become increasingly popular in recent years, providing an alternative to films and first-person survivor testimonies. Such testimonies are increasingly difficult to arrange as survivors age, become less mobile, and limit their in-person speaking engagements.[24]

One prominent example is the March of the Living, which since 1988 has brought more than 260,000 individuals to participate in an annual 3-kilometer memorial walk on Yom HaShoah from Auschwitz to Birkenau.[25] The initial educational trips to these sites were focused on the past, with educators and students dedicating themselves to preparing and studying for the experience. However, over time, the educational goal shifted toward eliciting emotional reactions among attendees and influencing their political, moral, and spiritual lives, rather than solely enriching knowledge and understanding of the Holocaust.[26]

An email that I recently received from a former student underscored this trend. After scheduling a tour to visit Holocaust memorial sites in Poland, the student wrote to me and shared the following:

> *The trip by the organization Nesivos is run by two of our Rebbeim from seminary, Rabbi Heller and Rabbi Kahane. I obviously want to be as well prepared for the trip as I can so I asked Rabbi Kahane what he recommends. He suggested I read Pearl Benish's book, which I was happy to say I did already, and also suggested I read Divine Madness by Rabbi Avigdor Miller. But most*

of all he suggested that as the trip is mostly Hashkafa based [around our feelings], the more history I know, the better understanding I'll have.[27]

Balancing Act: The Complexities of Teaching Empathy

While historical empathy is an important component of Holocaust education, this approach presents several challenges. Specifically, the strategies used to promote empathy and compassion among museum visitors have been critiqued because of the risks involved in humanizing such atrocities.[28] Critics argue that "visitors might be tempted to attribute these crimes simply to individual cruelty and blend out the political decisions, economic interests, or ideological motifs that created and still create the framework in which individual cruelty can thrive."[29]

Museum educators can take specific steps to address these concerns. One example can be found at Yad Vashem, where biographical information about Nazi leaders is placed in flat black bound boxes placed unobtrusively on the walls of the exhibit. This curatorial design, which originally addressed the moral dilemma of how and where to exhibit personal information about Nazi perpetrators—so as not to perpetuate their memory or encourage visitors to deface their images[30]—also mitigates the effects of humanizing their atrocities. Visitors must make an extra effort to open the boxes to read documentation about these specific perpetrators; it is not information that they just stumble across.

Another challenge is the issue of "presentism,"[31] the act of judging the past through the lens of the present. This tendency is natural and common among students, but it prevents them from contextualizing history and recognizing differences in norms between the past and the present. To combat this kind of reaction, I find it useful to introduce Lawrence Langer's concept of "choiceless choices":

> *After we peel the veneer of respectable behavior, cooperation, hope, mutual support, and inner determination from the surface of the survivor ordeal, we find beneath a raw and quivering anatomy of human existence resembling no society ever encountered before . . . These victims, who were plunged into a crisis of what might call "choiceless choice," where critical decisions did not*

reflect options between life and death, but between one form of "abnormal" response and another, both imposed by a situation that was in no way of the victim's own choosing.[32]

Langer offers stark examples of individuals who were forced to choose between seemingly impossible options: using their last drops of water for drinking or washing themselves; lying down to be shot or continuing to march to the gas chambers; or the grotesque "choice" of drowning a newborn infant in a pan of water to save the mother's life, versus risking discovery by the Nazis, who would surely kill both mother and newborn child. By explaining that during the Holocaust "words like dignity and choice had temporarily lost their traditional meaning because Nazi brutality had eliminated the human supports that usually sustain them,"[33] educators can help students achieve a delicate balance: creating connections to individual victims of the Holocaust without passing judgment on their actions or imposing present-day social norms on these impossible decisions.

Language also plays an important role in the teaching of the Holocaust, but poses challenges when it comes to historical empathy. In both classrooms and museums, curators and educators choose their language carefully to impart certain messages or narratives for their audiences. On a macro level, language is important in the building of large memorials or museums in different communities. When considering narratives for new Holocaust exhibitions, curators and developers carefully craft their messages for their intended audiences and specific locations. Memorial sites in Europe, museums in cities with large Jewish populations, and exhibitions created for rural populations in Midwestern states all talk about the same events while highlighting different points and using different storytelling techniques. For example, to evoke emotion in a population that frequently utilizes branding of cattle, the Holocaust museum in Texas highlights the practice of tattooing prisoners with identification numbers at Auschwitz-Birkenau.[34] This careful consideration of language also occurs on micro levels as well. In classrooms, teachers generally self-select what they consider age-appropriate language or texts for their students. Many gravitate toward positive terms as they grapple with teaching difficult subjects in the hopes of generating historical empathy. Using the term "survivor" instead of "victim" and "martyrdom" instead of "murder" creates positive messaging about the horrors of the Holocaust. Yet this technique has been criticized because it conceals and diminishes the intensity of the event for the learner who puts up "verbal fences between the atrocities of the camps and ghettos and what we are mentally willing or able to face."[35] This problem is even more acute in Hebrew when the phrase "Korban" (a sacrifice) is used to describe those who were murdered during the Holocaust.

Oftentimes, careful language selection about the memory of the Holocaust evokes a redemptive narrative. At the USHMM, emphasis is placed on American soldiers and liberators as rescuers during the Nazi genocide. This specific memory of the Holocaust is intended to sensitize people to other genocides worldwide and influence their moral judgment and actions.[36] The museum's origins reflect this intent: the initial commission formed by President Carter in 1978 recommended a living memorial for the American people that would serve as a "moral compass to keep America on course"[37] and prevent such atrocities from happening again. The proposed project included a "committee on conscience" that would alert the public and policymakers about (real or potential) genocide occurring anywhere in the world.[38] What followed were decades of American culture in which there was a propensity toward framing Holocaust testimonies with redemptive narratives that include heroics and forgiveness. The former director of the USHMM, Walter Reich characterized this bias as the "Schindlerization" of the Holocaust and critiqued the trend because it compromised the memory of the most horrific and gruesome aspects of the Holocaust in favor of generating historical empathy.[39]

A final common criticism is simply the lack of a systematic approach to the teaching of historical empathy. In the case of historical empathy and Holocaust education, teachers have the latitude to employ the resources that they believe will accomplish their goal. The decision to implement a course of Holocaust studies in a school to generate historical empathy must be accompanied by careful consideration about the way it is taught, its content and context, and the impact it will ultimately have on students. However, there is no consistency in the methods employed by educators who try to promote empathy in their Holocaust studies classes.[40]

Part of the issue is that the increase in thematic teaching and using the Holocaust for moral lessons about humanity has been accomplished not within the context of dedicated Holocaust studies courses but throughout various subjects and disciplines. A 2022 study conducted by New York State showed that while every public school in the state teaches about the Holocaust, only 19 percent offer a separate course on the subject. The study found that 99 percent teach about the Holocaust in social studies classes and 88 percent teach about it in English Language Arts classes.[41]

Drawing moral lessons and implications from the Holocaust and difficult texts is not unusual for these courses. This approach is frequently found in English literacy courses because English teachers strive to do more than just improve student reading, writing, and speaking; they also aspire to "improve [their] students as moral persons—what nineteenth-century literacy educators referred to, in religious terms, as the 'cure of souls' and in more secular terms, as 'personal cultivation.'"[42]

However, some researchers have suggested that empathy is a natural occurrence and not one that can be forced upon student learners—even (as we will discuss in the next chapter) by viewing survivor testimony[43]—and thus question whether all students will benefit emotionally from an intensive course about the Holocaust.[44] These scholars are concerned that using Holocaust education to inculcate positive values and attitudes among students may not always achieve its intended goals. Indeed, since scholars have expressed skepticism that these didactic goals can be achieved through the study of Jane Austen's novels, there are increasing calls for educators to temper their enthusiasm for creating moral compasses through the study of Holocaust literature and texts.[45]

When Empathy Meets Trauma: The Identity Card Dilemma

The deeper problems with using historical empathy become particularly apparent when viewed through the trauma-informed lens developed in Chapter 2. Just as museums must balance commemoration with emotional safety (as explored in Chapter 1), educators employing historical empathy face their own version of this challenge. One of the most well-known efforts to promote historical empathy illustrates this tension: the Identity Card project at the USHMM. Each visitor entering the permanent exhibition of the museum receives one of 600 identity cards of individuals who lived in Europe during the Holocaust. The cards, initially designed as US Passports, include a biographical sketch along with information about an individual's life/death during the Holocaust. This "phantom companion"[46] is meant to accompany the visitor throughout the exhibit and "help visitors to personalize the historical events of the time."[47] The cards proved so popular that the technology used to scan them throughout the exhibit broke within three months of the opening of the museum. More than thirty years later, paper versions continue to be given to visitors, and all the cards are available online for use in off-site Holocaust education programs.

Despite their popularity, the cards' initial design received criticism for historical inauthenticity and for suggesting falsified passports, which were mostly inaccessible during the Holocaust.[48] More fundamentally, scholars have increasingly argued that it is misguided to believe one can come to understand the experience of another by paralleling or comparing experiences in their lives. They view such actions as egotistical and lacking the multiple complexities required for genuine historical empathy.[49] In the case of the USHMM, researchers have noted that the victims' experiences are often described in the present tense, and that there is a "presumptuous intention" that "the identity's card's strategy of bonding can, indeed, write across chasms of the unknowable to arrive at some point of provisional fusion."[50]

In fact, there are good reasons to question whether the experience of living vicariously through others (in this instance, "others" being Holocaust victims and survivors) should remain a core component of Holocaust education.[51] Consider one common example seen in classrooms around the world: teachers assigning an essay where students must begin with the sentence "I am in a ghetto and . . ." or "I am in a concentration camp and . . ." These assignments encourage students to create fictional characters, describe imaginary tortures, and visualize the death of friends or family members. Students often finish the assignment believing that they have empathized and fully understood the situation of an individual in a ghetto or concentration camp when, in reality, this is likely not the case. Because one can never fully put themselves in "another's shoes" and because workshop activities lack the many real-life and sensory components of the original scenario, students will never be able to fully understand the choices made by individuals during the Holocaust. These activities will always fall short of recreating the circumstances under which a student can understand the many complex issues involved in the original scenario.

In some cases, educators on a quest to fulfill their agendas misappropriate historical realities to such an extent that they leave students vulnerable to encountering difficult or frightening information through oversimplification or in emotionally unsafe spaces. In fact, a study of more than 2,100 teachers conducted by the Institute of Education at the University of London found that more teachers taught about the Holocaust with the goal of teaching about the dangers of stereotyping, racism, and genocide than with historical aims such as deepening their students' knowledge of the Second World War history or the actions and reactions of people during a major historical event.[52]

However, ignoring the actual history of the Holocaust or using a methodology that focuses on specific agenda items chosen by the educator is increasingly viewed as a dangerous practice. Not only does this approach fall short of a factually accurate history lesson, but it also "leaves young people open to manipulation and coercion from those who use the past to push their own social, political or other agendas."[53] Scholars have even gone so far as to argue that the emotions produced by historical empathy at museums can inhibit a student's ability to contextualize the time and place that a historical event occurred. This limitation reduces their ability to think critically.[54]

When Empathy Meets Trauma: The Psychological Risks of Holocaust Education

Despite the prevalence of promoting empathy in Holocaust education, little research has been done on its effects and efficacy. Research about historical empathy at large primarily focuses on empathy within student engagement rather than how educators conceptualize and foster it.[55] And there has been almost no focus whatsoever on the outcomes of such an approach on students, leaving open the question not just of whether students can historically empathize with Holocaust victims, but what the effects are of even attempting to do so.

One possible result is that students may find that the chasm between their lives and the lives of the victims is too wide. If students cannot make the connections that the teacher is attempting to create, they may disassociate from the information and not engage with the materials, numbing them to the information being taught and "paralyzing" them in the process.[56] Research suggests that contemporary studies indicating a lack of Holocaust knowledge and awareness among young Americans have led to a proliferation of newly created Holocaust studies courses and materials, which in turn have overwhelmed and turned away young people.[57]

But perhaps most concerning of all—and the focus of this book—is the potential effect that this approach could have on students with trauma histories. These students may strongly identify with the materials and stories presented to them, and such strong associations and identification with Holocaust materials could provoke a range of responses, from physical or emotional distress to trivializing the significance of their own life experiences in the face of the more horrific and traumatic ones experienced by the Jewish people during the Holocaust.

It is not difficult to see how trauma becomes intertwined with historical empathy. Research shows that while students of Holocaust history and literature sometimes shift their views during the learning process, their prior identities continue to affect the way they hear and construct narratives.[58] They bring preexisting commitments that shape the way they absorb knowledge, and different students, hearing or reading the same narrative, will leave with different takeaways because of their backgrounds. This has led to debate among educators: some argue that students of Jewish descent, and especially those who are descendants of Holocaust survivors, should acknowledge personal connections when studying the Holocaust, while avoiding "the mantra of victimhood." Others contend that the Holocaust must be taught to them in a way that is not especially frightening because of their family backgrounds.[59]

Since visiting the Children's Holocaust Memorial in Whitwell, Tennessee, I've developed a new perspective on the everyday paper clip. Each time I see one, it reminds me of the millions who were murdered during the Holocaust and the remarkable task undertaken by middle school students to remember them. I have often expressed my hope for every student to participate in such an immersive learning experience, through which they learn about antisemitism, intolerance, and the dangers of leaving hate unchecked. However, I've received diverse reactions when sharing stories or pictures of the memorial, ranging from "They represented my grandfather with a paper clip?" and "Couldn't they have chosen a more meaningful way to commemorate actual lives lived?" to "Why put the paper clips—symbols of Jewish victims—back into a cattle car, the very method used to transport them to the deaths?" While having students connect to real people with authentic stories and experiences remains the primary method of Holocaust education today, the next chapter examines the most direct means of achieving that connection: experiencing the words and physical presence of a Holocaust survivor. Yet as that chapter will uncover, if the potential for historical empathy to trigger traumatic reactions exists even in a museum setting or during a historical site visit, the potential is even greater when encountering an actual Holocaust survivor.

Notes

1 "History of the Paperclip Project," *Whitwell Middle School*, https://www.whitwellmiddleschool.org/childrensholocaustmemorial/history (June 20, 2024).

2 Peter Novick, *The Holocaust in American Life* (New York: Houghton Mifflin, 2000), 4.

3 Shoshana Felman, "Education and Crisis, or the Vicissitudes of Teaching," *American Imago* 48, no. 1 (1991): 13–73, http://www.jstor.org/stable/26304031; Alan S. Marcus et al., "Holocaust Education in Transition from Live to Virtual Survivor Testimony: Pedagogical and Ethical Dilemmas," *Holocaust Studies* 28, no. 3 (2021): 279–301, https://doi.org/10.1080/17504902.2021.1979176.

4 Novick, *The Holocaust*, 4.

5 Leon Weissberg and Caren Schnur Neile, "Never Forget: March of the Living and Place-Based Holocaust Storytelling," *Storytelling, Self, Society* 11, no. 1 (2015): 126, https://doi.org/10.13110/storselfsoci.11.1.0121.

6 Aleida Assmann and Ines Detmers, "Introduction," in *Empathy and its Limits*, ed. Aleida Assmann and Ines Detmers (New York: Palgrave Macmillan, 2016), 1–17, https://doi.org/10.1057/9781137552372_1; Geerte M. Savenije and Pieter de Bruijn, "Historical Empathy in a Museum: Uniting Contextualisation and Emotional Engagement," *International Journal of Heritage Studies* 23, no. 9 (2017): 832–45, https://doi.org/10.1080/13527258.2017.1339108.

7 Kaya Yilmaz, "Historical Empathy and Its Implications for Classroom Practices in Schools," *The History Teacher* 40, no. 3 (2007): 331, http://www.jstor.org/stable/30036827.

8 Yilmaz, "Historical Empathy," 331.

9 Marcus et al., "Holocaust Education in Transition."

10 Rachel N. Baum, "'What I Have Learned to Feel': The Pedagogical Emotions of Holocaust Education," *College Literature* 23, no. 3 (1996): 44–57, http://www.jstor.org/stable/25112273.

11 Jason Endacott and Sarah Brooks, "An Updated Theoretical and Practical Model for Promoting Historical Empathy," *Social Studies Research and Practice* 8, no. 1 (2013): 41, https://doi.org/10.1108/ssrp-01-2013-b0003.

12 Andrea Witcomb, "Toward a Pedagogy of Feeling: Understanding How Museums Create a Space for Cross-cultural Encounters," in *The International Handbooks of Museum Studies*, 1st ed., ed. Andrea Witcomb and Kylie Message (Chichester: Wiley & Sons, 2015), 322.

13 Savenije and Pieter de Bruijn, "Historical Empathy."

14 Alan S. Marcus, Jeremy D. Stoddard, and Walter W. Woodward, *Teaching History with Museums: Strategies for K–12 Social Studies*, 2nd ed. (New York: Routledge, 2017), https://doi.org/10.4324/9781315194806.

15 Laurajane Smith, "Affect and Registers of Engagement: Navigating Emotional Responses to Dissonant Heritages," in *Representing Enslavement and Abolition in Museums: Ambiguous Engagements*, 1st ed., ed. Laurajane Smith, Geoff Cubitt, Kalliopi Fouseki, and Ross Wilson (New York: Routledge, 2011), 264–307, https://doi.org/10.4324/9780203808252.

16 Alan Rosen, ed., *Literature of the Holocaust* (Cambridge: Cambridge University Press, 2013), 2.

17 Endacott and Brooks, "An Updated Theoretical and Practical Model," 43.

18 "Stitching History From the Holocaust," Jewish Museum Milwaukee, https://jewishmuseummilwaukee.org/exhibit/stitching-history-from-the-holocaust/ (June 24, 2024).

19 "Stitching History From the Holocaust—Rental Information," Jewish Museum Milwaukee, https://jewishmuseummilwaukee.org/wp-content/uploads/2022/01/Stitching-History-From-the-Holocaust-Rental-Information.pdf (June 24, 2024).

20 Michael Gray, *Contemporary Debates in Holocaust Education* (Basingstoke, England: Palgrave Pivot, 2014), 60.

21 Amy Wallace, "A High-Tech Walk Down the Corridors of Bigotry: Museum: L.A.'s Wiesenthal Center Adopts Provocative Strategy to Document and Teach Lessons from Holocaust," *The Los Angeles Times*, January 30, 1993, https://www.latimes.com/archives/la-xpm-1993-01-30-mn-1892-story.html.

22 "Teaching with Testimony," *IWitness*, https://iwitness.usc.edu/home (February 19, 2022).

23 "Mini Course: Teaching Holocaust and Human Behaviour (Canada)," *Facing History and Ourselves*, https://www.facinghistory.org/learning-events/mini-course-teaching-holocaust-human-behaviour-canada (January 2, 2024).

24 Weissberg and Neile, "Never Forget."

25 International March of the Living, "About Page," *International March of the Living*, https://www.motl.org/about/ (January 25, 2022).

26 Nili Keren, "Teaching the Holocaust in Israel," *Internationale Schulbuchforschung* 22, no. 1 (2000): 95–108, http://www.jstor.org/stable/43057186; Weissberg and Neile, "Never Forget."

27 Personal communication, February 13, 2024.

28 Silke Arnold-de Simine, "The 'Moving' Image: Empathy and Projection in the International Slavery Museum, Liverpool," *Journal of Educational Media, Memory & Society* 4, no. 2 (2012): 23–40, http://www.jstor.org/stable/43049390.

29 Arnold-de-Simine, "The 'Moving' Image," 37.

30 Dorit Harel, *Facts and Feelings: Dilemmas in Designing the Yad Vashem Holocaust History Museum* (Tel Aviv: Yad Vashem Publications, 2010), 54.

31 Wineburg, as cited in Carolyn C. Casale, Adrainne Thomas, and Temika M. Simmons, "Developing Empathetic Learners," *Journal of Thought* 52, no. 3–4 (2018): 3–18, https://www.jstor.org/stable/90026734.

32 Lawrence L. Langer, "The Dilemma of Choice in the Death Camps," *Centerpoint: A Journal of Interdisciplinary Studies* 4, no. 1 (1980): 53–9.

33 Langer, "The Dilemma of Choice."

34 Personal communication from Michael Berenbaum, 2016.

35 Langer, "The Dilemma of Choice," 6.

36 S. K. Pinnock, "Atrocity and Ambiguity: Recent Developments in Christian Holocaust Responses," *Journal of the American Academy of Religion* 75, no. 3 (2007): 499–523, https://doi.org/10.1093/jaarel/lfm038.

37 Amy Sodaro, "The United States Holocaust Memorial Museum: The Creation of a 'Living Memorial,'" in *Exhibiting Atrocity: Memorial Museums and the Politics of Past Violence*, ed. Amy Sodaro (New Brunswick, NJ: Rutgers University Press, 2018), 31, https://doi.org/10.2307/j.ctt1v2xskk.6.

38 Elie Wiesel, "Report to the President," President's Commission on the Holocaust, September 27, 1979, https://www.ushmm.org/m/pdfs/20050707-presidents-commission-holocaust.pdf.

39 Walter Reich, "Unwelcome Narratives: Listening to Suppressed Themes in American Holocaust Testimonies," *Poetics Today* 27, no. 2 (2006): 463–72, https://doi.org/10.1215/03335372-2005-014; Noah Shenker, "Through the Lens of the Shoah: The Holocaust as a Paradigm for Documenting Genocide Testimonies," *History & Memory* 28, no. 1 (2016): 141–75, https://doi.org/10.2979/histmemo.28.1.141.

40 Endacott and Brooks, "An Updated Theoretical and Practical Model."

41 "Holocaust Instruction in NYS Public School Districts," *New York State Education Department*, https://www.nysed.gov/sites/default/files/programs/curriculum-instruction/holocaust-instruction-report-final-2022.pdf (July 2, 2024).42 Mary M. Juzwik, "The Ethics of Teaching Disturbing Pasts: Reader Response, Historical Contextualization, and Rhetorical (Con)Textualization of Holocaust Texts in English," *English Education* 45, no. 3 (2013): 303, http://www.jstor.org/stable/23364870.

43 Susanne Hillman, "Grim Expectations: Video Testimony in the College Classroom," *The History Teacher* 48, no. 2 (2015): 295–320, http://www.jstor.org/stable/43264406.

44 Eleni Karayianni, "Look before You Leap: Teaching about the Holocaust in Primary Schools," in *Holocaust Education: Contemporary Challenges and Controversies*, ed. Stuart Foster, Andy Pearce, and Alice Pettigrew (London: UCL Press, 2020), 95–113, https://doi.org/10.2307/j.ctv15d7zpf.11.

45 Juzwik, "The Ethics of Teaching."

46 Jonathan Rosen, "The Misguided Holocaust Museum," *New York Times*, April 18, 1993, https://www.nytimes.com/1993/04/18/opinion/the-misguided-holocaust-museum.html.

47 "Identity Card Project," United States Holocaust Memorial Museum, accessed July 16, 2024, https://www.ushmm.org/m/pdfs/20121024-idcards.pdf.

48 Weisel, "Report to the President"; Andrea Liss, *Trespassing Through Shadows: Memory, Photography, and the Holocaust* (Minneapolis: University of Minnesota Press, 1998).

49 Like Sophie Oliver, "The AESTH-Ethics of Empathy: Bakhtin and the Return to Self as Ethical Act," in *Empathy and its Limits*, ed. Aleida Assmann and Ines Detmers (New York: Palgrave Macmillan, 2016), 166–86, https://doi.org/10.1057/9781137552372_10.

50 Liss, *Trespassing Through Shadows*, 22–3.

51 Baum, "'What I Have Learned'"; Michalinos Zembylas, Loizos Loukaides, and Petroula Antoniou, "Teachers' Understandings of Empathy in Teaching about the Holocaust in Cyprus: The Emotional Risks of Identification and the Disruptive Potential of 'Empathic Unsettlement,'" *Teaching and Teacher Education* 89 (2020): 103007, https://doi.org/10.1016/j.tate.2019.103007.

52 Paul Salmons, "Universal Meaning or Historical Understanding? The Holocaust in History and History in the Curriculum," *Teaching History* 141 (2010): 57–63, http://www.jstor.org/stable/43260782.

53 Salmons, "Universal Meaning," 58.

54 Savenije and Pieter de Bruijn, "Historical Empathy."

55 Zembylas et al., "Teachers' Understandings of Empathy."

56 Liora Gubkin, "From Empathetic Understanding to Engaged Witnessing: Encountering Trauma in the Holocaust Classroom," *Teaching Theology and Religion* 18, no. 2 (2015): 103–20, https://doi.org/10.1111/teth.12273.

57 Vera Schwarcz, "To Catch the Echo: Rethinking Acts of Witnessing to the Shoah," *History and Theory* 54, no. 3 (2015): 429–40, https://doi.org/10.1111/hith.10770.

58 Karen Spector, "God on the Gallows: Reading the Holocaust through Narratives of Redemption," *Research in the Teaching of English* 42, no. 1 (2007): 7–55, http://www.jstor.org/stable/40171747.

59 David H. Lindquist, "Complicating Issues in Holocaust Education," *The Journal of Social Studies Research* 34, no. 1 (2010): 86, https://eric.ed.gov/?id=EJ887319.

4 Bearing Witness

Survivor Voices and Testimony

I remember the first time I met a Holocaust survivor from Auschwitz. I was eighteen years old, participating in a gap-year program, when a friend invited me to spend Shabbat at the home of an acquaintance in Ashdod, about 20 miles south of Tel Aviv. So many details of that Shabbat remain seared in my memory. We arrived Friday morning and spent a glorious day at the magnificent beach, soaking in the sun and jumping the waves. I thought this would be the beginning of a luxurious, picturesque weekend. In the late afternoon, we hailed a taxi to our hosts' home, but when we arrived at the given address, I was certain the driver had made a mistake. He had dropped us in front of an old, decrepit apartment building where several barefoot children played in the front courtyard. I turned to my friend, but she assured me we were at the correct address. With no elevator in sight, we lugged our suitcases up three flights of stairs to meet the family. Their apartment was small and bare; to accommodate us, we were given mattresses and slept in the apartment's *miklat* (bomb shelter), which also served as their storage room.

The family was quite poor, and there wasn't much food to share. At the Friday night dinner, one small chicken was divided into more than a dozen servings to feed everyone at the table. As an American from the land of plenty, this was like no other meal I had ever experienced. Yet despite the apparent scarcity around us, the home exuded joy, and when the mother lit candles on Friday night, peace and serenity seemed to descend upon its inhabitants. The faces of the small children, scrubbed clean for Shabbat, glowed in the candlelight around their dinner table. The father, dressed in traditional Hasidic garb, sat at the head of the table. He led the family in singing *zemirot* (Jewish hymns), while at the other end, an elderly grandmother with a simple headwrap sat in an oversized armchair. She was clearly the matriarch of the family, and I watched as everyone accorded her tremendous respect, deferring to her on almost every decision.

The following afternoon we sat and talked with the elderly grandmother. She spoke mostly in Yiddish, and while it was hard for me to understand everything she said, some communication needs no words. When I mentioned an upcoming trip to concentration camps in Poland and other Eastern European Holocaust sites, she unexpectedly pulled up her left sleeve to reveal a tattoo—a series of blue numbers blurred by her aging skin. The sight took my breath away. Although I had grown up in a community of Holocaust survivors (including my own grandparents), most had originally come from Germany and Western Europe, and none had been interned in the concentration camp that has become synonymous with the Holocaust: Auschwitz. Only prisoners arriving at Auschwitz were branded with these identification numbers.

Her openness in showing us her tattoo surprised me, and I was taken aback by how matter-of-factly she shared her story. Having only heard stories of Auschwitz secondhand, I felt there was something profound in what she was sharing with me. Even her very presence seemed to signal something sacred and inexpressible. I wanted to stand and applaud, to shout at the top of my lungs and cheer her for surviving the evil of Hitler and Mengele, but all I could do was nod and smile at this small woman in a dilapidated beachfront apartment. Perched on the edge of a rickety plastic chair, oblivious to the sweltering heat and buzzing flies around us, my mind racing and my heart thumping, I reacted in a way that would take me years to fully understand.

Though I wish I had caught every detail she shared about being rounded up by Nazis in a small town in Poland, much of it escaped me. I would like to recall the names of her parents and siblings who were murdered that day, but their identities elude me. I cannot recall many details of her wartime experience, but in the small act of lifting her sleeve and showing me her tattoo, this grandmother conveyed more horrific details about her time in Auschwitz than words or books could possibly describe. Although her action was a natural gesture that her family members had no doubt seen countless times, for me it was an extraordinary moment that drowned out everything else in the room.

For years, I have thought about the Ashdod grandmother and her story. Her image flashes through my mind whenever I visit Auschwitz or teach about its history. The sweet ordinariness of her postwar life, juxtaposed with how powerfully her very presence spoke to the most awful moments in history, shocked me at the time. More than raising or answering questions about

Auschwitz, her story ultimately taught me about the unique power of hearing firsthand testimony and meeting a Holocaust survivor in person.

Like visiting Holocaust museums or sites, the experience of hearing firsthand testimony raises important questions for Holocaust educators. My own experience of hearing that grandmother's story serves as a lens through which to explore how other students respond to the testimony of Holocaust survivors. What accounts for the differences in how listeners react to such testimony, and what causes those different reactions? How does the impact differ between recorded and firsthand testimony? Additionally, there is the question of how hearing testimony compares and contrasts with visiting a museum or Holocaust site—ultimately leading us to examine what hearing such testimony reveals about historical empathy and potential vicarious trauma.

The Power of Personal Narrative: Storytelling and Holocaust Education

My grandmother, a Danish Holocaust survivor who fled to Sweden with her entire family, spoke often about her life during the war. She was seventeen years old at the time and would describe the family's daring escape almost as an adventure. "Let me tell you my story," she would say. My grandfather, whose entire family was murdered in Nazi death camps, used to interject: "It's not a story." He rejected the word "story" because it often evokes warm, fairytale-like feelings or imaginative plots, which certainly did not reflect what happened to my grandmother.

However, storytelling is fundamental to Holocaust education and engaging audiences. As one might expect, survivor testimony is frequently used in Holocaust education, and teachers commonly invite survivors to tell their stories to students.[1] But what exactly happens when a survivor speaks and shares their story?

Research indicates that human beings are naturally predisposed to listen to stories, with story listening having been found to have a calming and meditative effect on students. Students report entering a "state of flow, losing sight of themselves, time, and space"[2] because of rituals associated with listening to stories. Moreover, stories are also proven to be an effective medium for conveying content to both children and adult learners.[3] I am often reminded of this when delivering academic or professional lectures; most audience questions afterward concern the stories I have used to support the research I cite.

But storytelling goes beyond merely an immersive and gripping experience. Researchers have defined storytelling as the art of using language to present a narrative in an interactive format. The interaction between speaker and listener(s) allows the audience to become co-creators in the story; through their perceptions and past experiences, they form their own image of the events being narrated.[4]

A key reason educators are drawn to survivor testimony is the oft-stated belief that they must "make something happen, and not just transmit passive knowledge."[5] Survivor testimony serves as a pedagogical tool to accomplish this goal. Teachers find survivor testimony particularly compelling because when students listen to oral histories, an *emotional* connection forms between speaker and listener.[6]

As Chapter 3 explained, Holocaust educators construct exhibits and plan trips to sites to create enduring memories that foster historical empathy for Holocaust victims. Yet no matter how visceral these narratives are—whether through recreated dress designs or trips to Holocaust memorial sites—nothing quite compares to the power of survivors' firsthand testimonies. Their testimony offers unique and personal insights, primarily because they speak "from inside a situation rather than from the outside in an objectifying manner."[7] If museum exhibits and visits to memorials attempt to personalize the Holocaust through narrative to generate historical empathy, no such narrative attempt is necessary when hearing a Holocaust survivor. Their very existence is itself the story.

But as noted above, although survivors are telling their personal narratives, once told the story becomes the "property" of the listener as well. This can result in some interesting outcomes. For example, researchers in Israel have observed that personal identification with Holocaust victims appears to create a deeper commitment to Holocaust memory. But to foster these connections, a "traumatic imperative" has been cultivated to influence students' reception of survivor testimony. One common approach is presenting survivor testimony in a sad and dramatic way so that listeners will personally identify with the victim.[8] In a study of students and their reactions to Holocaust Remembrance Day, some survivors reported being chastised for not expressing the appropriate kind of sadness during memorial events. As one student remarked about hearing testimony, "It doesn't matter how good their life is [now] . . . Holocaust survivors should at least look miserable."

For those who believe that effective Holocaust education relies more on creating emotional connections with present-day learners than on mastering historical details,[9] such a paradigm shift moves the educational focus from detached historical analysis to fostering historical empathy for Holocaust victims. Yet as noted previously, historical empathy demands a cognitive leap—envisioning the world through the eyes of historical figures without the taint of contemporary biases.[10] In the pedagogical realm, narratives steeped in historical empathy act as bridges, providing students with tools to understand the complex interplay of factors that shaped both sweeping historical narratives and individual destinies during the Holocaust.[11] Such historical empathy challenges students to engage with the visceral emotions stirred up by studying the Holocaust and to develop emotional kinship with its Jewish victims.[12]

While studies show that survivors of catastrophic and traumatic events often use linguistically favorable self-presentations, thereby casting doubt on the "historicity" of their oral testimony, their stories remain among the most persuasive "tools" in the Holocaust educators' toolkit.[13] Survivors' voices are authentic and urgent, with some scholars arguing that "in the end, the halting words of those who went through the death camps [are] all we have to counter the ignorance and disbelief spreading around the world."[14] However, educators must carefully create an environment where survivors are viewed not as superheroes or living artifacts but are valued for their personal life stories.[15] One researcher notes that this approach is essential to Holocaust education because "individuals who survived the Shoah were neither the dehumanized caricatures of Nazi ideology, nor are they the epitomes of the current obsession with redemptive survival." They add that "buying into either myth betrays an appalling intellectual laziness."[16] As a result, navigating how to use survivor testimony is neither obvious nor straightforward.

The complexity of survivor testimony became especially clear to me when Faye Skala spoke to a group of my students. Born in Łódź, Poland, she was almost ninety-nine years old when she visited Bais Yaakov Machon Ora in Passaic, New Jersey. Though wheelchair-bound, she possessed a magnetic personality and a commanding presence; the students hung on her every word. She candidly shared real-life stories of her survival in Auschwitz and Bergen-Belsen, including a humorous story of marrying her husband just one week after meeting him at the war's end because he owned a food shop.

However, her description of Mordechai Chaim Rumkowski, the head of the Judenrat (Jewish council) in the Łódź Ghetto, was jarring. Known as the "Elder" or "King" of the ghetto, Rumkowski held responsibility for maintaining order and organizing many aspects of Jewish life, including overseeing food rations, distributing housing, determining who would work in the factories, and ultimately who would be deported to concentration camps. Following his belief that those who worked and were useful to the German war effort would live longer, he chose to cooperate with the Nazis during deportations, selecting children and the elderly first to fill the required quotas.

Rumkowski remains a controversial figure in Jewish history, with some survivors and historians describing his leadership and moral choices as one of the darkest chapters of Holocaust history.[17] They consider him a Nazi collaborator and therefore complicit in the deaths of those sent from the ghetto. While the exact circumstances of his death remain obscured by history, nearly all eyewitness accounts indicate that immediately upon his own arrival at Auschwitz, he was lynched by former Łódź ghetto inhabitants and members of the Auschwitz Sonderkommando (groups of Jewish prisoners whom the Nazis forced to work in the gas chambers and crematoria) in revenge for his actions.[18]

Surprisingly, Faye, who had lived in the Łódź ghetto and seen Rumkowski in person, remembered him fondly. She called him "our boss" and "my king," viewing him as a protective rather than traitorous leader. It proved eye-opening to hear someone, especially a survivor from Łódź, speak so kindly about Rumkowski. It highlighted the need to think critically about the impact of survivor testimony, as survivors' stories can be surprising in terms of whom they bestow historical empathy upon.

Shifting Perspectives: The Eichmann Trial and the Rise of Survivor Testimony

While many museums now offer speaker bureaus featuring Holocaust survivors willing to speak on-site or at other locations, these offerings were not always available. In the postwar years, survivors were viewed as "mostly pitied, poor souls to be indulged on 'special occasions.'"[19] This attitude began to shift in the 1960s for several reasons. A primary catalyst was the trial of Adolf Eichmann, where more than 100 witnesses testified. This event, broadcast on American and European television stations, was "the first case of a trial in the aftermath of war to consider the emotions of victims as central to the practice of justice."[20] Though intended to educate the world about the horrific crimes the Nazis committed against the Jewish people, the trial ultimately challenged previously widely held "distinctions between reason and emotion and between the public and private spheres."[21]

Eichmann's trial stands in stark contrast to both the Nuremberg Trials immediately following the Second World War and the 2000 court case (featured in the movie *Denial*) where David Irving sued Dr. Deborah Lipstadt for publishing a statement identifying him as a Holocaust denier. Unlike Eichmann's trial, these two legal proceedings (held more than fifty years apart) emphasized using documents to establish historical facts. As described by William Zeck, a lawyer who prepared documents for the I.G. Farben trial, "I went to Nuremberg with the purpose of establishing certain law with respect to initiating and waging aggressive war."[22] In contrast, prosecutors at the Eichmann trial sought to convey memories and create an emotional impact when talking about the Holocaust, with researchers describing these efforts movingly:

> *The task of transmission is not only a matter of telling or proving, but also . . . a specific kind of communicative act that impresses on public memory "truth as event and as the shock of an encounter with events." The act of transmission is thus a means of passing on, through the drama of the human testimony, the impact of an unimaginable history.*[23]

Following Eichmann's conviction based on survivor testimony, many Jews throughout the world who had survived the horrors of the Nazi regime began to feel more comfortable sharing their stories with audiences. The Eichmann trial transformed not just survivors' mindsets but also attitudes toward survivors, with researchers noting that "beginning in the 1970s, they were increasingly celebrated as 'heroic witnesses' and exemplars of 'resilience' and 'the human spirit.'"[24]

This was just the opening of the floodgates of survivors sharing their testimony. Further increasing interest in Holocaust survivors and their experiences was a 1978 docudrama called "Holocaust" that was aired over four nights by NBC. "Holocaust" attempted to use one family's story to tell the larger story of the Holocaust. The nine-hour fictional series about the Jewish Weiss family from Berlin was so popular that "One in two Americans watched it, and in New York City, water pressure dropped to dangerously low levels during commercial breaks as viewers went to the bathroom or the kitchen all at the same time." The impact of this series was profound. It coincided with the invention of video recorders that provided tools for people to begin recording survivor testimonies. As Michael Berenbaum writes, "suddenly everyone seemed interested in the Holocaust and most especially, in the survivors."[25]

Following this increased interest in Holocaust history, many communities began establishing local Holocaust museums. The shift in perspective regarding survivors was so profound that in discussions about museum design, survivors were viewed as possessing "a semantic, historical, and moral authority that trumped psychologists, designers, historians, and other experts."[26] At the same time, these new spaces facilitated survivors sharing their stories with larger and more diverse audiences, with survivor testimony becoming foundational for Holocaust education[27] and central to generating historical empathy. As the USC Shoah Foundation states, "Through powerful, thought-provoking engagement with first-person stories from survivors and witnesses of genocide, students worldwide develop empathy, understanding, and respect."[28]

However, these museums have also created a distorting effect on the types of testimony that receive the most attention—those that use historical empathy to evoke a redemptive narrative. The USHMM exemplifies this approach through its opening exhibit's focus on American soldiers as liberators and its presentation of the Holocaust as a moral lesson against future genocides.[29] American Holocaust narratives have followed suit, emphasizing heroics and forgiveness rather than victims and survivors. This approach, which de-emphasizes the most horrific and tragic aspects of the Holocaust in favor of generating historical empathy, has become known as the "Schindlerization" of the Holocaust.[30] (See Figure 4.1)

Figure 4.1 Photograph of the opening exhibit at USHMM. The image shows America's troops discovering the charred remains of prisoners when they liberated the Ohrdruf concentration camp in Central Germany in April 1945. Photograph by author, May 6, 2025.

Creating Connections: How Survivor Testimony Fosters Historical Empathy

Encounters with survivor testimony help students form personal connections with difficult subjects and traumatic events. As with museum-based Holocaust history, students find it easier to comprehend a survivor's story than historical events in the abstract. However, unlike museums and memorial sites that must craft narratives highlighting individual stories, survivor testimony inherently does so. Their narratives provide a natural entry point into the larger historical narrative of the Holocaust, essential for fostering historical empathy. Researchers have noted that everything from the speaker's body language to their emotional expression during storytelling can impact the testimony's reception and help cultivate empathy among listeners.[31]

Personal testimonies often challenge prior knowledge or expectations of history. Consider the testimony of Bella Miller, originally from Boryslaw, Poland, who survived Auschwitz at the age of twelve with her mother. Bella grew up in a large, loving family in Boryslaw, a town in Eastern Poland rich with petroleum resources. Her area first fell under Soviet control during the German-Soviet Nonaggression Pact, but in 1942, when the Germans broke the agreement and invaded the area, Bella and her family went into hiding. Neighbors offered to hide them in a barn in exchange for large sums of money, but when their money ran out, they were promptly turned over to the Ukrainian authorities and soon transported to Auschwitz.

Upon arrival, Bella and her mother were separated from her father and brother, whom they never saw again. After claiming to be fifteen years old, Bella was sent to work with her mother, and together they managed to survive until the war's end. She recalled that shortly after the Soviet Army liberated the camp in January 1945, "I was roaming around Auschwitz and I went into one of the offices . . . they had a lot of blueprints hanging. Believe it or not I picked up one of the blueprints."[32] Bella had discovered a blueprint of the plumbing system at Auschwitz. She folded it, tucked it into her small sack of belongings, and took it to America. The map remains in her personal possession. (See Figure 4.2)

I've watched how Bella's telling of this story about her liberation brings up a host of complex questions for her audiences. They wonder how a twelve-year-old girl managed to just wander into the private offices of the Germans who just days earlier were murdering Jews *en masse*. They are disconcerted to find that the blueprint of a death factory looks remarkably similar to that of any other office building complex. And many are left wondering whether they would have had the courage, temerity, or foresight to take such a valuable, poignant, and disturbing piece of history—and preserve it as a reminder of such terrible events.

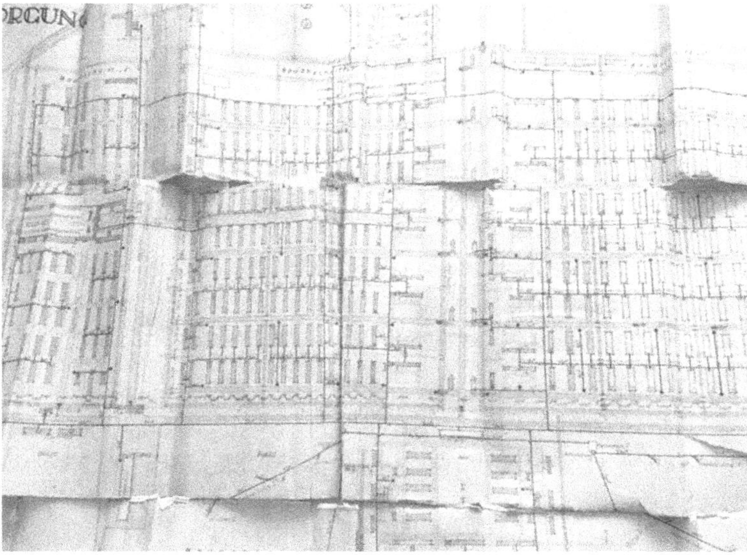

Figure 4.2 Section of the plumbing blueprint of Auschwitz. Courtesy: Bella Miller, May 15, 2019.

Through Children's Eyes: The Appeal and Challenges of Child Survivor Narratives

Today, almost the only remaining survivors still alive are those who were children during the Holocaust. This presents both opportunities and challenges for Holocaust educators as they work to foster historical empathy. Since childhood is a universal experience, mainstream Christian and other non-Jewish audiences can readily identify with Jewish victims through stories told by or about children. Two prominent examples of Holocaust literature with wide appeal are *The Diary of Anne Frank*, written by a teenage girl, and *Night*, a memoir narrated from a child's perspective. For years, I have surveyed my own students about what books they have read or movies they have watched about the Holocaust before they take my class. I am amazed to find that the most-read book is *The Boy in the Striped Pajamas*, a fictional story about a concentration camp commander's young son who dies in the gas chamber alongside Jewish prisoners. Despite lacking historical authenticity and generating controversy for creating sympathy for a Nazi leader's family, the story's young protagonist continues to resonate deeply with readers, making the book a perennial favorite even after its adaptation to film.

Many museums feature exhibits focused on children's experiences, with one notable example being *Remember the Children: Daniel's Story* at the USHMM. Daniel, a composite character, draws from the stories of children who lived in Germany, Auschwitz, and the Łódź Ghetto. Other institutions have developed temporary exhibits about children hidden during the Holocaust. The Museum of Jewish Heritage in Manhattan presented *Life in the Shadows: Hidden Children and the Holocaust* in 2006, while the Illinois Holocaust Museum and Education Center offers *Out of the Chaos: Hidden Children Remember the Holocaust*, a traveling exhibit showcasing "incredible stories of survival, strength, and courageousness in the face of unspeakable horrors."[33]

Because of their broad appeal, many museum professionals will turn to such narratives when designing workshops or short programming, as a simple online search will bring up numerous educational toolkits, books, and other educational materials about hidden children. This approach proved valuable when the Holocaust Museum & Center for Tolerance and Education in Rockland County, New York, needed a temporary exhibition while constructing a larger core exhibit on a local college campus, and chose to focus on hidden children during the Holocaust.

While planning a temporary exhibit about hidden children during the Holocaust at the Amud Aish Memorial Museum in Brooklyn, New York, a curator mentioned how valuable it would be to find a shoe that belonged to a child who hid during the Holocaust. I immediately thought of a shoe I had seen displayed in my good friend's childhood home. Her father, Hans Ettlinger, was born in The Hague and was only two years old when the Germans invaded the Netherlands. His family went into hiding before eventually escaping and emigrating to America. Initially, when I approached the Ettlinger family about loaning the shoe for a six-month exhibition, they declined. They couldn't understand why anyone outside their family would be interested in such a nondescript item and were hesitant to part with it. However, after much persuasion, they agreed. (See Figure 4.3)

The shoe became an immediate hit, emerging as the focal point of the exhibit. News coverage framed it as nothing short of extraordinary: "This is a shoe of life. It represents a child who was able to escape the Nazis."[34] One visitor, ninth-grader Mashi Lax, reflected on how learning about children during the Holocaust changed her perspective: "I just feel like it's important to know about this, because girls my age were going through so much and I

Figure 4.3 Child's shoe belonging to Hans Ettlinger being prepared for exhibit at the Amud Aish Memorial Museum. Photograph by author, September 13, 2016.

feel like now I shouldn't take life for granted."[35] What began as a simple artifact became a symbol for the entire exhibit, surprising the Ettlinger family with its power to connect with diverse audiences.

While the emphasis on child survivors' stories offers a welcoming window into Holocaust experiences, it carries a risk, as narratives from childhood perspectives can minimize rather than underscore the horrors that occurred. As one researcher notes, "However legitimate the end, however well-intentioned the motive, the invocation of young victims easily leads to rhetorical and ideological distortion."[36] This observation points to a fundamental issue: child survivors represent life, not death. The opening panel of *Remember the Children* illustrates this tendency when it states, "This is the story of a boy named Daniel and how he survived the Holocaust."[37] Though Daniel's story serves as an accessible entry point for young museum visitors—helping them relate to children who, like them, went to school, played sports, and had birthday parties—it shifts focus away from the six million Holocaust victims. Some scholars argue that hearing child survivors' personal histories can direct attention away from Nazi perpetrators, their allies, and those who remained silent during the genocide.[38]

I witnessed this dynamic firsthand when Rabbi Jacob Jungreis, a survivor from Derecske, Hungary, spoke to students about his experience aboard the Kasztner train. This rescue mission transported 1,684 Hungarian Jews from Hungary to Switzerland (via Bergen-Belsen) in 1944. Rudolf Kasztner, a Jewish leader in Hungary, negotiated this agreement directly with Adolf Eichmann. The train provided safe passage for many of Kasztner's family members, prominent Hungarian Jews, and approximately forty rabbis and their families, including the Jungreis family. Rabbi Jungreis, who was eleven years old during the escape to Switzerland, praised Kasztner as a *Tzaddik* (righteous person) and stated emphatically (and uncritically) that Kasztner believed, "after the war we have to rebuild the Jewish people. . . . The only ones who will rebuild the nation will be the rabbis." According to Jungreis, "He put on the list mainly rabbis."

However, Jungreis's testimony overlooks the fact that Kasztner's actions sparked "one of the most intense controversies of the Holocaust."[39] Many historians suggest that Kasztner, in pursuing his agreement with Eichmann, remained silent about the gassing of hundreds of thousands of Hungarian Jews at Auschwitz and withheld information that might have encouraged other Jews to hide or escape. Kasztner later faced accusations of Nazi collaboration after providing positive character references for several SS officers, leading a judge to declare that he had "sold his soul to the devil."[40] Though he was assassinated by Israeli veterans in 1957, the verdict against him was partially overturned in 1958. The Supreme Court of Israel concluded that he had tried to secure the release of as many individuals as possible, believing that revealing the Auschwitz atrocities to Jewish deportees would cause more harm than good.[41]

Historians continue to debate Kasztner's role, and many challenge Jungreis's characterization of him as a *Tzaddik*. Critics argue that Jungreis's survival and his childhood perspective of the war years have led him to unintentionally distort the historical record and offer uncritical praise of Kasztner's actions.

Preserving Memory: From Live Testimony to Digital Archive

A recent demographic study indicates that as of 2024, approximately 245,000 Jewish Holocaust survivors remain alive.[42] This number will diminish rapidly in the coming years, and finding Holocaust survivors to provide firsthand testimony has become increasingly difficult. In response, educators in classrooms and museums are developing new ways to bring oral testimonies to their audiences. Two major repositories of survivors' recordings are the Visual History Archive at the USC Shoah Foundation, containing over 55,000 survivor testimonies, and the Fortunoff Video Archive for Holocaust Testimony at Yale University, with more than 4,400 testimonies.[43] These video interviews preserve not only major historical events but also capture individual interpretations by probing "the depths of a person's life and documents for the historical record the normality and abnormality, the ordinary and extraordinary experiences of human circumstance."[44]

The systematic documentation of Holocaust survivors has shaped the genre of video testimony and influenced representations of other cultural traumas, such as the African experience of slavery.[45] The pressing need to record survivors before they die—ensuring their stories will educate future generations about these atrocities—has created an "anxiety of historical transmission."[46] This urgency is driving shifts in Holocaust education platforms, methodologies, and technologies, alongside changes in social and political discourse.

For example, research has shown that television and documentaries created for educational purposes significantly edit interviews and omit valuable raw data. This recognition has prompted the creation of new media archives that enable teachers to compare and analyze original, unedited testimonies with finished products.[47] Many interviews are quite lengthy, including off-camera moments between the interviewer and interviewee. These "unseen moments" offer additional context and reveal different perspectives than those captured in the official interview.[48]

However, live testimony and video testimony create distinctly different experiences. As education shifts toward recorded video testimony, students lose the personal connection of meeting survivors, shaking their hands, or sharing a hug. Research indicates that students become more critical and question the authenticity of testimony when survivors are not present.[49] I have observed students making fun of foreign accents and outdated clothing styles worn by Holocaust survivors in video testimony. Technical issues with older recordings (including grainy footage, poor audio quality, or equipment malfunctions) can create distracting pauses that diminish the power of the spoken word.

The USC Shoah Foundation's New Dimensions in Testimony Project represents the latest effort to preserve survivors' stories using modern technology. The project creates high-definition holographic recordings of virtual Holocaust survivors who can be "interviewed" anywhere, aiming to ensure that "now and far into the future, museumgoers, students, and others can have conversational interactions with these eyewitnesses to history to learn from those who were there."[50] These cinematic representations—described by some as "ghostlike"—allow viewers to "interact" with survivors posthumously. Audience members pose questions to the holograms, which respond with prerecorded answers possessing an "eternal resonance."[51]

Though Dimensions in Testimony began as an on-site museum experience, it is now available fully online. The interactive format engages viewers by allowing them to ask specific questions of interest, rather than watching passive full-length interviews. Yet the occasional technical glitch is revealed in capturing what is lost without a live person delivering testimony. When microphones fail to pick up questions or inquiries that fall outside the program's parameters, responses can be confusing. For instance, when asked, "Did you escape Germany?" the hologram of Edith Maniker, a Kindertransport survivor who fled to England in 1939, gives a lengthy, puzzling answer about never leaving the English orphanage because "I didn't have enough guts to really run away from anywhere." Similarly, when asked, "Did you ever meet a Nazi?" the hologram of Benjamin Ferencz—a Nuremberg Trials prosecutor who indicted twenty-four Einsatzgruppen members—inexplicably responds, "That's a great question, but I don't have an answer." Some scholars have offered more fundamental criticism, describing the project as a form of "mummification,"[52] and comparing it to the cultural commodification of Ancient Egypt in museum settings.

Living Witnesses: The Legacy of Holocaust Survivors

Many decades have passed since I met the Ashdod grandmother and learned about her survival in Auschwitz. In the years since, I have been blessed to meet numerous survivors of Auschwitz like Bella Miller, who continue to influence the way I think and teach about the Holocaust. Each survivor has deepened my understanding of how empathetic connections can link today's learners to historical trauma. Among these remarkable individuals, the story of Reb Yosef Friedenson stands out—one I have come to know intimately and through which I witnessed the impact of his Holocaust experience on others.

Reb Yosef was a survivor—or "graduate" as he preferred to say—of six different ghettos and concentration camps. Born in Łódź, he met and married his wife Gittel Leah Zilberman, in the Warsaw Ghetto. Though separated during the war, they both survived and found each other afterward. Reb Yosef, whose life is chronicled in *Faith Amid the Flames*,[53] was known for his religious devotion and steadfast faith in G-d. He dedicated himself to activism, prolific writing, and frequent lectures about the Holocaust and broader Jewish life. No less a figure than Elie Wiesel praised his efforts: "Reb Yosef Friedenson's memories from the Warsaw ghetto and the death camps are of extraordinary significance."[54] As patriarch of a large family—including one daughter who became my aunt through marriage—this personal connection allowed me to witness not just his influence on the Jewish world but also his impact on family members who regularly heard him speak about the Holocaust. (See Figure 4.4)

When I asked my cousin, Reb Yosef's granddaughter if she had ever visited Auschwitz, her response was immediate and emphatic: "Are you kidding me? When I was growing up every holiday party was a Holocaust party. I have

Figure 4.4 *Tefillin* (phylacteries) wrapped around Friedenson's arm over his tattoo from Auschwitz. Photo credit: Rabbi Yosef C. Golding.

no need to visit Auschwitz—sometimes it feels like I was practically there." Throughout his life, Reb Yosef grappled with his Holocaust trauma while striving to create meaning and purpose in his faith. He accomplished this by telling his life story and proclaiming his Jewish heritage as widely as possible. Each morning during prayer services, observers would watch as Reb Yosef deliberately wrapped his tefillin (phylacteries) around the arm bearing his Auschwitz tattoo—a daily ritual that symbolized his commitment to publicly sharing his story and maintaining his faith. Through these actions, he forged profound empathetic connections with those who regularly interacted with him. Yet his constant storytelling proved heartbreaking for his listeners, especially his direct descendants, who found themselves unable to escape these nightmarish narratives even during celebrations.

Hearing the granddaughter of a Holocaust survivor speak so emphatically about the impact her grandfather's storytelling naturally leads to important questions about Holocaust knowledge and vicarious trauma that merit further exploration. As museums increasingly incorporate survivor testimony through technology, understanding its impact becomes crucial—particularly the differences in response between visitors with no prior Holocaust knowledge, those who have personally met survivors, and those who have experienced their own trauma. The pressing need to record survivors before they die—ensuring their stories will educate future generations about these atrocities—has created an "anxiety of historical transmission" driving shifts in Holocaust education platforms, methodologies, and technologies. As we'll explore in the next chapter, museums face the challenge of not only preserving these testimonies but integrating them into thoughtfully designed spaces that balance historical accuracy with emotional impact. How do curators decide which artifacts most effectively convey traumatic history? What role do photographs and architectural design play in shaping visitor experiences? And perhaps most importantly, how can museums create spaces that honor the victims while protecting the psychological well-being of their visitors?

Notes

1 Andrew Preston, "An Authentic Voice: Perspectives on the Value of Listening to Survivors of Genocide," *Teaching History* 153 (2013): 62–9. http://www.jstor.org/stable/43260632.

2 Patrick Ryan and Donna Schatt, "'Can You Describe the Experience?'," *Storytelling, Self, Society* 10, no. 2 (2014): 145, https://doi.org/10.13110/storselfsoci.10.2.0131.

3 Renate Chancellor and Shari Lee, "Storytelling, Oral History, and Building the Library Community," *Storytelling, Self, Society* 12, no. 1 (2016): 39–54, https://doi.org/10.13110/storselfsoci.12.1.0039.

4 National Storytelling Network, "What is Storytelling?" accessed January 3, 2022, https://storynet.org/what-is-storytelling/.

5 Shoshana Felman, "Education and Crisis, or the Vicissitudes of Teaching," *American Imago* 48, no. 1 (1991): 68, http://www.jstor.org/stable/26304031.

6 Susanne Hillman, "Grim Expectations: Video Testimony in the College Classroom," *The History Teacher* 48, no. 2 (2015): 295–320, http://www.jstor.org/stable/43264406.

7 Silke Arnold-de Simine, "The 'Moving' Image: Empathy and Projection in the International Slavery Museum, Liverpool," *Journal of Educational Media, Memory & Society* 4, no. 2 (2012): 29, http://www.jstor.org/stable/43049390.

8 Lilach Naishtat Bornstein and Eyal Naveh, "From Empathy to Critical Reflection: The Use of Testimonies in the Training of Holocaust Educators," *Journal of International Social Studies* 8, no. 1 (2017): 4–36, https://eric.ed.gov/?id=EJ1173482.

9 Felman, "Education and Crisis"; Alan S. Marcus, Rotem Maor, Ian M. McGregor, Gary Mills, Simone Schweber, Jeremy Stoddard, and David Hicks, "Holocaust Education in Transition from Live to Virtual Survivor Testimony: Pedagogical and Ethical Dilemmas," *Holocaust Studies* 28, no. 3 (2021): 279–301, https://doi.org/10.1080/17504902.2021.1979176.

10 Kaya Yilmaz, "Historical Empathy and Its Implications for Classroom Practices in Schools," *The History Teacher* 40, no. 3 (2007): 331–7, http://www.jstor.org/stable/30036827.

11 Rachel N. Baum, "'What I Have Learned to Feel': The Pedagogical Emotions of Holocaust Education," *College Literature* 23, no. 3 (1996): 44–57, http://www.jstor.org/stable/25112273.

12 Marcus et al., "Holocaust Education in Transition."

13 Akiyo M. Cantrell, "The Management of Survivors' Guilt through the Construction of a Favorable Self in Hiroshima Survivor Narratives," *Discourse Studies* 19, no. 4 (2017): 377–401, https://www.jstor.org/stable/26377712.

14 Vera Schwarcz, "To Catch the Echo: Rethinking Acts of Witnessing to the Shoah," *History and Theory* 54, no. 3 (2015): 429, https://doi.org/10.1111/hith.10770.

15 Hillman, "Grim Expectations."

16 Hillman, "Grim Expectations," 315.

17 Simo Muir, "Rumkowski's Scapegoat? The Case of Łódź Ghetto Functionary Maks Szczęśliwy at a Rabbinic/Honor Court in Helsinki, 1949–1953," *Holocaust and Genocide Studies* 35, no. 2 (2021): 185–210, https://doi.org/10.1093/hgs/dcab035.

18 "Rumkowski in Auschwitz," *Commentary*, December 1979, https://www.commentary.org/articles/reader-letters/rumkowski-in-auschwitz/ (June 20, 2024).

19 Henry Greenspan, "The Humanities of Contingency: Interviewing and Teaching beyond 'Testimony' with Holocaust Survivors," *The Oral History Review* 46, no. 2 (2019): 361, https://doi.org/10.1093/ohr/ohz008.

20 Sonali Chakravarti, "More than Cheap Sentimentality: Victim Testimony at the Nuremberg Trials, the Eichmann Trial, and the South African Truth and Reconciliation Commission," in *Sing the Rage: Listening to Anger after Mass Violence* (Chicago: University of Chicago Press, 2014), https://doi.org/10.7208/chicago/9780226120041.003.0002.

21 Chakravarti, "More than Cheap Sentimentality."

22 William "Bill" Zeck, "William 'Bill' Zeck Describes the Role of the Nuremberg Trials in Establishing a Historical Record," *United States Holocaust Memorial Museum*, https://encyclopedia.ushmm.org/content/en/oral-history/william-bill-zeck-describes-the-role-of-the-nuremberg-trials-in-establishing-a-historical-record (August 22, 2024).

23 Cathy Caruth, "The Body's Testimony: Dramatic Witness in the Eichmann Trial," *Paragraph* 40, no. 3 (2017): 261, https://doi.org/10.3366/para.2017.0234.

24 Greenspan, "The Humanities of Contingency," 361.

25 Michael Berenbaum, "America and the Holocaust: Reflections on Three Quarters of a Century and the Development of Holocaust Consciousness in American Society," *The American Jewish Year Book* 121 (2021): 92, https://www.jstor.org/stable/48771582.

26 Deborah E. Lipstadt, *The Eichmann Trial* (New York: Schocken Books, 2011).

27 Marcus et al., "Holocaust Education in Transition."

28 "Teaching with Testimony," IWitness, https://iwitness.usc.edu/home (February 19, 2022).

29 S. K. Pinnock, "Atrocity and Ambiguity: Recent Developments in Christian Holocaust Responses," *Journal of the American Academy of Religion* 75, no. 3 (2007): 499–523, https://doi.org/10.1093/jaarel/lfm038.

30 Walter Reich, "Unwelcome Narratives: Listening to Suppressed Themes in American Holocaust Testimonies," *Poetics Today* 27, no. 2 (2006): 463–72, https://doi.org/10.1215/03335372-2005-014; Noah Shenker, "Through the Lens of the

Shoah: The Holocaust as a Paradigm for Documenting Genocide Testimonies," *History & Memory* 28, no. 1 (2016): 141–75, https://doi.org/10.2979/histmemo.28.1.141.

31 Brandon J. Haas, "Bearing Witness: Teacher Perspectives on Developing Empathy through Holocaust Survivor Testimony," *The Social Studies* 111, no. 2 (2019): 86–103, doi:10.1080/00377996.2019.1693949.

32 "Bella Miller: Holocaust Survivor and Speaker," *NJ State Bar Foundation*, https://www.youtube.com/watch?v=7ybZNSycC3Q (August 7, 2024).

33 "Out of Chaos: Hidden Children Remember the Holocaust," Illinois Holocaust Museum & Education Center, https://www.ilholocaustmuseum.org/wp-content/uploads/2022/11/IHM_TRAVELexhibit_CHILDREN-111422.pdf (August 23, 2024).

34 CBS News, "Museum in Brooklyn Shares Stories of Children Who Survived the Holocaust," January 26, 2017, https://www.cbsnews.com/newyork/news/brooklyn-museum-holocaust-exhibit/.

35 CBS News, "Museum in Brooklyn."

36 Mark M. Anderson, "The Child Victim as Witness to the Holocaust: An American Story?" *Jewish Social Studies* 14, no. 1 (2007): 19, http://www.jstor.org/stable/40207081.

37 "Remember the Children: Daniel's Story," United States Holocaust Memorial Museum, https://www.ushmm.org/information/exhibitions/museum-exhibitions/remember-the-children-daniels-story (August 23, 2024).

38 Bronislava Volková, *Forms of Exile in Jewish Literature and Thought: Twentieth-Century Central Europe and Migration to America* (Boston: Academic Studies Press, 2021), https://doi.org/10.2307/j.ctv2175r23.15.

39 Paul Bogdaner, *Kasztner's Crime* (New York: Routledge, 2016).

40 "On Trial," *Time*, July 11, 1955, https://web.archive.org/web/20081217113419/http://www.time.com/time/magazine/article/0,9171,807322-3,00.html.

41 "On Trial," *Time*.

42 "Holocaust Survivor Demographic Reports," *Claims Conference*, January 23, 2024, https://www.claimscon.org/demographics/.

43 Institute for Visual History and Education USC Shoah Foundation, "Institutions with Access to the Visual History Archive," accessed January 5, 2022, https://sfi.usc.edu/vha/access; Yale Fortunoff Video Archive for Holocaust Testimonies, "About the Fortunoff Archive," Yale University, https://fortunoff.library.yale.edu/about-us/our-story/ (Februry 9, 2022).

44 Chancellor and Lee, "Storytelling, Oral History," 44.

45 Arnold-de Simine, "The 'Moving' Image."

46 Marcus et al., "Holocaust Education in Transition," 281.

47 William Gaudelli, Margaret Crocco, and Alexandra Hawkins, "Documentaries Outtakes and Digital Archives in Teaching Difficult Knowledge and the Vietnam War," *Education and Society* 30, no. 2 (2012): 5–25, https://doi.org/10.7459/es/30.2.02.

48 Shenker, "Through the Lens of the Shoah."

49 Marcus et al., "Holocaust Education in Transition."

50 Institute for Visual History and Education, "Dimensions in Testimony," *USC Shoah Foundation*, https://sfi.usc.edu/dit (January 5, 2022).

51 Jenna Ng, "Holograms/Holographic Projections: Ghosts Amongst the Living; Ghosts of the Living," in *The Post-Screen Through Virtual Reality, Holograms and Light Projections: Where Screen Boundaries Lie* (Amsterdam: Amsterdam University Press, 2021), 185, https://doi.org/10.2307/j.ctv23985t6.8.

52 Maria Zalewska, "Holography, Historical Indexicality and the Holocaust," *Technologies of Knowing* 36, no. 1 (2016): 25–32, https://cinema.usc.edu/spectator/36.1/3_Zalewska.pdf.

53 Rabbi Yosef C. Golding, *Faith Amid the Flames* (New York: ArtScroll Mesorah Publications, 2019).

54 "Faith Amid The Flames," *The Lakewood Scoop*, July 18, 2019, https://thelakewoodscoop.com/news/faith-amid-the-flames-the-story-of-reb-yosef-friedenson-the-kiddush-hashem-he-witnessed-and-created%E2%80%8B%E2%80%8B-rabbi-yosef-c-golding/.

5 Unlocking the Past

The Promise and Perils of Museum Engagement

In May 2024, I went to visit the Nova Music Festival Exhibition titled *The Moment Music Stood Still*. Like the difficult exhibitions explored in earlier chapters, this installation faced the fundamental challenge of balancing commemorating an atrocity with the emotional well-being of visitors. But where Holocaust museums must bridge historical distance, this exhibition—which opened in Tel Aviv just two months after the October 7, 2023, terror attack—grappled with trauma that was still ongoing. The exhibition commemorates the day terrorists invaded Israel and brutally murdered some 1,200 people, including nearly 400 at the Nova music festival. As described on the exhibition website, it "set out to recreate an event dedicated to peace and love that was brutally cut short by Hamas's attack on Israel from Gaza on that fateful day."[1] Nearly 400 of those killed were at the Nova music festival. During its brief run in Manhattan, several colleagues warned me that it was overwhelming, describing it as "Auschwitz without glass."

The exhibit's size, scope, and detail were striking. Housed in a 50,000 square foot warehouse in the Wall Street district, the space felt sacred. The exhibition employed many of the techniques discussed earlier for cultivating historical empathy, but with an immediacy that risked overwhelming visitors. As I walked through, sand crunched beneath my feet in halls filled with tents, blankets, water bottles, shoes, and other items abandoned by festivalgoers fleeing the terrorists. Like the Holocaust artifacts explored in previous chapters, these objects served as powerful witnesses to tragedy. All were authentic, and signs throughout encouraged visitors to touch anything in the exhibition. Between burned-out cars and portable toilets riddled with bullets, the overwhelming scent of incense—recreating the festival's sensory experience—proved particularly powerful and somewhat nauseating. (See Figure 5.1)

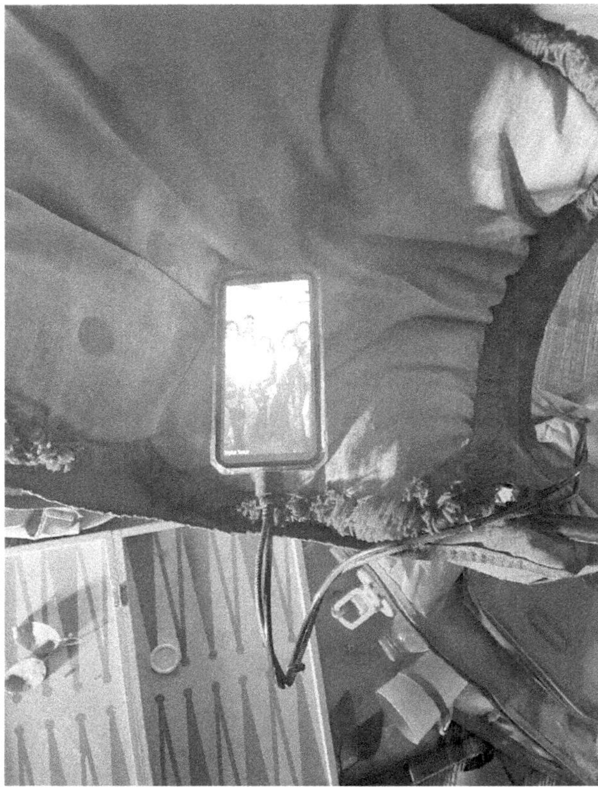

Figure 5.1 Games, backpacks, and a cell phone belonging to Nova festival attendees. Photograph by author, May 15, 2024.

The exhibition also utilized technology in ways that generated profound emotional connections. Throughout the space, screens displayed graphic videos captured from bodycams worn by terrorists, victims, and rescuers. Visitors could also pick up cell phones showing video footage and messages from festivalgoers who had hidden in the bushes during the attack. Reading the final words between victims and their loved ones was deeply moving, especially knowing that for so many, this was the last conversation they would ever have.

I visited the Nova Exhibit with Ari Scharf, director of Project Mesorah, who serves as a tour guide and has led hundreds of groups and private family tours to Holocaust sites in Eastern Europe. Our different perspectives—my expertise in museum spaces and his in site-based learning at Holocaust memorial sites—offered different perspectives regarding how the exhibition adapted established techniques for presenting traumatic history to address a very recent tragedy. Ari had personally visited the Nova Festival site in Israel twice since the attack. Standing near the burned-out cars, he showed me a picture of a field containing hundreds of burned vehicles, providing stark context that the handful of cars in the exhibit couldn't fully convey. He shared stories of meeting survivors and rescuers who had returned to the site to guide others. Yet what struck me most was his observation that this exhibit, here in the middle of Manhattan, created a more powerful experience than visiting the actual festival site.

The Moment Music Stood Still was not just carefully curated to educate visitors about the Nova music festival and Hamas's devastating attack on innocent festivalgoers. It illustrated in ways few exhibitions could how the principles of museum design explored in previous chapters could be applied to very recent trauma. The exhibition's raw and painful design forged intimate connections with the stories of individuals who were there that day. While visiting the actual site of a terror attack creates an experience that cannot be replicated elsewhere, as Ari explained, the museum experience affected visitors in a different way. The combination of objects, photographs, video footage, testimonies from survivors and first responders, and especially the pervading smell created a brief yet incredibly impactful encounter. I left the space contemplating what it takes for museums to successfully engage their audiences, particularly when presenting histories of such profound tragedy.

Form and Function: Architecture as Narrative in Holocaust Museums

In our modern world, museums take many forms. In some cities, they are ubiquitous, occupying full city blocks with grand architectural spaces of learning. In others, they are small and hard to locate, housing carefully curated exhibitions created by dedicated teams. Yet regardless of size or location, all contemporary museums serve a dual purpose: they are repositories for archival holdings charged with protecting and exhibiting historical collections, and they are teaching environments intended to promote learning for all ages. Museums across the globe are united by their commitment to creating learning experiences through documents, objects, and narratives. Through their collections of artifacts, photographs, and videos, history museums and cultural institutions connect history and modernity. And for those institutions that grapple with difficult histories, they must balance their roles as both archives of historical trauma and spaces that foster empathetic connections with the past.

Large museums utilize not just exhibition content but also spatial organization and building layout to guide, impact, and influence visitor attention. Museum exhibits incorporate media, text, markers, and signage in carefully considered arrangements to convey meaning and interpretation. Perhaps most significantly, they can use architectural design itself as a tool for managing visitors' emotional and psychological responses to how they grapple with the traumatic past. (See Figure 5.2)

The 2005 redesign of Yad Vashem, Israel's official Holocaust museum and memorial, exemplifies using architecture as a significant part of historical narrative. The striking design by architect Moshe Safdie combines historical significance with contemporary resonance, reflecting the trauma-informed approaches discussed in Chapter 2. The long triangular building tunnels into the earth and runs through the mountain on which Yad Vashem stands. Visitors cross a bridge to descend into the museum, creating a feeling of entering another world, before the journey ultimately ends with an upward opening toward a magnificent view of Jerusalem.[2] This careful orchestration of space reflects the museum's understanding of how physical environment shapes visitors' capacity to engage with traumatic content. Similarly, the exhibits at the National Museum of African American History & Culture in Washington, D.C., begin chronologically at the bottom of the building in the bowels of the earth, exploring the atrocities of slavery. As visitors move upward through the museum to the exhibits focused on African American contributions to culture and science, they enter a space with large windows where the "openness to light is symbolic for a museum that seeks to stimulate open dialogue about race and help promote reconciliation and healing."[3]

Shortly after the new museum at Yad Vashem opened, I learned of an even deeper significance behind the building's unique architecture from Ephraim Kaye, Director of the International Seminars at The International School for Holocaust Studies of Yad Vashem. According to Kaye, having the building cut through the mountain was inspired by Haim Gouri's poem "Heritage." Gouri, an Israeli poet and journalist who covered the Eichmann trial, used

Figure 5.2 View of the Jerusalem Forest seen from the balcony of Yad Vashem. Photograph by author, June 30, 2024.

the biblical Sacrifice of Isaac as a metaphor for the generational trauma and burden of the Holocaust on the Jewish people:

The ram came last of all. And Abraham
did not know that it came to answer the
boys question—first of his strength
when his day was on the wane.
The old man raised his head.
Seeing that it was no dream and that the angel
stood there—the knife slipped from his hand.

The boy, released from his bonds,
saw his father's back.

Isaac, as the story goes, was not
sacrificed. He lived for many years,
saw what pleasure had to offer
until his eyesight dimmed.

But he bequeathed that hour to his offspring.
They are born with a knife in their hearts.[4]

In discussing the complicated design and thinking behind the architectural concept, Avner Shalev, Chief Curator and Chairman of Yad Vashem, explained:

> *It is important to stress that we wanted to develop a balanced architectural concept that would match the contents and nature of the exhibition. On the one hand we did not want to make do with a box that would simply house an exhibit. On the other hand, we wanted to avoid a powerful, dominant and beautiful structure liable to overshadow the compelling contents. We believed that the contents to be exhibited were among the most difficult, sensitive, complex and undecipherable contents; there was no place for creating dramatic effects that might emphasize or undermine the actual narrative. At the same time we felt it was right that the building should have a unique presence to house the exhibits and conduct a quiet and restrained dialogue with them, rather than a gloomy one. I wanted the building to avoid totally severing the narrative from its surroundings because all the events occurred on solid ground, open to the sun and human eyes, and within a natural setting changing with the seasons of the year.*[5]

Silent Witnesses: The Power of Artifacts in Museum Spaces

While architectural design plays an important role, it is often the artifacts and objects housed in museum spaces that create the deepest emotional connection with visitors. Researchers suggest that "artifacts, material culture objects from the past, fascinate students,"[6] especially for young visitors for whom curiosity drives the museum experience. Students are prompted to think critically, research, and discover information about their identities when they encounter and touch unknown objects. This curiosity comes with both opportunities and risks—while objects can create profound historical understanding, they can also overwhelm visitors with their emotional weight. The power of these artifacts lies in their ability to simultaneously evoke empathy and trigger trauma responses. As portable objects that can be moved to different places, artifacts "store memories" and "allow us to live in the present while at the same time literally cling to the past."[7] Through them, stories about the past can be preserved long after their owners have moved on or died. Like survivor testimony, they serve as bridges between past and present, with their silent witness sometimes speaking more powerfully than words.

Artifacts serve a unique role in humanizing history.[8] Objects can embody the entire lives and histories of individuals, cultures, and nations.[9] Curating these objects requires careful consideration of both their historical significance and their psychological impact. Some researchers have coined the phrase "museum affect"[10] to describe how cultural artifacts become works of art through the viewers' eyes, serving as testimonials to the dead and the lives they led, rather than remaining static objects of the present.[11] This transformation from object to testimony echoes the way survivors' stories transform from personal memory to historical record. One notable research study found that using artifacts in literacy courses deepened connections between students and literature, demonstrating that objects enhanced engagement and motivated students to cultivate personal connections with literary characters.[12]

In history museums, exhibited objects play a particular role in the viewer's experience through their authenticity and connection to a specific time. They connect the viewer through a "special experience of history that cannot be attained in a cognitive, intellectual or discursive way,"[13] creating a visceral empathetic reaction rather than an intellectual understanding of the past. Artifacts—including letters, photographs, diaries, and other material items—are often featured in Holocaust museums and narratives, described as "incomplete but valuable portions of the story"[14] that become part of historical transmission. Like fragments of memory passed between generations, these objects carry both historical truth and emotional resonance. By providing contextualized narratives, artifacts offer an entryway for exploring lives lost and examining moral issues, allowing museum viewers to learn about individual stories and understand names and details within larger histories. They enable visitors to see history from other perspectives, particularly those of people who struggled to maintain their dignity in the face of adversity.[15]

The role of artifacts hit home for me when I read the announcement about the Museum of Jewish Heritage's first children's exhibit, "Courage to Act: Rescue in Denmark." The exhibit faced a challenge common to Holocaust education: how to convey a difficult historical truth while protecting young visitors from experiencing vicarious trauma. As the granddaughter of a Holocaust survivor who fled Denmark to Sweden during the famous rescue of Danish Jewry in October 1943, I was excited to see the museum featuring this important story. Even more intriguing from the perspective of a museum curator was how my grandmother's Holocaust-era artifacts would contribute to the exhibit. The possibility of being on the giving end of a museum loan instead of the receiving one was particularly meaningful. (See Figure 5.3)

The design team explained that "Courage to Act" was intentionally designed to limit the number of artifacts in the space. Instead, in creating a "family-friendly" exhibit about the Holocaust focused on middle school-age students, the exhibit relies heavily on cutting-edge technology rather than authentic artifacts and documents from the time.[16] Like many contemporary museums grappling with generational distance from the Holocaust, the exhibit attempts to address the issue by incorporating three hologram-like figures—composite characters inspired by different Danish Holocaust survivors' and rescuers' stories, allowing visitors to follow their narratives throughout the exhibit. As noted in the press, "Each is on an emotional, personal, and, eventually, literal journey as they escape Denmark or aid in the escape of Denmark's Jews. The museum and the exhibition's creative team believes children will relate more to these figures and find the story of the Danish rescue even more personal and impactful."[17] This emphasis on personal connection over historical artifacts represents a significant shift

Figure 5.3 Objects on exhibit, including my grandmother's purple siddur. Photograph by author, March 27, 2025.

in how museums cultivate historical empathy. The exhibit even includes a model of the Gerda III, one of the fishing boats that ferried Danish Jews to safety, accompanied by a dramatic video installation telling its story.

Yet while "Courage to Act" emphasizes "state-of-the-art technology and creative storytelling,"[18] carefully selected artifacts remain for visitors to explore. Like the survivor testimonies that ground abstract historical narratives in lived experience, these objects anchor the hi-tech narrative and create a physical link to history. Among these carefully curated items is my grandmother's siddur (prayer book) with its striking purple velvet cover and ornate silver nameplate. Seeing my family heirloom rendered as a historical artifact brought home for me the important work museums do to create a bridge between personal and collective memory.

Sacred Objects: The Ethics of Displaying Human Remains

Not all museum items are the same. The display of certain objects, particularly hair from people who were murdered during the Holocaust, raises complex ethical questions. These items occupy an unsettling space between artifact and human remains—between educational tool and sacred object. Since ancient times, hair has been viewed as a symbol of immortality, and in Victorian culture, families saved locks of hair of loved ones after their deaths. This ritual established hair as an enduring symbol of life that could be preserved and woven into artwork, portraiture, or jewelry,[19] while the preservation of Holocaust victims' hair transforms this intimate cultural practice into something far more haunting. (See Figure 5.4)

Through my work, I have frequently observed visitors who seem particularly drawn to exhibit cases containing hair. This was evident during a recent visit to Yad Vashem, where I spent time observing visitors in the exhibit hall containing the hair of twelve-year-old Lili Hirsch, who was murdered in Auschwitz. Just before deportation, her mother cut off her long braids (which had not been cut since her childhood) and gave them to a neighbor for safekeeping. This maternal act of preservation becomes even more poignant against the backdrop of genocide. While standing in the exhibit hall that housed this hair, I noticed that many visitors lingered at this display longer than at other ones.

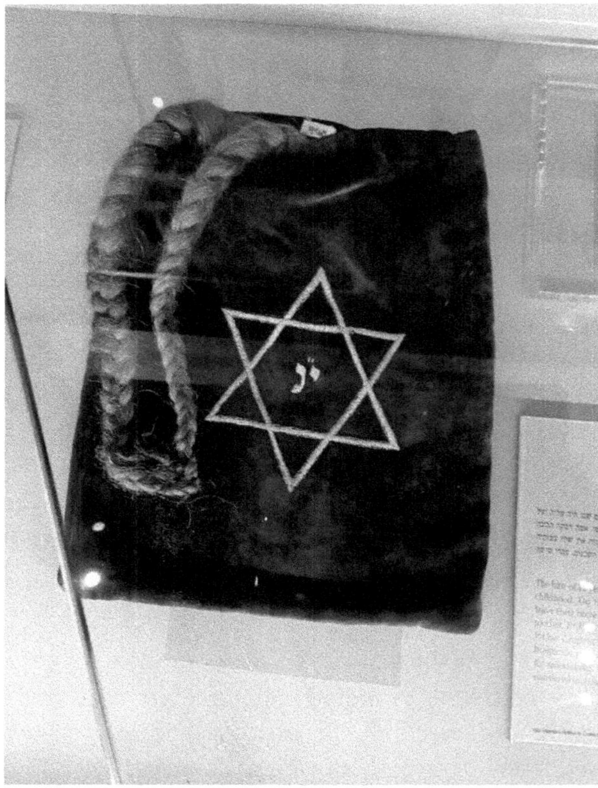

Figure 5.4 Lily Hirsch's hair on display at Yad Vashem. Photograph by author, June 30, 2024.

The exhibition of human remains emerged as a major debate among the content committee at the USHMM, particularly regarding hair from Auschwitz—some still plaited or braided after being shaved off victims upon their arrival at the concentration camp. The hair provoked a visceral reaction among museum committee members, who questioned whether these items should be considered human remains or historical artifacts, and the ensuing debate over historical accuracy and psychological impact exemplified the core tension facing Holocaust museums: how to display evidence of atrocity without re-traumatizing visitors. In a memo, museum project director Michael Berenbaum noted that the hair was not considered human remains "either according to Jewish law or to common sense."[20] However, Alice Greenwald, lead design consultant, argued against exhibiting the hair, suggesting that memorial sites and concentration camps in Europe were more suitable places, noting that "what might be logically true is not always emotionally true + this museum will be affecting people's emotions."[21] Although two-thirds of the committee voted to display the hair, it was ultimately excluded from the final museum design, following testimony from women survivors who noted that their own hair might be in the bundles.[22] (See Figure 5.5)

Similar discussions surrounding other objects at the USHMM, including shoes and boxcars, addressed questions of their tactility and their function as evidence of these crimes. These everyday objects, transformed by historical circumstance into evidence of atrocity, carry their own psychological weight. Raul Hilberg argued that "some aspects [of the Holocaust] cannot be shown because they are not represented in objects. When we do have specific objects, we should show them. The hair and [a dissecting] table are elements of ultimate rationality amidst [a] process no one can understand." The shoes were included in the final museum design as witnesses to the Holocaust, and the narrative above the display features a quote from Yiddish poet Moshe Schulstein:

Figure 5.5 Shoes belonging to victims of the Holocaust on exhibit at the United States Holocaust Memorial Museum. Photograph by author, May 6, 2025.

We are the shoes, we are the last witnesses.
We are shoes from grandchildren and grandfathers,
From Prague, Paris and Amsterdam,
And because we are only made of stuff and leather
And not of blood and flesh, each one of us avoided the hellfire.

These debates reflect a fundamental question about museum ethics: When does the educational value of an artifact outweigh its potential to traumatize? Bernard-Donals reviewed thousands of visitors' comments left after visits to the museum and found that some objects troubled their connections to the Holocaust. Comments included "I was overcome with nausea" and "it was quite hard to take all of it in."[23] He suggests this occurs when items like shoes do not function in a metonymic sense (standing in for, or linking to, a historical event) but rather in a synecdochic manner (becoming a substitution for a larger event). This distinction helps explain why certain artifacts overwhelm visitors' capacity for historical empathy, short-circuiting understanding rather than enhancing it. These synecdochic representations can trouble viewers' relationships with the past, and their focus on a particular item can distance them from the event and distract them from the larger historical narrative. (See Figure 5.6)

The power of personal objects to evoke both empathy and trauma was starkly resonant at the end of the Nova Festival Exhibit, where visitors encountered a lost and found containing many different items abandoned during the terror attack: water bottles, prayer books, sweatshirts, shoes, and more. This display served to reunite as many objects as possible with their owners, with each item bearing a barcode linking to a website where people could claim their belongings. Among these displays, one table drew more attention than any other: a table full of shoes, some single and some in pairs, that had been left behind in tents or had fallen off as people ran for their lives. Omri, a staff member, told me that he had personally spent a month at the Nova Festival site working to gather these abandoned belongings. Over several months, he had researched their provenance and successfully returned some items—including a diary and a hula hoop—to their rightful owners. "These shoes attract the most attention," he observed. "Many people linger in this area, picking up and touching the shoes on the table. I think that they remind visitors of similar ownerless shoes that they have seen at Holocaust museums."

Figure 5.6 Lost and found containing shoes from the Nova Exhibit in New York. Photograph by author, May 15, 2024.

Bearing Witness: Photography and Visual Memory in Holocaust Museums

Several years ago, I purchased an educational kit from Yad Vashem titled "But the Story Didn't End That Way." The kit was developed "to provide teachers and students with up-to-date and readily available didactic tools, adapted for educational needs."[24] It includes a comprehensive folder containing eighteen large posters that create a timeline of the Kristallnacht events, providing a photo essay that can be used in many ways for educational and commemorative purposes. Each time I display these posters, different students engage with these frozen moments of history differently. Some lean in close, studying every detail, while others maintain their distance, as if the images might overwhelm them. When teaching about Kristallnacht, I display several of the posters and provide activities and educational prompts to encourage my students to interact and think critically about the images presented. It takes nearly an hour for my students to work through the activity as they delve deeply into the subject and learn from the many nuances of the photographs. While student responses differ each year, often influenced by current world events or other unique factors, these photographs remain a valuable tool to communicate this specific memory.

The captivating nature of photographs helps explain why almost all museums use them in their galleries and promotional materials. Researchers explain that "photographic, cinematic, and video images are the raw materials used to construct personal histories: events remembered because they were photographed, moments forgotten because no images were preserved, and unphotographed memories that work in tension with camera memories."[25] However, within the hierarchy of items that curators choose to exhibit, photographs occupy the lowest rank, often used to accompany or authenticate other items on display instead of being treated as artifacts themselves. Yet these images carry their own psychological weight, particularly in Holocaust museums where they must bridge not just historical distance but emotional barriers.

Like hair and shoes, photographs reflect broader questions about how to present the historical record while being sensitive to the potential for trauma. Some researchers argue that photographs in Holocaust museums often fail to accomplish their intended goal of "return[ing] the humanity to all the people murdered in the chaos of war when the numbers discussed are literally incomprehensible."[26] This argument oftentimes rests on the belief that black and white, grainy photographs and film footage taken during the war lack the power to bridge the gap between history and the modern museum visitor. It is argued that the same qualities that make these images feel "historical"—their coarse resolution and monochrome palette—can create an emotional distance that prevents an authentic connection from occurring.

Interestingly, modern color photographs taken of the same places are often disconcerting to viewers who expect all images of concentration camps to be in black and white. One photographer who took a series of photographs of twelve different concentration camps decades after the war recalled how during a lecture a heated argument ensued when an enraged member of the audience screamed, "You can't photograph Nazi concentration camps in color, on sunny days. There weren't any deep blue skies or puffy white clouds during the Holocaust. Don't you know that the Holocaust happened in black and white?"[27] His reaction reveals how deep certain expectations shape not just how we see but feel about such photographs.

Black and white photography also encourages outside emotions, such as nostalgia, sadness, or yearning, to influence the viewer, making it a preferred technique for modern photography studios seeking to encourage these sentiments.[28] Similarly, many artists choose to depict Holocaust scenes in black and white because of the familiar disconnect and feelings evoked by such historical imagery. While this style of photography can protect viewers from being overwhelmed, it can also create barriers to connecting and empathizing with the experiences of those who endured these events. I once met an artist who told me that as she began drawing and painting artwork about the Holocaust, her default choice was always black and white. That was how she had always imagined the Holocaust taking place. This continued until, one day, a Holocaust survivor stopped by to view her artwork and questioned her technique, saying, "our lives were not in black and white. We were real people, with real colored lives. If you really want to show what life was like during the Holocaust, use color and bring back our lives as we lived them." Her remarks were meant as a reminder that presenting the Holocaust should not just document atrocities but reflect the humanity of those who experienced it.

Advances in technology are making it possible to colorize and redevelop negatives to produce crisper, colorized images from historical photos. These technological capabilities offer new possibilities for connecting viewers with historical events, yet also raise questions about authenticity and emotional impact. For example, contemporary colorization methods add a new dimension to visual experiences but are not without controversy. Seeing images in color emphasizes the human element and allows viewers to see the world as people lived it. Some researchers suggest that colorizing photographs intensifies emotions such as pity, horror, disgust, and empathy because it "challenges us to respond to history not simply as accountants and analysts, but as human beings, capable of the same fear, confusion, passion, ambition, anger, and love as those whose images we see."[29] While deepening the emotional connection may create a deeper understanding, it can also overwhelm viewers unprepared for such a vision of the past. Critics also argue that colorization methods distort the historical context in which the photographs were taken and downplay film history. As a result, many archival policies require a statement to alert viewers when an image has been altered from its original form.[30]

This debate emerged during the design and development of the Soldiers Holocaust Education Center, a small educational facility and exhibit created by Yad Vashem specifically for soldiers in the Israeli Defense Force. While many of the museum curators and designers wanted to utilize technology to colorize the photographs used in the exhibition, others argued that it would interfere with the images, distorting their authenticity and historical context. A compromise was reached whereby the backgrounds of the pictures were colorized while the subjects of the photos (including faces and buildings) were not. The result is a vivid and visually striking exhibition that seemingly takes advantage of the benefits of color photography while appearing to remain faithful to the photographs' accuracy. But it also reveals how museums constantly navigate between making history accessible and maintaining its emotional impact.

The use of photographs and videos in Holocaust museum exhibitions is further complicated by their lack of what might be called "objectivity." Most photos found in museums documenting the Holocaust were taken by Germans for propaganda purposes and to document their victories. The introductory panel to the special exhibition "Flashes of Memory: Photography during the Holocaust" aptly captures the concern in abstract terms:

> *The camera, with its manipulative power, has tremendous impact and far-reaching influence. Although photography purports to reflect reality as it is, it is essentially an interpretation of it, since elements such as worldview, values and moral perception influence the choice of the object to be photographed as well as how it is presented. When visual documentation is also used as a historical document, the elements require even greater attention.*[31]

Can museums use images that once dehumanized victims and instead return the focus to their humanity? One researcher suggests that to "restore the victims as subjects, not objects, of history," we must refrain from studying images of victims of the Holocaust from the perpetrator's perspective.[32] Instead of focusing on people heading to their deaths, one should try to identify them and speak their names. Rather than examining methods of mass murder, one should investigate and expose killers' motives and hate to understand how "networks of complicity made the Holocaust possible."[33] Her research into the identification of a family photographed during the mass murder in Miropol, Ukraine, demonstrates this philosophy through the discovery of an additional (previously obscured) child seen just moments before being shot and cast into a mass grave.

Equally worrisome is how certain images risk becoming iconic representations of mass murder, leading visitors to view them with indifference over time. "The problem is not that people remember through photographs, but that they remember only the photographs. This remembering through photographs eclipses other forms of understanding and remembering."[34] When images become too familiar, they can lose their power to move us, creating a different kind of distance between the viewer and the image. Therefore, it is seen as crucial for Holocaust museums to emphasize the context in which each photograph was taken.[35]

A notable example is the analysis of four famous photographs of the Auschwitz crematoria taken by members of the Sonderkommando, which were smuggled out of the camp in a tube of toothpaste. These images do many things: they offer evidence of atrocity, serve as acts of resistance, and function as a bridge between the past and the present. Their existence serves as both historical evidence of crimes against humanity and the ban on photography in concentration camps, while also illustrating the "conflict between the *mediated* and the *immediate*."[36] Although these images capture a single moment in time, when exhibited they create a temporal link to historical atrocities, with the images serving as a mediator of social relationships between the victims and the viewers.

This raises crucial questions that museums must consider when presenting images that capture traumatic events: Are they primary evidence of horrific violence or merely witnesses to it? Are they aesthetic objects or historical documents? Is it ethical to make violent history accessible in sanitized spaces? One scholar perhaps captured the complexity of photographic exhibits in modern museums best:

> *what remains invisible in this context is not the original experience of suffering, but the social relations of production whose invisibility is both expressed as and expresses the overwhelming experience of individual trauma.*[37]

Engaging the Visitor: Curation, Learning, and Emotional Response

Visitors to museums generally assume they will experience a "one-way flow of information from museum exhibit to visitor."[38] Yet when presenting difficult histories, museums must not only inform but also guide visitors through potentially overwhelming emotional terrain. This creates opportunities for museums to promote specific ideas or agendas.

When developing an exhibit, designers consider three elements: categories, narratives, and engagement. The foundations of the exhibit are the categories of information selected for display. The narrative shapes visitor perceptions and ideas about this information. Together, categories and narratives provide interpretive language and exhibits that engage visitors in the space.[39] And as a result, each choice they make informs not just what visitors learn, but how the material impacts them.

The role of a museum curator thus is to connect the various museum elements with one another and ultimately connect the exhibit to the visitor. Indeed, as one scholar notes, "The act of curating at its most basic is simply about connecting."[40] Yet doing so is no easy task. A study conducted at the National Museum of African American History & Culture found it difficult to predict where visitors would have strong emotional responses. The report cataloged where and why visitors said they cried in the exhibit. Some reacted because "design and narrative were powerful enough to open that possibility; others mentioned aspects of the exhibit that held personal significance and associations."[41] Other museums take a more passive approach to curating with an eye to generating an emotional reaction. At the Holocaust Gallery in Warsaw, near the Rapoport Memorial to the Ghetto Heroes, the curatorial team relies heavily on a minimalistic technique. By limiting the text within the exhibit, they aim to force visitors to engage closely with the information and enter a dialogue to develop personal meaning during their visit.[42] They seek to evoke memories and recollections of personal events, relationships, and issues less mediated by a curatorial agenda.

Understanding the motivation of museum visitors is also crucial for creating exhibits that capture their attention, and grasping their reason for visiting is particularly important when presenting difficult histories. Some visitors are seeking an emotional connection, while others need a protective distance. Five styles of motivated visitors have been identified, including the "explorer," who is generally curiosity-driven, the "facilitator," who organizes and enables group visits, the "professional/hobbyist," who feels a close personal or professional connection to specific content, the "experience seeker," who views the museum as an important destination for a one-time visit, and the "recharger," who seeks "contemplative, spiritual restorative experiences [and] use the museum as a refuge from the work-day world."[43]

Learning styles also influence the visitor experience at a museum. According to scholars, "museum learning is unique, multi-faceted and inspires higher-order affective and cognitive development."[44] Researchers have divided museumgoers into three different types of learners: "idea preference visitors" who seek information, facts, and statistics; "people preference visitors" who are primarily interested in emotions, stories, biographies, and photographs; and "object preference visitors" who seek reflective moments while viewing artifacts. Some researchers maintain that as a result of these different motivations and learning styles, visitors "get" what they expect out of a visit, not necessarily what curators and museum staff hope to achieve.[45]

However, there is equally compelling evidence to suggest that museum visitors appreciate when their standard method of thinking is challenged and they are compelled to learn when presented with competing narratives. Such conflicting displays (which could be intentional or merely generated as a result of the push and pull of artifacts and photographs) have the potential to create a "dissonance of a cacophony" that challenges "people to think again about their stereotypes, and to emerge from their museum experience feeling that they have had some profound encounter with the subject."[46] Unsurprisingly, these encounters can take on particular significance in Holocaust museums, where challenging preconceptions (like whether the Holocaust can be "colorized") can be fraught.

Schools that recognize the value of these educational spaces schedule visits to meet academic goals, often seeking to complement or supplement school-based curricula. Educators bring students for focused programming and one-time field trips, and even attend teacher training workshops offered by museums. However, the relationship between museums and schools is complex. In recent decades, attendance numbers and visitor statistics have often dictated the direction of exhibits and program offerings. This pressure to maintain attendance can conflict with museums' responsibility to present difficult histories thoughtfully and ethically. One response has been to "align more closely to academic content standards, to teach math, science, history, and language arts through art in the hopes that connecting to academic standards would provide the relevance needed to increase program numbers."[47] An example of this is seen in the educational programs offered by the Intrepid Sea, Air & Space Museum. The Intrepid is a legendary American aircraft carrier that had a dark history during its 31 years of service. It was responsible for sinking two Japanese warships and being hit by five kamikaze and one torpedo attack during the Second World War, and serving in the Cold War and the Vietnam War.[48] As of 2019, the museum had approximately 14,000 students visiting the museum and engaging in "inquiry rich discussions [that] allow students to see how their world was shaped by the past and consider what role they may play in the future."[49] Yet today, the museum offers more field trip options related to STEM (science, technology, engineering, and math) than in social studies or history.[50] Many museum educators disagree with this approach, believing that "objects have the power to illuminate so many of the dark regions of our minds and beings beyond those addressed in the classroom, and it is [their] responsibility to advocate for that power."[51] Some museums have shifted to focus on fostering creativity and developing critical thinking skills to avoid being seen as "playing handmaiden to schools and curriculum standards."[52]

Several museums have adopted a constructivist approach for authentic learning, suggesting that a "teacher's or curator's job is not to impart information but to make it possible for the learner to construct their own understanding of the topic."[53] For example, I have created numerous museum workshops with focused activities requiring students to act as curators and develop their own mini-exhibitions using the institution's resources. By placing students in the role of curator, these workshops force them to grapple with the same challenges museums face: how to present difficult histories in ways that both inform and honor their emotional weight. This workshop style can be designed to meet state standards, such as the New York State Social Studies Framework,[54] while using a constructivist learning approach that encourages students to think critically about the knowledge they are encountering. Similar programs that engage visitors by teaching the challenges of narrating history are valuable because they "invite a new generation of visitors to help us take up the task."[55]

Museums also utilize marketing platforms, such as social media sites, podcasts, and blogs, to encourage participation both during and after visits. These digital spaces create new opportunities but also new challenges when it comes to engaging with difficult histories. One of the best examples of using marketing platforms in the learning process is the Holocaust Museum & Center for Tolerance and Education (HMCTE),[56] where I worked with the design team during the design and installation of a new permanent exhibition on the Rockland Community College campus. While the design of the exhibit is purposeful, intentionally making the museum's resources, artifacts, and stories of local survivors accessible in alignment with the museum's mission and vision, one aspect of the storytelling varies and remains unscripted: the visitor response videos. At the end of the exhibit and tour, visitors to HMCTE can record their reflections on their experience at the museum. This installation is similar to the visitor reflection booths at the National September 11 Memorial Museum where visitors can record their reactions to the 9/11 Memorial and Historical Exhibition. Some visitor responses are emotionally moving, while others are controversial. Some are predictable and clearly reflect the tour or workshop content, while others appear to be based on preconceived ideas or expectations. "It's like social media without a handle. Anyone can put data in it. We want good data, of course, but its almost like an open chat room," says Andrea Winograd, executive director of HMCTE.[57] "In fact, we recently had a visitor who recorded himself saying 'Hitler should have finished the job.'" The varied responses reveal how differently people engage with difficult histories based on their own experiences. These videos are ultimately integrated into the exhibit and play on a large screen for future audiences, creating an ongoing dialogue between past and present visitors about how to process historical events.

While these initiatives have made museum access and participation easier for many in the twenty-first century, "there is a parallel need to examine its potential for challenging museums authority and legitimacy and also the risk of disenchanting the museum-going experience."[58] Some scholars note increasing similarities between museums and entertainment spaces, and use the term "edutainment" to describe the hybridization of museum learning and amusement-park-style attractions and shows that are increasingly utilized to attract and grow audiences.[59] This trend reflects a broader cultural shift in which institutions traditionally associated with education and scholarship change in response to consumer-driven preferences, blending educational content with immersive and interactive experiences to remain relevant and attract large audiences. For example, *Van Gogh: The Immersive Experience* is a light and sound exhibition where visitors can "step into a painting" and experience artwork through projections and other visual mediums. It has toured multiple cities since 2017 and has attracted more than five million visitors.[60] *National Geographic Encounter: Ocean Odyssey* used similar audio-visual tools to create an immersive underwater experience. When I visited the exhibition in Times Square, it felt like a trip to a spectacular aquarium (albeit without any live animals or fish). As one review explained, the exhibit "is not a museum, aquarium or virtual reality; instead, the producers consulted with dozens of technologists and scientists to create a new kind of immersive experience that guests can physically walk through to share stunning ocean encounters with friends and family."[61] Needless to say, museums dedicated to difficult histories must tread carefully to avoid such a reductionist path lest they trivialize the experience they are trying to convey.

While museums continue evolving their digital and interactive offerings to increase accessibility, this transformation raises important questions about institutional authority and the potential dilution of the museum experience. As institutions traditionally focused on education increasingly incorporate entertainment elements, the emerging "edutainment" approach represents a significant shift in how cultural institutions engage with visitors. Museums now frequently blend educational content with immersive experiences to maintain relevance in a consumer-driven marketplace, creating environments that prioritize engagement ahead of informative scholarship. As we'll explore in the next chapter, these developments pose particular challenges for institutions presenting difficult histories like the Holocaust. When museums adopt more immersive, technology-driven approaches to Holocaust education, how do they maintain the appropriate emotional tone? How can curators balance the desire for engaging experiences against the risk of trivializing trauma? And ultimately, how can we ensure that innovations in museum design serve to deepen visitor understanding rather than overwhelming them with vicarious trauma?

Notes

1. Nova Exhibition, "Nova Exhibition," *Nova Exhibition*, 2023, https://www.novaexhibition.com.
2. "Architecture," *Yad Vashem*, 2025, https://www.yadvashem.org/museum/holocaust-history-museum/architecture.html.
3. National Museum of African American History and Culture, "The Building," *The Smithsonian Institution*, https://nmaahc.si.edu/about/building.
4. "Seven Poems, Seven Paintings," *Yad Vashem*, 2025, https://www.yadvashem.org/education/educational-materials/lesson-plans/poems-paintings.html.
5. Dorit Harel, *Facts and Feelings: Dilemmas in Designing the Yad Vashem Holocaust Memorial Museum* (Jerusalem: Yad Vashem, 2010).

6 Lois Hendrickson, "Teaching with Artifacts and Special Collections," *Bulletin of the History of Medicine* 90, no. 1 (2016): 136, https://www.jstor.org/stable/26310794.

7 Yael Zerubavel, *Time Maps: Collective Memory and the Social Shape of the Past* (Chicago, IL: University of Chicago Press, 2003), 43.

8 Hendrickson, "Teaching with Artifacts and Special Collections."

9 Laura Schiavo, "What to Do with Heritage: The Museum of Jewish Ceremonial Objects, 1931–43," in *Radical Roots: Public History and a Tradition of Social Justice Activism*, ed. Denise D. Meringolo (Amherst, MA: Amherst College Press, 2021), 395–426, http://www.jstor.org/stable/10.3998/mpub.12366495.18.

10 Alpers, as cited in Kate Lawless, "Memory, Trauma, and the Matter of Historical Violence: The Controversial Case of Four Photographs from Auschwitz," *American Imago* 71, no. 4 (2014): 393, https://www.jstor.org/stable/26305100.

11 Victoria Aarons and Alan L. Berger, *Third-Generation Holocaust Representation: Trauma, History, and Memory* (Evanston, IL: Northwestern University Press, 2017), http://www.jstor.org/stable/j.ctt22727kb.

12 Dawan Coombs and Rachel Knecht Freeze, "Lives on Display: Examining Artifacts of Hope," *The English Journal* 108, no. 2 (2018): 20–30, https://www.jstor.org/stable/26610252.

13 Steffi de Jong, *The Witness as Object: Video Testimonies in Holocaust Museums* (New York: Berghahn Books, 2018), 113, https://doi.org/10.2307/j.ctv3znzsd.

14 Aarons and Berger, *Third-Generation Holocaust Representation*, 226.

15 Robert M. Ehrenreich and Jane Klinger, "War in Context: Let the Artifacts Speak," in *Does War Belong in Museums?: The Representation of Violence in Exhibitions*, ed. Wolfgang Muchitsch (Wetzlar, Germany: Transcript Verlag, 2013), 145–54, http://www.jstor.org/stable/j.ctv1wxr1z.14.

16 Conversation with Ellen Bari and Sara Softness, December 12, 2022.

17 Tom Teicholz, "Denmark's Safe Harbor Is a Children's Exhibit at NY's Museum of Jewish Heritage," *Forbes*, October 27, 2023, https://www.forbes.com/sites/tomteicholz/2023/10/27/denmarks-safe-harbor-is-a-childrens-exhibit-at-nys-museum-of-jewish-heritage/.

18 "Courage to Act: Rescue in Denmark," Museum of Jewish Heritage—A Living Memorial to the Holocaust, 2025, https://mjhnyc.org/exhibitions/courage-to-act-rescue-in-denmark/.

19 Rachel Harmeyer, "Objects of Immortality: Hairwork and Mourning in Victorian Visual Culture," Proceedings of the Art of Death and Dying Symposium, The University of Houston Libraries, 2018, http://hdl.handle.net/10657/3003.

20 Michael Bernard-Donals, "Synecdochic Memory at the United States Holocaust Memorial Museum," *College English* 74, no. 5 (2012): 417–36, http://www.jstor.org/stable/23212923.

21 Greenwald, as cited in Bernard-Donals, "Synecdochic Memory at the United States Holocaust Memorial Museum," 431.

22 Personal communication with Alice Greenwald, 2016.

23 Bernard-Donals, "Synecdochic Memory at the United States Holocaust Memorial Museum," 418.

24 "But the Story Didn't End That Way," The International School for Holocaust Studies, Yad Vashem Information Systems, 2000, https://www.yadvashem.org/download/education/units/crystal.pdf.

25 Sturken, as cited in Olga Gershenson, "Meta-Memory: About the Holocaust in New Israeli Video Art," *Jewish Film & New Media: An International Journal* 6, no. 1 (2018): 70, https://doi.org/10.13110/jewifilmnewmedi.6.1.0067.

26 Ehrenreich and Klinger, "War in Context," 146.

27 James Friedman, "The Holocaust Didn't Happen in Black and White," *Shofar* 37, no. 1 (2019): 4, https://doi.org/10.5703/shofar.37.1.0001.

28 "Why Do We Love Black and White Photography?" *Headshot London*, February 9, 2015, https://www.headshotlondon.co.uk/blog/why-do-we-love-black-and-white-photography/.

29 Marina Amaral and Dan Jones, *Colour of Time: A New History of the World, 1850-1960* (Chicago: Head of Zeus Ltd, 2018), 9.

30 Liz Watkins, "The Politics of Nostalgia: Colorization, Spectatorship and the Archive," *Comparative Cinema* 9, no. 17 (2021): 123–45, https://doi.org/10.31009/cc.2021.v9.i17.07.

31 "Introductory Panel—Flashes of Memory: Photography during the Holocaust," *Yad Vashem*, Jerusalem, June 30, 2024.

32 Wendy Lower, *The Ravine: A Family, a Photograph, a Holocaust Massacre Revealed* (New York: Mariner Books, 2021), 26.

33 Susie Linfield, "When Genocide Is Caught on Film," February 21, 2021, https://www.nytimes.com/2021/02/16/books/review/the-ravine-holocaust-photo-wendy-lower.html.

34 Sontag, as cited in Ursula Böser, "'A Film Unfinished': Yael Hersonski's Re-Representation of Archival Footage from the Warsaw Ghetto," *Film Criticism* 37, no. 2 (2012): 52, http://www.jstor.org/stable/24777861.

35 Marea Piotrowska, Kamila Ferenc, Radecka-Mikulicz, and Justyna Majewska, "Curatorial and Educational Challenges in Creating the Holocaust Gallery," in

New Directions in the History of the Jews in the Polish Lands, ed. Antony Polonsky, Hanna Węgrzynek, and Andrzej Żbikowski (Boston: Academic Studies Press, 2018), 29–39, https://doi.org/10.2307/j.ctv7xbrh4.10.

36 Lawless, "Memory, Trauma, and the Matter of Historical Violence," 404.

37 Lawless, "Memory, Trauma, and the Matter of Historical Violence," 411.

38 Lisa King, "Rhetorics in a Museum Space: Connecting Exhibit Spaces, Contexts, and Audiences," *JAC* 33, no. 3/4 (2013): 671, http://www.jstor.org/stable/43854572.

39 Corinne A. Kratz, "Where Did You Cry? Crafting Categories, Narratives, and Affect through Exhibit Design," *Kronos* 44 (2018): 229–52, https://www.jstor.org/stable/26610867.

40 Hans Ulrich Obrist, *Ways of Curating* (London: Penguin Books, 2015), 1.

41 Kratz, "Where Did You Cry?," 249.

42 Piotrowska et al., "Curatorial and Educational Challenges in Creating the Holocaust Gallery," 37.

43 Laureen Trainer, Marley Steele-Inama, and Amber Christopher, "Uncovering Visitor Identity: A Citywide Utilization of the Falk Visitor-Identity Model," *The Journal of Museum Education* 37, no. 1 (2012): 103, http://www.jstor.org/stable/41705813.

44 Ben Garcia, Michael Murawski, and Ralph Cordova, "What We Do Best: Making the Case for the Museum Learning in Its Own Right," *The Journal of Museum Education* 37, no. 2 (2012): 47, http://www.jstor.org/stable/41705823.

45 James B. Schreiber, Andrew J. Pekarik, Nadine Hanemann, Zahava Doering, and Ah-Jin Lee, "Understanding Visitor Engagement and Behaviors," *The Journal of Educational Research* 106, no. 6 (2013): 462–8, http://www.jstor.org/stable/43824302.

46 Jonathan Webber, "Jewish Tourism to Poland: The Opportunities for New Museum Narratives to Recontextualize Jewish Histories," in *New Directions in the History of the Jews in the Polish Lands*, ed. Antony Polonsky, Hanna Węgrzynek, and Andrzej Żbikowski (Boston: Academic Studies Press, 2018), 142, https://doi.org/10.2307/j.ctv7xbrh4.21.

47 Jessimi Jones, "Examining Why: Our Work with Teacher and Schools," *The Journal of Museum Education* 39, no. 2 (2014): 176, http://www.jstor.org/stable/43305024.

48 Intrepid Museum, "75 Years since USS Intrepid's Darkest Day," 2019, https://intrepidmuseum.org/75-years-uss-intrepids-darkest-day.

49 Intrepid Museum, "Support Intrepid: Spotlight on School Programs," YouTube video, November 19, 2019, https://www.youtube.com/watch?v=eBn_po8iDcI.

50 Intrepid Museum, "Field Trips," 2024, https://intrepidmuseum.org/plan-your-visit/group-visits/field-trips.

51 Garcia et al., "What We Do Best," 48.

52 Jones, "Examining Why," 176.

53 Nicholas Grindle and Ben Thomas, "Curating Connections in the Art History Curriculum," in *Developing the Higher Education Curriculum: Research-based Education in Practice*, ed. Brent Carnell and Dilly Fung (London: UCL Press, 2017), 106, https://doi.org/10.2307/j.ctt1xhr542.13.

54 "Social Studies," *New York State Education Department*, n.d., https://www.nysed.gov/standards-instruction/social-studies.

55 Hilary Iris Lowe, "Dwelling in Possibility: Revisiting Narrative in the Historic House Museum," *The Public Historian* 37, no. 2 (2015): 60, https://doi.org/10.1525/tph.2015.37.2.42.

56 Holocaust Museum & Center for Tolerance and Education, "Holocaust Museum & Center for Tolerance and Education," September 30, 2022, https://www.holocauststudies.org.

57 Personal communication with Andrea Winograd, April 1, 2025.

58 Mathilde Pulh and Rémi Mencarelli, "Web 2.0: Is the Museum–Visitor Relationship Being Redefined?" *International Journal of Arts Management* 18, no. 1 (2015): 44, http://www.jstor.org/stable/24587086.

59 Pierre Balloffet, François H. Courvoisier, and Joëlle Lagier, "From Museum to Amusement Park: The Opportunities and Risks of Edutainment," *International Journal of Arts Management* 16, no. 2 (2014): 4–18, http://www.jstor.org/stable/24587153.

60 "Van Gogh Philadelphia, PA Exhibit: The Immersive Experience," *Van Gogh Expo*, 2021, https://vangoghexpo.com/philadelphia/?utm_source=landing&utm_medium=landing_vangoghexperience_nyc&utm_campaign=96017_nyc&cp_landing=cta_hero&cp_landing_term=cta_hero&cp_landing_source=vangoghexpo.

61 Beth Beckman, "Under the Sea Times Square: A National Geographic Encounter," *Little Kid Big City*, October 6, 2017, https://littlekidbigcity.com/national-geographic-encounter-ocean-odyssey/.

6 Teaching with Compassion

Trauma-Informed Approaches in Holocaust Education

"My mother did it backward," Tali told me with quiet certainty. "If only she had gone to the Empire State Building first, everything would have been different."

I was intrigued by this unexpected opener from the twenty-two-year-old Canadian pre-med student. She wasn't prone to dramatics or exaggeration. But when she heard about my research on psychological experiences in Holocaust museums, she insisted I hear her story, convinced it held an important lesson about how they can unknowingly create trauma through the intensity of their presentations. "When I talk to people about my experience," she explained, "they often dismiss it. They say things like 'everyone gets upset at the 9/11 Museum' or 'of course you were scared, you were just a kid.' But this was different."

When Tali was eleven years old, her mother organized what was meant to be a perfect mother-daughter trip to New York City. But what began as an educational visit would become a lesson in how trauma can emerge in unexpected ways, particularly when encountering difficult histories in museum spaces.

The 9/11 Memorial Museum was designed to allow visitors to access the story of the terror attacks in different ways. In the footprint of the North Tower is the historical exhibition where the story of 9/11 is told through artifacts, images, and video and audio recordings, while the personal stories of the victims are explored in the memorial exhibition beneath the footprint of the South Tower. "In our planning, what we call the interstitial spaces, which is basically everything which is not within the footprint of the two towers, and which are quite dramatic both architecturally and narratively—those spaces do not raise the most difficult and challenging elements of the story," says Clifford Chanin, executive vice president and museum director.[1] "So you could walk through that part of the museum and get the story, but you would not get it in the detail that you would get it in the historical exhibition or in the South tower, the memorial exhibition." Those spaces were designed in consultation with trauma specialists to help visitors avoid emotional overload and include "emotional breathers" like silent reflection spaces.[2]

Like many visitors to the city, Tali and her mother included the 9/11 Memorial & Museum on their itinerary, hoping to pay their respects at the site where nearly 3,000 people lost their lives in the 2001 terror attacks. The museum had carefully designed its spaces to balance education with emotional impact, which, according to psychologist Billie Pivnick, keeps it "feeling alive and present without making it so alive and present that it's unbearable."[3] Like many modern museums dealing with tragic histories, it employed sophisticated multimedia presentations to help visitors understand the events of that day and reflection spaces to stop and process the learning experience.

Tali and her mother first visited the Memorial Pools, and then descended into the subterranean exhibition space beneath them where they spent several hours exploring the horrific details of 9/11 in the historical exhibition. "I remember avoiding a lot of the screens in the museum," Tali recalled, "but you end up absorbing it anyway." Though the exhibit was designed with small alcoves with warning signs that housed the most graphic images, providing a buffer for visitors who might want to avoid such content, Tali found herself drawn in despite her best efforts. She didn't want to get separated from her mother, who was moving through these spaces, and so she followed—inadvertently exposing herself to photographs of people jumping from the burning towers to their deaths. "The thing about museums," Tali observed, "is that they create this immersive environment. You're surrounded by the sounds, the images, the artifacts. There's no pause button like when you're watching videos at home."

After lunch, they headed to their next destination: the Empire State Building. Standing in the lobby waiting for the elevator, Tali began feeling anxious. She refused to take a headset for an audio tour and could not bring herself to walk out onto the observation deck. Her mother encouraged her to "look at the view," but Tali could not bring herself to even glance in that direction. "We had just learned how two gigantic buildings could fall, and then we went to the top of another one," Tali explained. "It was not a great idea. I'm pretty sure that's where my fear of heights came from, since I don't remember having it before." This transformation—from a child comfortable with heights to an adult who can't approach a window in a tall building—illustrates how powerfully museum experiences can reshape our relationship with the world around us.

In the moment, Tali couldn't articulate to her mother why she was so upset. It would be years before she could explain how the sequence of their visits had triggered such intense anxiety. In my office, Tali articulated how even the smallest details from the trip caused vicarious traumatization and had a lasting effect on her mental health. "It's not like I hadn't seen that footage before," she reflected. "I remember Googling it as a kid. But it's not the same as the immersive experience of a museum." The carefully curated exhibits, cutting-edge technology, and visceral proximity to the events had created an impact that mere images on a screen never could. And when combined with their subsequent visit to the Empire State Building, the whole experience was too much for Tali.

Tali's experience crystallized a fundamental challenge facing museum educators who guide visitors in spaces that present difficult histories: How do we help visitors process traumatic content without inadvertently creating new trauma? As she suggested, sometimes the solution can be as simple as thoughtful sequencing. But her story also points to deeper questions about how we cope with challenging historical knowledge and how to better support visitors in that process.

As discussed in previous chapters, the potential for vicarious trauma at Holocaust museums and other sites dedicated to difficult histories is very real. Yet these histories must be taught because their lessons are too important to leave untold. The challenge lies in developing frameworks that support visitor experiences while maintaining emotional safety. What signals indicate when historical knowledge becomes too overwhelming? How can educators anticipate and respond to signs of distress? Most importantly, how can we create spaces where visitors can meaningfully engage with difficult histories while preserving their psychological well-being? The answers lie in understanding both the ways people cope with traumatic knowledge and how those who work in museum spaces and guide trips to Europe or memorial sites can better support these coping processes.

The complexity of managing vicarious trauma and STS suggests that a systematic approach is needed to support both educators and visitors in trauma-informed learning spaces. While many frameworks exist for trauma-informed practice, the ABC framework originally developed by Saakvitne and Pearlman for therapists working with traumatized clients offers particularly valuable insights for Holocaust museums and memorial sites.[4] This model speaks directly to their unique dynamics through three key principles. Awareness addresses the need to recognize both individual trauma histories and collective memory. Balance speaks to the fundamental tension between historical accuracy and psychological safety. Connection acknowledges how meaningful Holocaust education depends on creating empathetic links to the past without triggering trauma responses in the present. The National Child Traumatic Stress Network has already adapted this framework for educators working with traumatized students.[5] Through a detailed examination of each element—Awareness, Balance, and Connection—Holocaust educators can develop strategies that support visitors while maintaining the educational integrity of these crucial historical narratives.

Recognizing and Responding: The Role of Awareness in Trauma Prevention

Encounters with difficult histories in classrooms and museums confront students with previously unimaginable events that can have profound psychological effects.[6] In these situations, educators serve as front-line responders who can help mitigate potential trauma.[7] The first step in preventing vicarious trauma is awareness—awareness of students' trauma histories, appropriate age and settings for Holocaust education, and effective trauma-informed teaching models.

Museum educators face a particular challenge in identifying previously traumatized students. Unlike classroom teachers, they rarely receive information about visitors' mental health challenges or trauma backgrounds. Without knowing students' baseline emotional states, it becomes difficult to gauge their psychological reactions during tours. One simple but effective approach I've implemented is asking schools during registration if there are any specific group dynamics or individual circumstances we should be aware of. A basic question on the registration form—"Have any students experienced loss or trauma that might be triggered during their visit?"—often yields invaluable information that might otherwise go unshared. The importance of this awareness extends from seemingly trivial sensitivities to extremely traumatic experiences. For example, it struck home when a teacher called and informed me that a particular student had severe anxiety about being photographed. By knowing this in advance, we could ensure no cameras or phones were used in the vicinity of the student. The student had an uneventful visit and participated in all the programming, and the teacher thanked us after the visit for being sensitive to this issue.

Museum staff face additional challenges beyond identification. Without ongoing relationships with visitors, they cannot provide long-term support or help process emotional difficulties that arise and assist them in moving beyond "the sensational experience of trauma and toward a restorative grasp of themselves and [the] world."[8] This limitation makes it crucial to minimize both primary and vicarious trauma during the brief span of a museum visit. Additionally, educators must recognize their own limitations in relating to Holocaust trauma—those who did not experience the Holocaust and the pain of the victims do not have the right to speak in place of survivors or claim to share their trauma. Such presumptions risk trivializing genuine survivor experiences while potentially serving educators' own emotional needs rather than visitors' educational ones. The sense or desire that they do should be resisted because it gives them the potentially self-serving illusion of empathetic understanding.[9]

The use of graphic images presents another area where awareness is crucial. While some educators believe such materials effectively evoke student empathy, extreme care must be taken in how and when these materials are introduced. The International Holocaust Remembrance Alliance's (IHRA) 2019 guidelines suggest that using graphic Holocaust images is problematic, as this approach can reinforce negative stereotypes about Jews, degrade victims, and disturb viewers' sense of modesty. The IHRA maintains that "the Holocaust can be taught effectively without using graphic photographs or film footage."[10] Others argue that since Holocaust atrocity images already circulate widely, they should be included in educational settings where teachers can provide historical context and support students' emotional reactions.[11] Increasingly, educators are providing trigger warnings about potentially traumatic materials, though the effectiveness of such warnings remains debatable.[12] (See Figure 6.1)

Figure 6.1 Pots and pans seized from Jews arriving in Auschwitz. Photo courtesy: Mordechai Golding.

Awareness extends critically to identifying age-appropriate settings for Holocaust education. "It's never too late to visit Poland. But it can be too early," observed David, a veteran guide I met who has led more than thirty student groups to Holocaust memorial sites. Though he guides these educational tours, David has no role in recruiting or vetting participants—a limitation that has led to challenging situations. Twice he has witnessed students experience panic attacks at Auschwitz. The first occurred in Bloc 5, where displays include personal items seized from murdered Jews like suitcases, shoes, pots, and pans. The student required medical assistance, and an ambulance had to be called. In another incident, a student disappeared during a tour of the prisoner barracks. After an intense search, they found him curled in a fetal position beneath one of the bunks. These experiences have led David to conclude that although schools and educational programs may offer Poland trips, not every teenager is emotionally or psychologically prepared for such intense encounters with historical trauma. He emphasizes that parents must realistically assess their children's readiness because "Once they are on the trip, it is left to the staff on the ground to deal with their emotional needs, and we are not always aware or adequately equipped to deal with panic and anxiety attacks brought on by these visits."

Awareness of the impact of such visits needs to extend to after the encounter with the difficult history, as an experience with a young woman named Noa brought home for me. After returning from a large group heritage tour to Poland with her seminary, she began experiencing panic attacks and flashbacks. Initial therapy sessions proved unhelpful, as she felt the therapist didn't truly understand her experience. Two months later, she still needed support processing what had happened. A teacher suggested she speak with me as someone who would be interested in her experience; I made it clear that I was not a therapist but would still be willing to listen to her. During our conversation, Noa revealed several important details that contributed to her lingering feelings: the overwhelming size of her tour group, an insufficient number of chaperones, and the recent death of a close relative that she believed she had "gotten over." When I later discussed Noa's case with her teacher, who leads journeys to Poland, she offered a crucial insight that helped explain what likely had happened: "From my experience and from the many journeys I have led, Poland rarely causes trauma, but can trigger traumatic memories."

The teacher's observations resonate with my friend Laura's experience visiting Theresienstadt at age fourteen. Her parents had organized a family legacy tour to Hungary and Prague, bringing their young children along. "Our tour guide was a Holocaust survivor, and it was very traumatizing to me," Laura recalled. The guide showed them where she had been interned, including the bed where prisoners had to sleep "the short way instead of the long way" to maximize capacity. "I remember vividly the guide saying that when one person would roll in the middle of the night, everybody had to roll." When the guide described the crematorium, including the smell of burning bones and flesh, the experience became overwhelming. For Laura, these graphic details combined with memories of her own grandmother's Holocaust-related nightmares to create lasting trauma. Years later, she still questions her parents' decision to expose her and her siblings to Theresienstadt and has avoided organized tours of concentration camps ever since.

With growing recognition of how ACEs affect learning, trauma-informed educational practices have become increasingly important.[13] These approaches focus on both healing vulnerabilities and building strengths,[14] with successful models integrating culture, collaboration, empowerment, peer support, and trust[15] to create trauma-sensitive schools and classrooms that provide safe environments where students can thrive.[16] However, it's important to recognize that no educational space can be entirely stress-free. Rather than attempting to eliminate all discomfort, trauma-informed spaces aim to encourage "a way of thinking, feeling, and acting that fosters students' critical rigor."[17] Children who have experienced trauma often benefit from specific accommodations like reminders, advance warnings, and information about schedule changes that disrupt routines.[18] But as demonstrated by the unexpected student reactions to *A Night at the Garden* discussed in Chapter 2, even experienced Holocaust educators must remain alert to how changing political and social circumstances can reshape visitors' interpretations of familiar material.

Creating trauma-informed spaces requires educators to fundamentally shift their approach to teaching and learning. Some teachers struggle with the expanding expectations of their role, feeling caught between traditional academic responsibilities and new demands to act as mental health advocates[19] and function as "front-line trauma workers for young people who do not have access to clinical care."[20] While training in trauma response is essential for creating secure learning environments, staff are often are asked to manage trauma-influenced behaviors with little to no training.[21] As one seasoned Holocaust educator gruffly said to me when I asked her about identifying and working with traumatized students in her classroom: "Of course there are students who can't handle learning about the Holocaust. But there's nothing I can really do about it." But the ABC model suggests that there is; as Noa's teacher observed, tour leaders, teachers, and museum educators need both awareness and "the humility of being teachers who are teachable." To heighten awareness, she stressed the importance of teacher preparation, including pre-trip meetings, ongoing discussions throughout the journey (whether a tour or a museum visit), and debriefing afterward to ensure that everyone involved is as prepared as they can be for the experience and its aftereffects. (See Figure 6.2)

Finding the Middle Ground: Balancing Historical Accuracy with Psychological Safety

Creating meaningful encounters with difficult histories requires a careful balance between historical accuracy and psychological safety. Museums and educators must weigh multiple competing demands: presenting traumatic content authentically while protecting visitors' emotional well-being, encouraging engagement while respecting individual coping needs, and promoting learning without triggering trauma responses.

The USHMM exemplifies these complex curatorial challenges. During the museum's design phase, curators grappled with how to accurately portray the Holocaust's most horrific elements while maintaining an emotionally safe space for visitors, particularly young ones. Their solution included installing privacy walls in front of monitors displaying the most graphic and disturbing images, allowing visitors to choose whether to view such content. This decision, though well-intentioned, had unexpected consequences. Rather than providing psychological protection, the privacy walls sometimes heightened visitors' voyeuristic curiosity about the "hidden" content. These screened-off spaces paradoxically became an attraction to what some visitors perceived as "the good stuff."[22]

A 1993 essay published shortly after the museum's opening captured this tension, describing the exhibits in stark terms: "Peep-show format. Snuff films. Naked women led to execution. People being shot. Into the ditch shot, spasms, collapse, dirt thrown in over. Crowds of naked people. Naked people standing about to be killed, naked people lying down dead."[23] The author likened the museum to a theme park, questioning whether such a graphic presentation served the institution's stated goals of encouraging authentic understanding and moral education.

Yet this critique proved to be an outlier. Most reviewers praised the museum as a "pedagogical masterpiece" for achieving balance in its narrative presentation and thoughtfully incorporating "provision for shock"[24] through spaces like the Hall of Remembrance. This carefully designed six-sided limestone chamber serves as a testament to architectural balance: "a chaste

Figure 6.2 Videos taken during liberation by the Soviet, British, and American armies hidden behind a privacy screen. Photograph by author, May 6, 2025.

vacancy, seventy feet high, unencumbered by iconography, washed in a kind of halting light, in a light that seems anxious about its own appropriateness."[25] The hall provides visitors a silent space for reflection after experiencing the main exhibition, exemplifying how thoughtful design can help visitors process difficult historical content. (See Figure 6.3)

USHMM's careful attention to visitor experience reflects a broader understanding of how people engage with sites of historical trauma. Most visitors to dark tourist sites who encounter difficult knowledge and histories exhibit a range of predictable behaviors. Research at Rwandan genocide memorials reveals three kinds of visitor responses. These center around etiquette, lessons, and emotions: visitors engage in ritualized behaviors of respect—taking photographs, making donations, signing guestbooks, and paying tribute to the dead; they also seek to extract meaning through political, educational, and humanitarian lessons; and they experience and express powerful emotions both during and after their visits. These patterns, though largely unspoken, form a near-universal visitor experience.[26]

Beyond these observable behaviors, when confronting the horrific experiences of Holocaust victims, individuals often resort to various

Figure 6.3 Hall of Remembrance. Photograph by author, May 6, 2025.

psychological coping mechanisms. These include "techniques of aversion, suppression, erasure, detachment, minimalization, sentimentalization, and eventually 'normalization' of victims' suffering and experience."[27] The encounter with historical injustice frequently triggers intense emotional responses—sadness, anger, outrage.[28] As one researcher notes, "when a student's sensibility about the world is disquieted, the disquieted individual seeks to steady themselves and their now-turbulent footing in the way they experience the world. This steadying is not always pleasant."[29] If visitors feel pressured to experience specific emotional responses, they may react with resistance or anger,[30] sometimes expressed in the form of accusations of racism or institutional bias.

These patterns of visitor response—both the observable behaviors and underlying psychological mechanisms—directly inform the ongoing challenge of maintaining balance in Holocaust museums. While curators and designers bear primary responsibility for creating balanced exhibit narratives that both engage visitors and maintain emotional safety, this work continues through the ongoing efforts of museum staff. Educators leading tours and programs must constantly navigate these same tensions between engagement and protection, learning and trauma prevention. Understanding how individuals process and cope with difficult histories becomes essential for maintaining this delicate balance in practice.

Understanding Individual Responses: Coping Mechanisms and Support Strategies

The Holocaust consistently evokes profound sadness in visitors, and confronting this emotional weight can be deeply uncomfortable.[31] Students encountering difficult historical content typically display clear signs of discomfort and unease,[32] requiring educators to help them maintain psychological balance throughout their visit—before, during, and after. But this emphasis on balance is really about helping students cope. As the Oklahoma Department of Mental Health and Substance Abuse Services notes, "B is for Balance. And when we talk about B, what we're really talking about is safe coping skills and self-care."[33]

What then does it mean to cope? Lazarus and Folkman define coping as "constantly changing cognitive and behavioral efforts to manage specific external and/or demands that are appraised as taxing or exceeding the resources of the person."[34] Coping strategies thus emerge both in response to long-term trauma and during acute moments of crisis, serving as personal resources for stress management.[35]

Effective coping serves a dual purpose: addressing objective challenges and managing emotional responses. It helps individuals tackle both concrete problems and modify or reduce the cognitive, emotional, and physical stress of difficult situations.[36] Research shows that emotional regulation and self-awareness—cognitive components of empathy—can be developed as protective factors against vicarious traumatization.[37] Particularly for young visitors, coping represents a normal stress response; children often employ behavioral coping mechanisms to maintain a sense of safety and control in challenging situations.[38] (See Figure 6.4)

Figure 6.4 Stairs in Anne Frank's Secret Annex. Photo courtesy: Anne Frank House, Amsterdam.

The search for effective coping strategies in the face of trauma has deep historical roots within Holocaust history itself. Anne Frank's diary provides a powerful example of active coping during extreme circumstances. While hiding in an Amsterdam attic for more than two years, living under constant threat of discovery or death from air raids, Anne developed creative strategies to manage her fears. In one of her final diary entries, written just two months before the family's discovery and deportation to concentration camps, she described her method for dealing with bombing raids:

> *I have a brand-new prescription against gunfire: During particularly loud bangs hasten to the nearest wooden stairs, run up and down a few times and make sure that you fall gently downstairs at least once. What with the*

scratches and the noise of the running and falling, you are too busy to listen to the gunfire let alone worry about it. The writer of these lines has certainly used this ideal recipe with success![39]

Contemporary students, like their historical counterparts, employ various coping mechanisms—both positive and negative—to manage their emotional responses to Holocaust sites. Many struggle with anxiety about potential uncontrollable emotional reactions during their visits. Isabella Friedman's account of her school trip to Poland illustrates these common concerns. She "counted down the days with dread until I'd have to leave my sunny kibbutz for cold, gloomy Eastern Europe" and worried about her emotional response after hearing about others' experiences. "I had heard the horror stories of what it felt like to visit a concentration camp," she recalled.

> *My friend Rayna, who visited Auschwitz the previous summer, told me that she felt nauseous, weak, and dizzy the entire time she was there. Even though our school's staff repeatedly told me and my peers that there was no wrong way to react to the sites we were going to see, I feared being too sad, not sad enough, anxious, or worst of all, laughing.*[40]

While all individuals develop coping mechanisms when confronting difficult histories, the effectiveness of these strategies varies significantly. Some coping mechanisms lead to positive outcomes, while others, such as substance abuse, can be destructive.[41] Research consistently shows that effective coping correlates with positive psychological outcomes, while negative coping tends to increase anger and distress.[42] This distinction becomes particularly important in educational settings, where educators must learn to recognize students' coping styles and help guide them toward more constructive approaches.

Negative coping strategies often manifest as avoidance and disengagement, behaviors frequently associated with high anxiety levels.[43] Studies have established clear links between avoidance behaviors and negative psychological attitudes,[44] with research demonstrating strong connections between trauma exposure and maladaptive coping mechanisms. Individuals with trauma histories frequently exhibit poor coping styles, particularly avoidance, which can lead to adverse mental health outcomes.[45] This pattern appears consistently across different populations; for instance, a study of mothers experiencing parental distress found that disengagement and other negative coping strategies strongly correlated with increased psychological distress, regardless of preexisting mental health conditions.[46]

In Holocaust museum settings, avoidance behaviors can manifest in multiple ways: complete refusal to participate in visits, selective avoidance of specific exhibitions, or mental disengagement during guided tours. The case of Yael, a high school senior, illustrates the complexity of these responses. Despite being a motivated student who had demonstrated deep engagement with Holocaust education—even winning first place in a national student art competition about Holocaust resilience—Yael experienced intense anxiety about visiting the Museum of Jewish Heritage. On the morning of her school field trip, she refused to board the bus, later explaining that Holocaust imagery triggered sensations of "having been there before" and "reexperiencing something that happened to me personally." These feelings had emerged two years earlier after reading a Holocaust-related book. Through careful negotiation, Yael was able to partially participate in the museum experience, viewing pre-war and postwar exhibitions while bypassing sections about ghettos and camps.

Research demonstrates that active coping strategies generally prove more effective than avoidance for managing trauma responses. Studies of terror attack victims show that willingness to forgive and problem-focused coping correlate with reduced PTSD symptoms, while avoidance coping does not.[47] Active forms of coping—methods employed to deal directly with a problem or event—are consistently associated with better stress management and lower stress levels, though there may be times when temporary avoidance is necessary.[48] Moreover, active coping approaches and the use of instrumental supports have been linked to post-traumatic growth and increased self-compassion among trauma survivors.[49] These findings are supported across diverse contexts, from parents with infants in neonatal intensive care units who cope through talking and scrapbooking[50] to Israeli Defense Force soldiers who report that faith-based coping strategies prove more beneficial than purely emotional responses.[51] (See Figure 6.5)

The effectiveness of active coping often depends on finding personally meaningful strategies. Photographer James Friedman's experience documenting Nazi concentration camps in the 1980s provides a compelling example. While creating some of the first color photographs of these sites—taking an approach he described as "brazenly passionate and 'hot' rather than detached and 'cool'"[52]—Friedman developed an innovative coping

Figure 6.5 Flossenbürg concentration camp, near Bayreuth, Germany, 1981. Photo credit: James Friedman.

mechanism. Feeling overwhelmed by "the remnants of evil and murder that pervaded each site," he deliberately included personal objects in his photographs to maintain his psychological equilibrium:

> *I included in many of the photographs personal objects that I had brought with me or some of my tools and equipment. Doing so somehow connected me to home and provided a sense of protection from the evil at these sites. For example, my photograph "Site where prisoners were shot in mass, Flossenbürg concentration camp, near Bayreuth, Germany, 1981" shows in the foreground some marker pens and a small camera I carried, with a note about the location and date. The well-tended lawn in the background had been a killing field; the stone marker informs visitors that "prisoners were shot in mass here."*[53]

The process of engaging with Holocaust sites often requires more than just immediate coping strategies—it demands a deeper integration of the experience. Mental health professionals typically recommend that trauma victims work to integrate difficult experiences into their life history as part of the healing process.[54] Such integration involves developing comfort with oneself rather than dissociating from challenging situations. In trauma-sensitive learning spaces, this means fostering an atmosphere where participants can recognize and process how confronting difficult histories affects them. One tour leader for student groups to Holocaust sites in Poland and Eastern Europe, who happens to be a clinical social worker and psychotherapist, emphasizes this perspective by deliberately referring to his tours as "journeys" rather than "trips"—a distinction that acknowledges the personal and emotional growth inherent in these experiences. As he explained to me, "It's not a trip that your tour guide gets personal with you, but a journey that you get personal with you."[55]

Coping mechanisms can sometimes manifest in ways that appear inappropriate or disrespectful, particularly in settings dedicated to historical trauma. Educators need to understand these varied responses and develop nuanced approaches to addressing them. A notable example occurred on Martin Luther King Day in 1994, when a screening of *Schindler's List* in Oakland, California, sparked national controversy. During the film, a group of African American and Latino students from Castlemont High School began laughing at Holocaust scenes, prompting outrage from other audience members. The screening was halted, and the students were asked to leave the theater.[56] The incident drew widespread condemnation, with critics arguing that "clearly, these students experienced the wrong emotions. To laugh at images of human torture and violence exposes oneself as insensitive at best, immoral and depraved at worst."[57]

Yet a more complex understanding emerged through Mark Rader, the teacher who organized the field trip. In response to the controversy, which had attracted national attention and even prompted a visit from Steven Spielberg himself, Rader offered a different perspective. As reported in the New York Times,[58] Rader interpreted the laughter as a defensive response—adolescents using humor to shield themselves from overwhelming emotions, particularly in front of peers who might judge them for displaying sadness about the Holocaust. This interpretation finds support in broader research on laughter as a coping mechanism. Scholars have identified various forms of situational laughter, distinguishing between cruel and reparative laughter, examining laughter as a response to unexpected narrative shifts, and understanding laughter as "a response to the utter absurdity of the situation."[59] Such analysis suggests that apparent inappropriate responses may often mask deeper emotional processes.

Coping in Holocaust museums and dark tourism sites requires active attention to visitors' self-care needs, both during and after their encounters with difficult histories. While photographs and videos allow visitors to engage with historical events from a physical distance, these media can still provoke intense psychological responses. Some visitors may exhibit heightened anxiety or panic behaviors, while others may freeze, appear defiant, or employ other coping mechanisms to manage their stress.[60] Rather than viewing these behaviors as disciplinary issues, educators need to adopt a trauma-informed perspective that recognizes such responses as natural reactions to encountering difficult histories.

Research on STS among human rights investigators provides valuable guidance for managing exposure to disturbing content in museum settings.[61] Studies show that visual and auditory materials typically generate stronger emotional impacts than written documentation. Effective mitigation strategies operate on multiple levels: practical viewing techniques (such as limiting exposure time, taking frequent breaks, working in groups, and following difficult content with lighter material), community support (engaging with friends, family, fellow students, or mental health professionals), and personal self-care practices (including exercise, meditation, mindfulness, and adequate sleep).

The availability of these coping resources proves crucial for both visitors and their guides. Research on secondary traumatization among Israeli students following terror attacks demonstrates that access to support resources correlates directly with reduced post-traumatic distress.[62] As researchers note, "an ethic of empathy and caring is necessary to provide a safe place for students to examine, challenge, and change their cherished beliefs and assumptions."[63] This understanding has transformed how Holocaust museums approach visitor care, with staff showing greater awareness of varied trauma responses and developing clear pathways to additional support when needed.[64] By recognizing that emotional responses to Holocaust history—whether expressed through tears, laughter, or apparent detachment—reflect genuine attempts to process difficult knowledge, museums can better fulfill their dual mission of historical education and psychological support.

From Personal to Collective: Building Meaningful Connections

On June 11, 2003, Sarri Singer boarded Jerusalem's #14 bus, unaware that her life was about to change forever. The daughter of New Jersey State Senator Robert Singer, Sarri had recently moved to Israel from New York City, driven by her experience during 9/11. That September morning, she had overslept and missed being at her Lower Manhattan job just blocks from the Twin Towers. Feeling both grateful for her survival and compelled to act, she "felt an urge to make a difference."[65] Within three months, she "had quit [her] job and moved to Israel to volunteer with organizations that assisted victims of terror and their families."[66] But as she went to meet a friend for dinner on that warm June evening, her life changed forever.

As the bus made its way through Jerusalem, a massive explosion rocked the vehicle. An eighteen-year-old Hamas terrorist had detonated a suicide vest, killing sixteen people and injuring more than seventy others. Though sitting just two rows behind the terrorist, Sarri miraculously survived while those around her instantly died. The attack left her with extensive burns, shattered eardrums, and a body riddled with shrapnel—some pieces so deeply embedded that they could not be removed despite multiple surgeries and months of rehabilitation.

Rather than let the trauma define her, Sarri chose to transform her pain into purpose. Drawing inspiration from the kindness she received during her recovery, she founded Strength to Strength, an international organization supporting terror attack victims and their families. The organization facilitates peer-to-peer support meetings that empower "victims of terrorism to share experiences and empowers them to live life to their best potential."[67] Understanding that trauma ripples through families, the program extends support to children and spouses who experience the aftermath vicariously.

When I asked Sarri about the most crucial element of healing and trauma prevention, her answer was immediate and unambiguous: "connections." As she explained, Strength to Strength's programs focus on connecting victims because

> *someone who has been through a similar experience to you can understand better than anyone else what you are going through. If you see somebody who is ahead of you in terms of their healing process, they are the people who can show you that you can get there. People want to see that there is a light at the end of the tunnel and that they are not going to be this way forever.*[68]

This emphasis on human connection aligns with research on managing STS. As the third and final step in the ABC process, connections—whether to oneself, to others, or to a higher power—play a vital role in mitigating vicarious trauma. This is especially true in educational settings, where a child who feels a sense of connection to educators and peers "will be a lot more open to learning and will really thrive," says Dr. Carly Namdar, Director of Resilience Programs and School-Based Services at Ohel Children's Home and Family Services. "For a child to be able to open themselves up to learn difficult concepts, there needs to be that sense of safety. There needs to be that sense of trust and connection. So that if they are struggling, they don't have to stick with that discomfort."[69] Educators therefore can and should shape experiences that forge these healing connections in meaningful ways.

Creating Safe Spaces: The Power of Community and Shared Experience

Building connections takes many forms, and the physical environment plays a crucial role. When introducing a survivor giving testimony in a classroom, I deliberately arrange the room so that the survivor sits in a circle with the students—not as a lecturer in the front of the room. I learned this technique from Moshe Sternberg, a psychotherapist who worked with Holocaust survivors at Yad Vashem, who promoted this approach because it helps survivors speak more comfortably and conversationally with their listeners.[70] This arrangement does more than comfort the speaker—it also creates feelings of connection and safety among those who are listening. Sitting together at eye level and creating a safe space for the survivor to share their testimony in turn creates a feeling of safety among the listeners. Many times, I have observed how this simple seating arrangement lowers the anxiety in the room and creates feelings of connection between the speaker and the listeners.

The importance of creating space for connection extends beyond the classroom to memorial sites. When visiting Holocaust sites, it is important to build in time for visitors to debrief and share their reflections with their peers. These moments of shared processing allow program participants to share their feelings and reflections with one another, creating deep and often lasting relationships with others on the trip. While participants often find it hard to share the intense emotions they experience after visiting a concentration camp or mass grave, creating a setting that normalizes expressing emotions and feelings of vulnerability is essential in mitigating vicarious trauma.

There are many touchpoints during such programs; checking in on the pulse of the group and giving them an opportunity to process the experience would be valuable. They include moments when they are leaving a specific site, like a ghetto or concentration camp, at the end of the day, before participants head to their rooms to go to sleep, and especially at the end of the trip before getting on a plane to return home. Checking in a few days or weeks later to see what lessons or questions remain with them is also important.

Ben, a tour guide who leads about ten student groups to Poland each year, emphasizes that the debriefing sessions he runs each evening are the most important part of the day. As they check into the hotel each night, he runs a session where students are asked to share one takeaway from the program that day. Ben does not distribute room keys until after the session because he wants to make sure that everyone comes to the program and does not head to their room to process their feelings alone.

Even in time-constrained settings like museums, educators can create opportunities for connection. I often find that school groups are rushed when they come to museums, often leaving little time to process what they learned in a formal session. If they do not have time for a question-and-answer or reflective session with museum staff, I like to provide resources for teachers to use back in the classroom to review and process their students' experiences. Using the 3-2-1 assessment method—where students are asked to provide three pieces of information that they learned, two questions that they still have, and the one most important part of the day for them—teachers can address lingering feelings and help students process what they are thinking. When this process is conducted in the classroom, students interact with one another and feel connected to their peers who also experienced intense emotions that day, often in a way that they could not do during a guided tour.

Faith, Loss, and Meaning-Making: Spiritual Dimensions of Holocaust Education

Beyond peer connections, many find strength in a spiritual connection with a higher being through faith-based coping. Religious coping has been identified as an effective method for dealing with trauma because it gives meaning to the situation and provides a sense of control.[71] Like coping in general, religious coping takes two forms. Positive religious coping is associated with better outcomes and includes seeking spiritual support and praying. Negative religious coping manifests as discontent or doubt about religious beliefs and is associated with increased depression and anxiety.[72]

The struggle with faith during and after the Holocaust is well-documented in survivors' diaries and memoirs. One of the most powerful examples is Elie Wiesel's journey from rejection to reconciliation with his faith. In his memoir *Night*, Wiesel describes his arrival in Auschwitz as a pivotal moment that shattered his religious beliefs. His anguish is captured in his haunting words:

> *Never shall I forget that night, the first night in the camp, which has turned my life into one long night, seven times cursed and seven times sealed. Never shall I forget the smoke. . . . Never shall I forget the nocturnal silence which deprived me, for all eternity, of the desire to live. Never shall I forget those moments which murdered my G-d and my soul and turned my dreams into dust.*[73]

Yet more than 50 years later, Wiesel's relationship with faith evolved. In a profound 1997 op-ed in the New York Times, he wrote:

> *Auschwitz must and will forever remain a question mark only: it can be conceived neither with God nor without God. At one point, I began wondering whether I was not unfair with you. After all, Auschwitz was not something that came down ready-made from heaven. It was conceived by men, implemented by men, staffed by men. And their aim was to destroy not only us but you as well. Ought we not to think of your pain, too? Watching your children suffer at the hands of your other children, haven't you also suffered?*
>
> *As we Jews now enter the High Holidays again, preparing ourselves to pray for a year of peace and happiness for our people and all people, let us make up, Master of the Universe. In spite of everything that happened? Yes, in spite. Let us make up: for the child in me, it is unbearable to be divorced from you so long.*[74]

This complex relationship with faith continues to echo through generations. Many descendants of Holocaust survivors also use faith-based connections to process Holocaust history. Research has revealed that individuals with high levels of spirituality and religiosity tend to develop problem-focused coping styles through their religious practice. Conversely, those with low levels of spirituality and religiosity more often turn to avoidant coping strategies.[75] The impact of these coping mechanisms is significant, with negative religious coping having been found to increase stress by "adding to the burden already placed on someone grappling with a stressful situation."[76]

The same thing can happen in reverse, with students using encounters with Holocaust material to process personal issues. I can recall clearly a student named Michelle who visited my office repeatedly throughout the year, each time circling around the same profound question, though she phrased it differently in every conversation: "If something like the Holocaust happened to Jews, and antisemitism still persists, what's the point of maintaining Jewish identity?" she would ask, her voice carrying an undercurrent of deeper uncertainty.

Sensing there might be more beneath her philosophical questioning, I eventually asked if any particular aspects of our Holocaust studies had unsettled her or if she was processing a personal loss that might be surfacing in these discussions. That's when the fuller picture emerged. Michelle revealed that just months before, her family had suffered the devastating loss of her baby sister, who died shortly after birth. The grief had created a quiet fracture in her home. Her father coped by hanging pictures of the baby throughout the house, while her mother couldn't bear to speak the child's name or discuss the loss. Behind Michelle's persistent questions about Jewish identity and historical suffering lay a more immediate spiritual struggle: she was grappling with fundamental questions about G-ds role in personal tragedy. Her doubts about divine presence in the face of loss were finding expression through our discussions of antisemitism and the Holocaust, as she sought to make sense of both historical and personal suffering.

In appropriate educational settings, educators can frame Holocaust lessons through a spiritual or religious lens to help students process difficult knowledge. This approach resonates deeply with some students. As a student once told me, at her private religious school, she wants the teacher to focus on teaching spiritual and religious aspects of the Holocaust in the classroom because "history can always be found in a textbook." To explore this connection between spirituality and Holocaust education, I designed an experiential lesson that would help students connect to something larger than themselves—something sacred and transcendent that could help them find meaning in what they were learning.

The lesson began simply: I brought two potatoes, some oil, matches, an old article of clothing, and a dull knife to class. When I announced we would be learning outside that day, students followed me with curiosity. Together, we read about Jewish inmates in Bergen-Belsen who, despite their desperate circumstances, were determined to light a menorah during Chanukah. Using threads from their threadbare clothing as wicks and scraps of potatoes and oil from their meager food portions, they created a makeshift menorah for the first night of the holiday.

Though we were studying life in the concentration camps, this unexpected intersection with Chanukah—months away from the actual holiday—captured my students' attention. When I revealed the supplies in my bag and explained that we would recreate the Bergen-Belsen menorah ourselves, their engagement deepened. They began questioning every detail: how thick to slice the potato, how to fashion wicks from clothing, and whether our oil matched what the prisoners would have had. (See Figure 6.6)

The activity took a powerful turn when the wicks we made from the old clothing wouldn't light. Without prompting, students began pulling threads from their own shirts to try instead. Once the menorah was finally lit, we read about the Bluzhever Rebbe, who stood in Bergen-Belsen and recited the traditional blessing: "Blessed are you G-d, King of the Universe . . . who has sustained us, kept us alive and brought us to this moment."[77] The Rebbe then posed a haunting question to his fellow prisoners: "Is it not anomalous to thank God for miracles that he had wrought for our ancestors long ago, while He seemingly performs none for us in our tragic plight?"[78] His answer resonated across time: "By kindling this Chanukah candle we are symbolically identifying ourselves with the Jewish people everywhere. Our long history records many bloody horrors our people have endured and survived. We may be certain that no matter what may befall us as individuals, the Jews as a people will—with the help of God—outlive their cruel foes and emerge triumphant in the end."[79]

The impact of this experience was visible as my students sat quietly, protecting the flames from the wind, showing visible emotion when the lights finally flickered out. Their reflections revealed deep connections: "Seeing the flame burning as we were shielding it from the wind really touched me—it symbolized survival in the face of adversity," one student shared. Another noted that "there is something about hands-on activities that make spirituality seem much more real," while a third reflected on "how much love, energy, and actual resources had to be given to do a mitzvah."

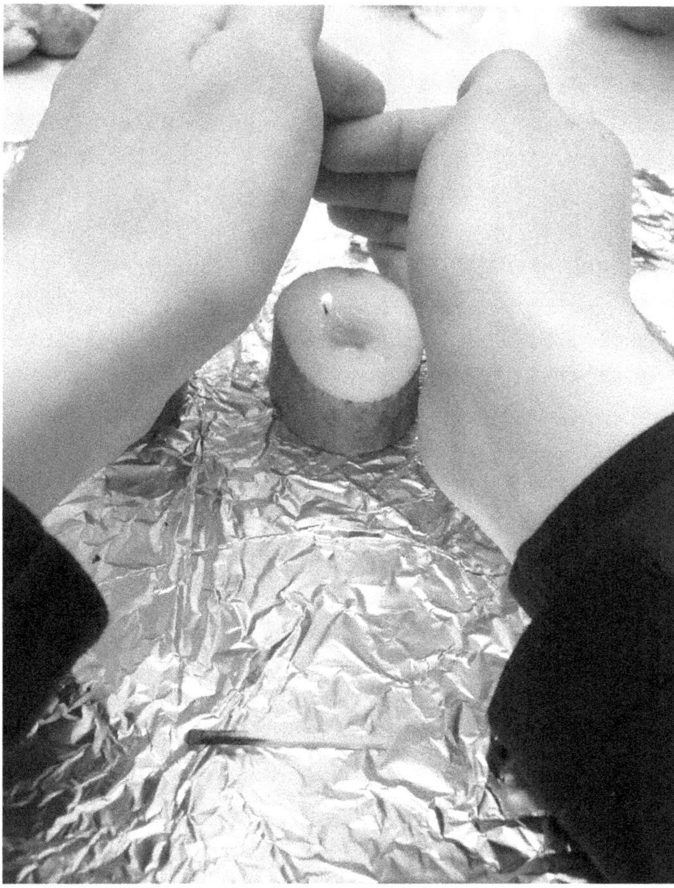

Figure 6.6 A student shields the flames of a menorah made from potatoes, April 26, 2018. Photograph by author.

Notes

1 Personal communication with Clifford Chanin, March 31, 2025.

2 The Associated Press, "9/11 Memorial Museum Design to Lessen Emotional Impact," *CBC News*, May 21, 2014, https://www.cbc.ca/news/world/9-11-memorial-museum-design-to-lessen-emotional-impact-1.2649302.

3 The Associated Press, "9/11 Memorial Museum Design to Lessen Emotional Impact," *CBC News*, May 21, 2014, https://www.cbc.ca/news/world/9-11-memorial-museum-design-to-lessen-emotional-impact-1.2649302.

4 Karen W. Saakvitne and Laurie Anne Pearlman, *Transforming the Pain: A Workbook on Vicarious Traumatization* (New York: W.W. Norton & Company, 1996), 75.

5 National Child Traumatic Stress Network, "Taking Care of Yourself," *NCTSN*, https://www.nctsn.org/resources/taking-care-of-yourself (February 20, 2025).

6 Aparna Mishra Tarc, "'I Just Have to Tell You': Pedagogical Encounters into the Emotional Terrain of Learning," *Pedagogy, Culture and Society* 21, no. 3 (2013): 383–402, https://doi.org/10.1080/14681366.2012.759132.

7 Beverly Ray and Martha Hocutt, "Learning From and Teaching About Disaster: The Case of the April 2011 Tornado Outbreak," *American Secondary Education* 44, no. 2 (2016): 66–84, http://www.jstor.org/stable/45147975.

8 William Gaudelli, Margaret Crocco, and Alexandra Hawkins, "Documentaries Outtakes and Digital Archives in Teaching Difficult Knowledge and the Vietnam War," *Education and Society* 30, no. 2 (2012): 23, https://doi.org/10.7459/es/30.2.02.

9 Colin Davis, *Traces of War: Interpreting Ethics and Trauma in Twentieth-Century French Writing* (Liverpool: Liverpool University Press, 2018).

10 International Holocaust Remembrance Alliance, "Recommendations for Teaching and Learning about the Holocaust," *International Holocaust Remembrance Alliance*, https://www.holocaustremembrance.com/sites/default/files/inline-files/IHRA-Recommendations-Teaching-and-Learning-about-Holocaust.pdf (January 25, 2022).

11 Ruth-Anne Lenga, "Seeing Things Differently: The Use of Atrocity Images in Teaching about the Holocaust," in *Holocaust Education: Contemporary Challenges and Controversies*, ed. Stuart Foster, Andy Pearce, and Alice Pettigrew (London: UCL Press, 2020), 195–220, https://doi.org/10.2307/j.ctv15d7zpf.16.

12 Francesca Laguardia, Venezia Michalsen, and Holly Rider-Milkovich, "Trigger Warnings: From Panic to Data," *Journal of Legal Education* 66, no. 4 (2017): 882–903, https://www.jstor.org/stable/26453524.

13 Vanessa Sacks and David Murphey, "The Prevalence of Adverse Childhood Experiences, Nationally, by State, and by Race or Ethnicity," *Child Trends*, last modified February 12, 2018, www.childtrends.org/publications/prevalence-adverse-childhood-experiencesnationally-state-race-ethnicity.

14 Tom Brunzell, Helen Stokes, and Lea Waters, "Trauma-Informed Flexible Learning: Classrooms That Strengthen Regulatory Abilities," *International Journal of Child, Youth and Family Studies* 7, no. 2 (2016): 218–39, https://doi.org/10.18357/ijcyfs72201615719.

15 Sheryl H. Kataoka, Pamela Vona, Alejandra Acuña, Lisa Jaycox, Pia Escudero, Claudia Rojas, Erica Ramirez, Audra Langley, and Bradley D. Stein, "Applying a Trauma Informed School Systems Approach: Examples from School Community-Academic Partnerships," *Ethnicity & Disease* 28 (2018): 424, https://www.jstor.org/stable/48667763.

16 Brian Cavanaugh, "Trauma-Informed Classrooms and Schools," *Beyond Behavior* 25, no. 2 (2016): 41–6, http://www.jstor.org/stable/26381827.

17 Michalinos Zembylas, "'Pedagogy of Discomfort' and Its Ethical Implications: The Tensions of Ethical Violence in Social Justice Education," *Ethics and Education* 10, no. 2 (2015): 166, https://doi.org/10.1080/17449642.2015.1039274.

18 Cavanaugh, "Trauma-Informed Classrooms."

19 Salvatore Terrasi and Patricia Crain de Galarce, "Trauma and Learning in America's Classrooms," *The Phi Delta Kappan* 98, no. 6 (2017): 35–41, http://www.jstor.org/stable/26386969.

20 Brunzell et al., "Trauma-Informed Flexible Learning," 220.

21 Elizabeth M. Anderson, Lisa V. Blitz, and Monique Saastamoinen, "Exploring a School-University Model for Professional Development with Classroom Staff: Teaching Trauma Informed Approaches," *School Community Journal* 25, no. 2 (2015): 113–34, https://files.eric.ed.gov/fulltext/EJ1085667.pdf.

22 Robert M. Ehrenreich and Jane Klinger, "War in Context: Let the Artifacts Speak," in *Does War Belong in Museums?: The Representation of Violence in Exhibitions*, ed. Wolfgang Muchitsch (Wetzlar, Germany: Transcript Verlag, 2013), 145, http://www.jstor.org/stable/j.ctv1wxr1z.14.

23 Gourevitch, as cited in Zehavit Gross, "The Process of the Universalization of Holocaust Education: Problems and Challenges," *Contemporary Jewry* 38, no. 1 (2018): 5–20, http://www.jstor.org/stable/45209113.

24 Leon Wieseltier, "After Memory," *The New Republic*, May 3, 1993, 20, https://static1.squarespace.com/static/55955834e4b00f5f813573d5/t/56be5c4d356fb031229f4f0d/1455316046428/After+Memory.pdf.

25 Wieseltier, "After Memory," 20.

26 Annalisa Bolin, "On the Side of Light: Performing Morality at Rwanda's Genocide Memorials," *Journal of Conflict Archaeology* 7, no. 3 (2012): 199–207, https://www.jstor.org/stable/48601744.

27 Michalinos Zembylas, Loizos Loukaides, and Petroula Antoniou, "Teachers' Understandings of Empathy in Teaching about the Holocaust in Cyprus: The Emotional Risks of Identification and the Disruptive Potential of 'Empathic Unsettlement,'" *Teaching and Teacher Education* 89 (2020): 2, https://doi.org/10.1016/j.tate.2019.103007.

28 Michalinos Zembylas and Claire McGlynn, "Discomforting Pedagogies: Emotional Tensions, Ethical Dilemmas and Transformative Possibilities," *British Educational Research Journal* 38, no. 1 (2012): 41–59, http://www.jstor.org/stable/23211443.

29 H. James Garrett, "Difficult Knowledge: Encounters with Social Trauma in Pedagogy," *Counterpoints* 506 (2017): 31, http://www.jstor.org/stable/45136321.

30 Lisa Jenny Krieg, "'Who Wants to Be Sad Over and Over Again?' Emotion Ideologies in Contemporary German Education about the Holocaust," *Journal of Educational Media, Memory & Society* 7, no. 2 (2015): 110–28, http://www.jstor.org/stable/44319958.

31 Krieg, "Who Wants to Be Sad."

32 Garrett, "Difficult Knowledge."

33 Oklahoma Department of Mental Health and Substance Abuse Services, "Vicarious Trauma," Oklahoma Department of Mental Health and Substance Abuse Services, https://oklahoma.gov/content/dam/ok/en/odmhsas/documents/a0004/vicarioustrauma-transcript.pdf (January 9, 2024).

34 Ann Chunyan Peng, Laura T. Riolli, John Schaubroeck, and Everett S. Spain, "A Moderated Mediation Test of Personality, Coping, and Health among Deployed Soldiers," *Journal of Organizational Behavior* 33, no. 4 (2011): 513, https://doi.org/10.1002/job.766.

35 O. A. Grinstein-Cohen, A. Katz, and O. Sarid, "Religiosity: Its Impact on Coping Styles Among Women Undergoing Fertility Treatment," *Journal of Religion and Health* 56, no. 3 (2017): 1032–41, http://www.jstor.org/stable/26749277.

36 Josep Gustems-Carnicer and Caterina Calderón, "Coping Strategies and Psychological Well-Being among Teacher Education Students: Coping and Well-Being in Students," *European Journal of Psychology of Education* 28, no. 4 (2013): 1127–40, https://doi.org/10.1007/sl0212-012-0158-x.

37 M. Alex Wagaman, Jennifer M. Geiger, Clara Shockley, and Elizabeth A. Segal, "The Role of Empathy in Burnout, Compassion Satisfaction, and Secondary Traumatic Stress among Social Workers," *Social Work* 60, no. 3 (2015): 201–9, http://www.jstor.org/stable/24881483.

38 Bessel van der Kolk, *The Body Keeps the Score: Brain, Mind, and Body in the Healing of Trauma* (London: Penguin Books, 2015).

39 Anne Frank, *The Diary of Anne Frank: The Critical Edition*, ed. David Barnouw and Gerrold Van Der Stroom, trans. Arnold J. Pomerans and B. M. Mooyaart (New York: Doubleday, 1989).

40 Isabel Hoffman, "Prayers in Majdanek," *Jewish Women's Archive*, October 16, 2019, https://jwa.org/blog/risingvoices/prayers-majdanek.

41 Pashtoon Murtaza Kasi, Haider Ali Naqvi, Abaseen Khan Afghan, Talha Khawar, Farooq Hasan Khan, Umber Zaheer Khan, Urooj Bakht Khuwaja, Jawad Kiani, and Hadi Mohammad Khan, "Coping Styles in Patients with Anxiety and Depression," *ISRN Psychiatry* (June 2012): 1–7, https://doi.org/10.5402/2012/128672.

42 Robert R. Wright, Cynthia D. Mohr, Robert R. Sinclair, and Liu-Qin Yang, "Sometimes Less Is More: Directed Coping with Interpersonal Stressors at Work," *Journal of Organizational Behavior* 36, no. 6 (2015): 786–805, https://doi.org/10.1002/job.2002.

43 Paul Boxer and Elizabeth Sloan-Power, "Coping With Violence: A Comprehensive Framework and Implications for Understanding Resilience," *Trauma, Violence, & Abuse* 14, no. 3 (2013): 209–21, https://www.jstor.org/stable/26638314.

44 Gustems-Carnicer and Calderón, "Coping Strategies and Psychological Well-Being."

45 Tiffany Jenzer, Samuel N. Meisel, Jessica A. Blayney, Craig R. Colder, and Jennifer P. Read, "Reciprocal Processes in Trauma and Coping: Bidirectional Effects over a Four-Year Period," *Psychological Trauma: Theory, Research, Practice, and Policy* 12, no. 2 (2020): 207–18, https://doi.org/10.1037/tra0000500.

46 Tali Malka, Ilanit Hasson-Ohayon, Gil Goldzweig, and David Roe, "Coping Style Is Associated with Parental Distress beyond Having a Mental Illness: A Study among Mothers with and without Mental Illness," *Psychiatric Rehabilitation Journal* 43, no. 2 (2020): 170–3, https://doi.org/10.1037/prj0000381.

47 Michael Weinberg, Sharon Gil, and Ora Gilbar, "Forgiveness, Coping, and Terrorism: Do Tendency to Forgive and Coping Strategies Associate with the Level of Posttraumatic Symptoms of Injured Victims of Terror Attacks?" *Journal of Clinical Psychology* 70, no. 7 (2013): 693–703, https://doi.org/10.1002/jclp.22056.

48 Teresa Mayordomo-Rodríguez, Juan Carlos Meléndez-Moral, Paz Viguer-Segui, and Alicia Sales-Galán, "Coping Strategies as Predictors of Well-Being in Youth Adult," *Social Indicators Research* 122, no. 2 (2014): 479–89, https://doi.org/10.1007/s11205-014-0689-4.

49 Melanie Munroe, Mohamed Al-Refae, Helen W. Chan, and Michel Ferrari, "Using Self-Compassion to Grow in the Face of Trauma: The Role of Positive Reframing and Problem-Focused Coping Strategies," *Psychological Trauma: Theory, Research, Practice, and Policy* 14, no. 1 (2022): 157–64, https://doi.org/10.1037/tra0001164.

50 Ellen Huenink and Susan Porterfield, "Parent Support Programs and Coping Mechanisms in Nicu Parents," *Advances in Neonatal Care* 17, no. 2 (April 2017): E10–E18, https://doi.org/10.1097/anc.0000000000000359.

51 Uzi Ben-Shalom and Yizhaq Benbenisty, "Coping Styles and Combat Motivation During Operations: An IDF Case Study," *Armed Forces & Society* 42, no. 4 (2016): 655–74, https://www.jstor.org/stable/48669898.

52 Sarah Rose Sharp, "The Disturbing Force of Early Color Photos of Nazi Camps," *Hyperallergic*, October 26, 2017, https://hyperallergic.com/407605/james-friedman-holocaust-angela-meleca-gallery/.

53 James Friedman, "The Holocaust Didn't Happen in Black and White." *Shofar* 37, no. 1 (2019): 5, https://doi.org/10.5703/shofar.37.1.0001.

54 Henry Greenspan, "The Humanities of Contingency: Interviewing and Teaching beyond 'Testimony' with Holocaust Survivors," *The Oral History Review* 46, no. 2 (2019): 360–79, https://doi.org/10.1093/ohr/ohz008.

55 Personal communication, January 8, 2024.

56 Christine Spolar, "The Kids Who Laughed Till It Hurt," *The Washington Post*, March 10, 1994, https://www.washingtonpost.com/archive/lifestyle/1994/03/10/the-kids-who-laughed-till-it-hurt/61462b5b-4c73-46f3-97e7-5e01e4c7f138/.

57 Rachel N. Baum, "'What I Have Learned to Feel': The Pedagogical Emotions of Holocaust Education," *College Literature* 23, no. 3 (1996): 47, http://www.jstor.org/stable/25112273.

58 "Laughter at Film Brings Spielberg Visit," *The New York Times*, April 13, 1994, 33.

59 John Bruns, "Laughter in the Aisles: Affect and Power in Contemporary Theoretical and Cultural Discourse," *Studies in American Humor* 7 (2000): 9, http://www.jstor.org/stable/42573389.

60 Anna Berardi and Brenda M. Morton, "Maximizing Academic Success for Foster Care Students: A Trauma-Informed Approach," *Journal of At-Risk Issues* 20, no. 1 (2017): 10–16, https://files.eric.ed.gov/fulltext/EJ1148240.pdf.

61 Elise Baker, Eric Stover, Rohini Haar, Andrea Lampros, and Alexa Koenig, "Safer Viewing: A Study of Secondary Trauma Mitigation Techniques in Open Source Investigations," *Health and Human Rights* 22, no. 1 (2020): 293–304, https://www.hhrjournal.org/2020/05/safer-viewing-a-study-of-secondary-trauma-mitigation-techniques-in-open-source-investigations/.

62 Hasida Ben-Zur, Sharon Gil, and Yinon Shamshins, "The Relationship Between Exposure to Terror Through the Media, Coping Strategies and Resources, and Distress and Secondary Traumatization," *International Journal of Stress Management* 19 (2012): 132–50.

63 Zembylas and McGlynn, "Discomforting Pedagogies," 56.

64 Ellen Galinsky, "Words Matter: Moving from Trauma-Informed to Asset-Informed Care," *YC Young Children* 75, no. 3 (2020): 46–55, https://www.jstor.org/stable/26979164.

65 Sarri Singer, *Written Testimony Before the House Committee on Oversight and Government Reform*, February 2, 2016, https://oversight.house.gov/wp-content/uploads/2016/02/2016-2-2-Written-Testimoney-for-Sarri-Singer1.pdf.

66 Singer, *Written Testimony.*

67 "Our Mission," *Strength to Strength*, https://www.stosglobal.org (January 27, 2025).

68 Personal communication with Sarri Singer, December 16, 2024.

69 Personal communication with Carly Namdar, January 10, 2025.

70 "A Workshop with Psychotherapist Moshe Sternberg and Three Holocaust Survivors," *Learning to Make a Difference: Teaching the Shoah, Antisemitism, and Contemporary Israel*, Jewish Educators Seminar, Yad Vashem, Israel, December 31, 2007.

71 Laura McIntire and Renae Duncan, "Associations among Religious Coping, Daily Hassles, and Resilience," *Archive for the Psychology of Religion* 35, no. 1 (2013): 101–17, https://doi.org/10.1163/15736121-12341252.

72 Gil Zukerman, Liat Korn, Ephraim Shapiro, and Leah Fostick, "Avoidance Behavior Following Terror Event Exposure: Effects of Perceived Life Threat and Jewish Religious Coping," *Journal for the Scientific Study of Religion* 55, no. 3 (2016): 516–30, http://www.jstor.org/stable/26651594.

73 Elie Wiesel and Marion Wiesel, *Night* (New York: Penguin Classics, 2004), 44.

74 Elie Wiesel, "A Prayer for the Days of Awe," *New York Times*, October 2, 1997.

75 Christian U. Krägeloh, Penny Pei Chai, Daniel Shepherd, and Rex Billington, "How Religious Coping Is Used Relative to Other Coping Strategies Depends on the Individual's Level of Religiosity and Spirituality," *Journal of Religion and Health* 51, no. 4 (2010): 1137–51, https://doi.org/10.1007/s10943-010-9416-x.

76 Mayordomo-Rodríguez et al., "Coping Strategies," 486–7.

77 David C. Gross, "Holocaust Survival," *Aish.com*, 2002, http://www.aish.com/h/c/s/h/48956896.html (January 2, 2025).

78 Gross, "Holocaust Survival."

79 Gross, "Holocaust Survival."

7 Vicarious Resilience

I stood alone in the climate-controlled storage room, cradling a nondescript, round wooden case between my hands. While the case itself had little historical significance—a typical product picked up by a tourist on the streets of Jerusalem—inside lay what many consider the crown jewel of the HMCTE: the Jakubowicz Family Megillah. In the quiet of that moment, I couldn't help but marvel at the journey this sacred scroll had taken—from a small Ukrainian town where it was once read to a congregation of 400, to being hidden in an attic during the darkest days of the Holocaust, and finally to this museum in Rockland County, New York. When Andrea Winograd, the museum's executive director, called asking if I could curate a special exhibit of Judaica from their collection, I knew immediately this scroll would be its centerpiece. (See Figure 7.1)

The physical presence of the megillah was arresting. The calfskin parchment had become brittle and yellowed with age, yet the Hebrew letters still stood bold and black against the surface. As I carefully unrolled a small section, I could almost hear the voices of those who had once gathered to hear its story of survival against impossible odds—a story that would take on painful new meaning during the Holocaust.

In Brod, a town in the sub-Carpathian region of Ukraine, this was the only megillah in the entire Jewish community. Each year on Purim, it is read aloud in the synagogue to commemorate the biblical tale of the Jews' narrow escape from annihilation in ancient Persia. Then came a modern Haman. When the Nazis arrived, nearly all of Brod's Jewish residents were transported to Auschwitz and murdered. Only two people from the entire community survived: Herman Jakubowicz and his brother.

When Herman returned to his hometown after liberation, he found nothing but ghosts where Jewish life had once thrived. But searching through the ruins of his family home, he discovered a small sack hidden in the attic. Inside were a few precious objects that had escaped the systematic Nazi looting, including the family megillah.

Figure 7.1 The author preparing the Jakubowicz Family Megillah for exhibition, August 22, 2022.

As I prepared to feature it in what would become the "Sacred Scrolls of the Holocaust" exhibit, the parallel was impossible to ignore: a scroll containing the story of the Jewish people's escape from destruction had itself escaped destruction. I found myself wondering what Herman must have felt in that moment of discovery. Did his fingers tremble as he unrolled the familiar parchment? Did he hear the echoes of voices that would never again gather to hear their words? Or was he feeling some kind of relief—or even resolve—as he realized that the family megillah survived? As I designed the exhibit, these questions lingered with me. I wanted visitors to feel the weight of loss—and how the scroll embodied the power of resilience.

For this megillah tells a story more complex than mere survival. The exhibit I created guided visitors through chambers of destruction and despair, but culminated in a space of rebirth. Alongside the Jakubowicz megillah were other rescued sacred items—a fragment of a Torah scroll with letters still visible, a pair of *tefillin* wrapped in faded cloth, and *mezuzot* pried from doorposts before families were taken away. Also displayed were photographs of newly written scrolls, commissioned after the war by survivors determined to rebuild. "They responded to death by recreating life," read the text on the exhibition wall. "Jewish life. In the greatest act of revenge imaginable, determined survivors rebuilt their shattered lives. They married, started new families, and reestablished Jewish communities."

On the exhibit's opening day, I watched visitors approach the megillah with a reverence that matched my own first encounter with it. Some leaned in close, their faces inches from the protective glass as they examined the beautiful calligraphy of Hebrew letters. Others stood back, their expressions suggesting they were overwhelmed by what this object represented. "It's like the last witness from another world," remarked one visitor, his voice barely above a whisper. He had traveled three hours to view the exhibit, telling me he was a child of Holocaust survivors. "My parents came emptyhanded to America—everything had been destroyed. Just looking at this megillah gives me a sense of just how much they must have lost." In his eyes, I saw both grief for what was gone but also wonder at what had survived.

This is what makes the Jakubowicz megillah so powerful—it represents not just itself but an entire world of Jewish ritual objects that were targeted specifically because of their religious significance. The Nazis didn't just seek to murder Jews; they sought to eradicate Judaism itself, to ensure that no one would ever again gather to hear these ancient words. Yet here it was, its letters still "gleaming impressively black," as one reporter noted at the exhibit's opening. "Its words tell one tale of survival," she wrote. "It tells another just by being there to be seen."[1]

I've often returned to sit quietly with the megillah during off-hours. In its presence, the themes we've explored throughout this book—trauma and resilience, memory and witness, education and empathy—seem to converge. How do we teach about such horror without traumatizing new generations? How do we balance historical truth with psychological well-being? How do we honor the dead while serving the living?

Perhaps this small scroll, rescued from an attic in Ukraine and now displayed in a museum in New York, offers one answer: resilience means not merely persevering through hardship, but allowing ourselves to be fundamentally transformed by it. The megillah poignantly expresses this principle—after witnessing destruction, it now serves a purpose its creators could never have imagined, teaching visitors about both loss and renewal. We honor the past when we allow it to reshape our present and future. In this way, resilience becomes more than persistence; it becomes transformation—the capacity to emerge from trauma not unchanged, but remade with purpose.

What Is Resilience?

The chapters of this book have focused on how museums, exhibitions, and memorials wrestle with competing imperatives: to document atrocities while safeguarding visitors' emotional well-being; to convey historical truth while acknowledging the limitations of representation; and to honor the dead while serving the needs of the living. From the box of ashes I discovered at my local Holocaust museum to the innovative technologies that attempt to bridge generational distance, these spaces navigate the delicate balance between memory and trauma. The preceding pages have grappled with how to safely explore horrific stories of pain and suffering without becoming emotionally or psychologically hurt in the process—in short, how to comprehend the incomprehensible.

What emerges from this exploration is not a set of definitive answers, but rather a framework for approaching difficult histories with both intellectual rigor and emotional intelligence. By understanding the psychological mechanisms of trauma, the pedagogical challenges of teaching about atrocity, and the curatorial complexities of displaying evidence of genocide, we can create more effective yet sensitive educational experiences. Such approaches acknowledge the individual's capacity not broken by encountering difficult histories but transformed by them—while recognizing that such transformation requires careful scaffolding, thoughtful presentation, and an awareness of how personal histories shape our reception of collective trauma.

As I always tell my students, we teach about the Holocaust not to tell them about how people died, but about how people lived. Artifacts like Hedy Strand's dresses and Herman Jakubowicz's family megillah speak not just to tragic loss, but to perseverance and the determination to maintain dignity and tradition despite the atrocities surrounding them. These objects bear witness to lives lived with purpose—lives that refuse to be defined solely by their ending. The stories of individuals like R Yosef Friedenson and Faye Skala remind us that even within narratives of unspeakable suffering, there exist powerful testimonies to human resilience and the enduring choice for life over death, for memory over forgetting, for meaning over despair.

What does it mean to be resilient? How did Jews under Nazi rule find the strength to resist and respond? The term "resilience" is often linked with overcoming a challenge or moving on from a difficult situation. But as Sherri Mandel[2] writes in *The Road to Resilience: From Chaos to Celebration*, resilience is not so much about overcoming as it is about becoming. It is about accepting those challenges and moments of trauma as new realities, choosing to embrace vulnerabilities, and finding within them the seeds of renewal.[3] It is captured in what Viktor Frankl famously described in his Holocaust memoir *Man's Search for Meaning*: "When we are no longer able to change a situation . . . we are challenged to change ourselves."[4] Resilience, then, is the strength we find to channel our thoughts and actions in a positive way, no matter what is happening around us—how we respond to events that we cannot control and our ability to adapt positively to adversity.

Although some people are naturally more inclined toward adaptability, resilience is a skill that can be learned and strengthened with practice.[5] While the core concept of resilience involves the internal resources an individual uses to adapt to adversity, there are also external social factors—such as family and community interactions—that contribute to and influence our ability to adapt and become resilient.[6]

The exhibit *Resilience: Children, Families, and Communities During the Holocaust* that I curated for HMCTE explores this multi-layered quality of resilience. While the Scrolls Exhibit centered on one family's artifact as a lens to explore larger experiences, the Resilience Exhibit invited the viewer to witness how Jews adapted to devastating new realities during the war—whether living in ghettos, hiding, or escaping to unfamiliar lands. (See Figure 7.2)

One of the most tragic themes of the Holocaust is the forced separation of individuals from their families. The photograph in the exhibit of a young girl arriving on the Kindertransport to Great Britain, asleep in a chair and clutching her doll, captures this pivotal moment experienced by thousands of other children like her. That transition from being cared for at home to

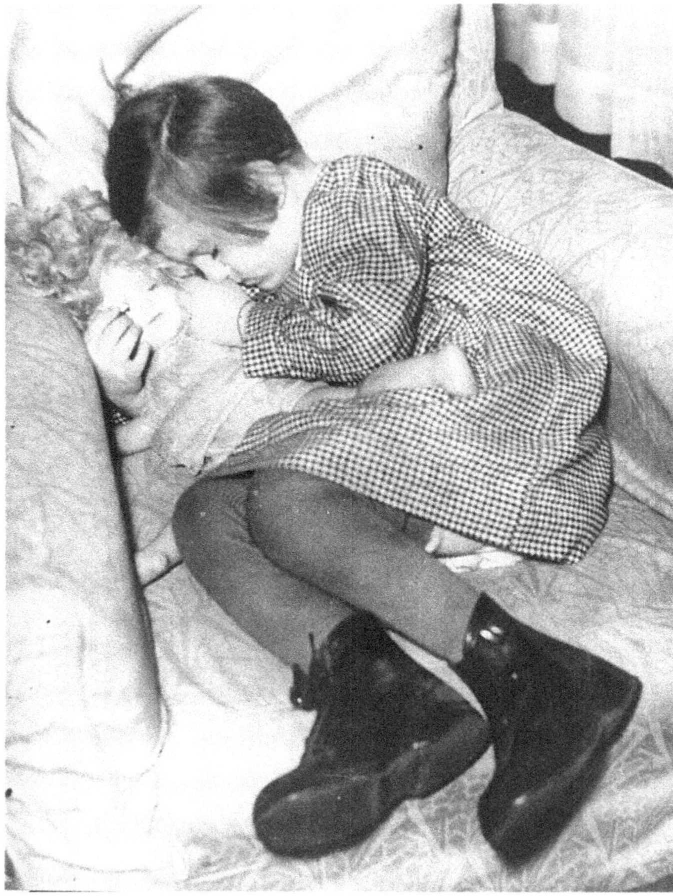

Figure 7.2 Close-up of a newly arrived refugee girl sleeping with her doll. United States Holocaust Memorial Museum, courtesy of Lydia Chagoll.

becoming a refugee in a strange land marked the first of many instances where she would need to draw upon inner reserves of resilience to adapt to a new reality.

After the war, survivors built new families, oftentimes bearing little resemblance to what they had known before. Perhaps the most poignant illustrations of familial resilience were the garments survivors fashioned from whatever materials were available to them. Lily Lax Friedman created her wedding dress from off-white parachute material, which she wore on her wedding day in the Bergen-Belsen Displaced Persons Camp. As evidenced by the multiple seams and stitches along its sides, many brides borrowed and re-fitted the dress for their own weddings. These young women embraced their new realities with determination and faith, fulfilling the words of Psalms (118), "The stone the builders discarded has become the very cornerstone of the building."

Equally moving is a tiny blouse sewn by Ida Schwartz in Mauthausen in 1945, just weeks after the American Army liberated the camp. Ida, who weighed 70 pounds and was twenty years old at the time, had endured and survived the Plaszów concentration camp, Auschwitz-Birkenau, and Bergen-Belsen. Using blue-checkered bedsheets issued by the US Army hospital, Ida created for herself a new shirt. Ida also married and later immigrated to America with her husband and son. They brought with them her blouse, a tangible symbol of their resilience and determination to create new lives on the very foundation of those shattered in the Holocaust. (See Figure 7.3)

The exhibit also explored how communal instances of resilience both paralleled and contrasted with individual and family experiences. Throughout the Holocaust and its aftermath, communities formed, dissolved, and reformed. Acts like ghetto uprisings, the secret Oneg Shabbat archive documenting ghetto life, Shavuot prayer services conducted just weeks after liberation, and public Pesach sedarim held in the years following the Holocaust all demonstrate this communal spirit of renewal. The strength of individuals within these communal structures created ripple effects, inspiring courage on a larger scale. Many survivors drew vital strength from their reconstituted communities, finding purpose to persevere another day. As our exhibit catalog explained, "Individuals strengthened their families and communities, but also drew fortitude from them as well."[7]

Vicarious Resilience

The strength of individuals and communities during the Holocaust continues to create ripple effects, inspiring resilience on a larger scale that extends to those who encounter their stories. As I wrote in an essay about the Resilience Exhibit,

> *Visiting the Resilience Exhibit is a process of self-reflection and a starting point for personal growth. Many of our students have experienced, or are*

Figure 7.3 Blouse sewn by Ida Schwartz in the Mauthausen Displaced Persons Camp using US Army hospital bed sheets. Photograph by author, October 12, 2018.

> *currently experiencing, challenges in their lives, but have become experts at masking their vulnerabilities through outward signs of strength and self-protection. What they need to know is that when everything is falling apart, these trials may serve as events that can eventually propel them to greatness. By immersing students in stories of Holocaust resilience, stories not always of survival or happy endings but ones of hope and possibilities, we empower them to begin the process of adapting and becoming resilient. They learn to persevere for themselves, their families and communities, offering strength while drawing fortitude from others as well.*

I witnessed this transformative impact firsthand when conducting a workshop for approximately 400 eighth-grade students at a public school in upstate New York that had temporarily hosted the Resilience Exhibit. After the session, the school principal approached me with profound gratitude, explaining how particularly meaningful the Kindertransport stories were for their student body, many of whom were immigrants who had come to America without their entire families. These students, separated from their own support networks and navigating unfamiliar cultural terrain, found in these historical accounts not just educational content but also inspiration.

What they experienced represents what researchers call "vicarious resilience," a concept introduced in 2007 by Hernández, Gangsei, and Engstrom in their studies of psychotherapists working with victims of violence. The term describes the positive transformation and growth professionals may experience through engaging with their clients' stories of overcoming trauma.[8] While little empirical data exists about this phenomenon,[9] vicarious resilience is the counterbalance to vicarious trauma, compassion fatigue, and STS discussed in earlier chapters.[10]

Like vicarious trauma, vicarious resilience is part of the complex emotional landscape of trauma work. The crucial difference is that while vicarious trauma can be mitigated, vicarious resilience can be intentionally cultivated and strengthened.[11] This raises intriguing questions for Holocaust education: If those who work with trauma survivors can successfully integrate their secondary experiences to foster their own growth,[12] might museum visitors and students of difficult histories do the same? If vicarious trauma stems largely from our capacity for empathy, can that same empathy enable us to absorb resilience vicariously? When confronting difficult histories, can we identify and harness coping skills that strengthen our ability to adapt during challenges in our own lives?

This certainly was the intention of some courageous Jews during the Holocaust. Abraham Sutzkever—the renowned Yiddish poet who survived the Vilna Ghetto—captured one such remarkable act of resilience in his poem "Grains of Wheat." The poem honors the clandestine work of the "Paper Brigade"—the nickname for a group of Jews who worked for Einsatzstab Reichsleiter Rosenberg (ERR), the operation that oversaw the looting of cultural treasures from Jews during the Holocaust. The Germans had plans to establish a "Museum of an Extinct Race" and, under Operation Rosenberg, books and manuscripts from the massive Strashun Library in Vilna were identified, sorted, and sent back to Germany in crates for this purpose. A group of Jews was forced to sort valuable books and manuscripts for Nazi looters. Rather than merely complying, these brave individuals risked their lives, secretly salvaging thousands of literary treasures, hiding them in the hopes that one day after the war, these books would be discovered by Jews who had survived.[13] In Sutzkever's powerful metaphor, these rescued texts were like ancient Egyptian wheat kernels buried with a Pharaoh, waiting silently for millennia until discovered and planted—sprouting "stalks like the sun" despite their long dormancy. The rescued Jewish manuscripts would likewise await liberation, when "the words that defiantly bloom" would once again "feed and sustain the folk in its eternal walk."[14]

Perhaps the most visible symbol of resilience-as-resistance stands at the entrance to Auschwitz. Nearly every guide who brings visitors to this infamous concentration camp stops beneath the iron gate bearing the cruelly ironic phrase "Arbeit Macht Frei" ("Work Makes One Free")—a mockery suggesting that hard labor might lead to freedom when, in reality, most prisoners were worked to death. (See Figure 7.4)

Yet looking closely at this infamous sign reveals a subtle act of defiance: the letter "B" in "Arbeit" is deliberately inverted. The prisoners forced to craft this sign risked their lives to embed this small but profound message of resistance. Today, this upside-down letter has become an enduring symbol of courage, replicated in Holocaust memorials worldwide as a testament to those who dared to resist even under the most oppressive circumstances.

Both the members of the Paper Brigade and the metalworkers at Auschwitz exemplify how victims used the very tools of their oppression to resist Nazi dehumanization. They took profound risks not merely for themselves, but to convey messages of hope and continuity to future generations. Their actions invite us to consider how we too might discover resilience through connecting with these historical acts of courage, finding in them not just stories of past trauma, but lessons in human dignity that can strengthen our own capacity to face adversity.

The Enduring Call of Resilience

Countless stories of faith, hope, and resilience emerge from victims and survivors of the Holocaust, showing that despite the depravity and inhumanity surrounding them, many individuals responded with remarkable acts of courage and humanity. These stories—whether visualized in the inverted "B" at Auschwitz, expressed through Sutzkever's exquisite poetry, or embedded in artifacts displayed in museums—offer profound lessons about the human capacity for resilience in the face of enormous suffering.

After the Great Deportation in the summer of 1943, when more than 300,000 Jews were deported from the Warsaw Ghetto and gassed at Treblinka, Rachel Auerbach emerged as one of the ghetto's few surviving members.

Figure 7.4 The gate at the entrance to Auschwitz, November 18, 2024. Photo credit: Shaindy Landerer.

Walking through streets littered with the abandoned belongings of their dead owners, she wrote in her diary: "Oh, the crying of things abandoned forever by their owners, becoming degraded in strange hands like corpses not buried who have no one to do right by them. He who has not seen the weeping of dead things, he has not seen or heard in his life any sad things."[15] Her powerful words capture why the artifacts in museums today have the power to affect our emotions and bridge connections to the past—they are not mere objects but witnesses to both destruction and survival.

Throughout this book, we have explored the many reasons people visit Holocaust museums and memorial sites—dark tourism, education, family research, combating Holocaust denial, and more. We have examined how encounters with difficult histories affect those who choose to learn about them, balancing the risks of vicarious trauma with the potential for vicarious resilience. And we have investigated how museums, educators, and visitors navigate the complex terrain between historical truth and psychological well-being. What emerges from this study is not merely a deeper understanding of how to teach about traumatic histories, but also an appreciation for why engaging with the Holocaust is so important. When we approach difficult histories with awareness, mindful of the emotional responses they can provoke, we transform potentially traumatizing encounters into opportunities for growth.

The stories of those who survived the Holocaust remind us that resilience is not about returning unchanged to a previous state, but about being transformed by adversity and finding meaning in that transformation. As we stand at the intersection of past traumas and present challenges, we can honor the memory of those who suffered by cultivating our own capacity for resilience—finding in their stories not just the darkness of what humans can inflict upon one another, but also the remarkable light of what we can endure, overcome, and transform. In doing so, perhaps we fulfill the deepest hope of those who preserved books in the Vilna Ghetto, who inverted letters at Auschwitz, who created wedding dresses from parachutes, and who fashioned new lives from the fragments of shattered worlds. Their resilience becomes ours, their strength our inheritance, their testimony our call to action—ensuring that these histories, difficult though they may be, continue to illuminate our path forward with wisdom, compassion, and resolve.

Notes

1 Hannah Rubin, "A People and Its Parchments," *Tablet Magazine*, August 24, 2022, https://www.tabletmag.com/sections/community/articles/people-parchments-exhibit-scrolls.

2 Sherri founded the Koby Mandell Foundation after her son was brutally murdered by terrorists in a cave near her home in Israel.

3 Julie Golding, "Resilience in Holocaust Education: A Museum Based Approach," *Jewish Educational Leadership* 18, no. 2 (Spring 2020), https://www.lookstein.org/journal-article/spring-2020/resilience-in-holocaust-education/.

4 Viktor E. Frankl, *Man's Search for Meaning: An Introduction to Logotherapy* (Boston: Beacon Press, 2006), 112.

5 U.S. Department of State, "What is Resilience?" *Deployment Stress Management Program*, https://2009-2017.state.gov/m/med/dsmp/c44950.htm (March 10, 2025).

6 Francesca Giordano, Shannon Lipscomb, Petra Jefferies, Kyong-Ah Kwon, and Margherita Giammarchi, "Resilience Processes Among Ukrainian Youth Preparing to Build Resilience with Peers During the Ukraine-Russia War," *Frontiers in Psychology* 15 (February 20, 2024): 1331886, https://doi.org/10.3389/fpsyg.2024.1331886.

7 "Resilience: Children, Families, and Communities During the Holocaust," exhibit produced by the Holocaust Museum & Center for Tolerance and Education, Abigail E. Miller, Isabella Costa, and Julie Golding, 2018.

8 Pilar Hernández, David Gangsei, and David Engstrom, "Vicarious Resilience: A New Concept in Work with Those Who Survive Trauma," *Family Process* 46, no. 2 (June 2007): 229–41, https://doi.org/10.1111/j.1545-5300.2007.00206.x.

9 Andrea Heather Bennett, *Exploring the Lived Experience of Vicarious Resilience among Canadian Psychotherapists Treating Complex Trauma* (PhD diss., University of British Columbia, 2025), https://doi.org/10.14288/1.0447327.

10 Orit Nuttman-Shwartz, "Shared Resilience in a Traumatic Reality: A New Concept for Trauma Workers Exposed Personally and Professionally to Collective Disaster," *Trauma, Violence & Abuse* 16, no. 4 (2015): 466–75, https://www.jstor.org/stable/26638374.

11 Hernández et al., "Vicarious Resilience."

12 Nuttman-Shwartz, "Shared Resilience in a Traumatic Reality," 467.

13 David E. Fishman, *The Book Smugglers: Partisans, Poets, and the Race to Save Jewish Treasures from the Nazis* (Lebanon, NH: University Press of New England, 2017).

14 Abraham Sutzkever, "Grains of Wheat," in *Geveb*, trans. James Adam Redfield (January 2025) https://ingeveb.org/texts-and-translations/grains (March 5, 2025).

15 Samuel D. Kassow, *Who Will Write Our History?: Rediscovering a Hidden Archive from the Warsaw Ghetto* (Bloomington: Indiana University Press, 2007).

Appendix

The Auschwitz Exhibit: A Case Study

This chapter explains a research case study I conducted at the exhibit *Auschwitz: Not Long Ago, Not Far Away* that investigates vicarious trauma experienced by students during school visits to a Holocaust museum and how educators and museum professionals can maximize the educational impact of such visits.

Auschwitz is the German name for Oświęcim, a city in southern Poland approximately 40 miles from Krakow. Oświęcim has been home to a bustling Jewish community since the sixteenth century; it was a minor footnote on a map before the Second World War, yet it represents the epitome of evil during the Nazi regime. Between 1940 and 1945, more than 1.1 million people were murdered in Auschwitz (including nearly one million Jews), and entire Jewish communities that had existed for centuries in Europe were decimated in a matter of hours. Located in German-occupied Poland, Auschwitz was the largest Nazi concentration camp. It consisted of three main complexes: the main camp (Auschwitz I), Birkenau (Auschwitz II), and Monowitz (Auschwitz III), and more than forty sub-camps where prisoners were exploited as slave laborers. Pearl Benisch, a survivor of Auschwitz, described her memory of the place as "a huge camp, spread over several miles and encompassing barracks for men and women, warehouses, workshops, factories and, as we soon discovered, gas chambers and crematoria."[1]

Today, Auschwitz is a popular "dark tourist" destination, with more than 2 million people visiting the site in its first ten years since it was opened for visitors and 2.3 million visitors in 2019 alone.[2] The award-winning museum exhibit, *Auschwitz: Not Long Ago, Not Far Away*, is a traveling exhibition jointly produced by Musealia (an independent Spanish traveling museum exhibition company) and the Auschwitz-Birkenau State Museum and is the "most comprehensive" presentation about Auschwitz "ever shown in North

America."[3] In 2019, the exhibit traveled to the Museum of Jewish Heritage in New York City, where this study was conducted.

Auschwitz: Not Long Ago, Not Far Away is an immersive Holocaust educational experience recommended for visitors ages twelve and older. It contains more than 700 artifacts, 400 photographs, and a number of unpublished memoirs. The artifacts are loaned by more than twenty institutions and individuals from around the world and include the ordinary items of victims, such as eyeglasses, shoes, and suitcases, along with religious objects, including a shofar (ram's horn) that was blown by a Jewish inmate in Auschwitz on the holiday of Rosh Hashanah. The exhibit also features artifacts belonging to the perpetrators, including a gas mask used by the SS and concrete posts that supported the barbed wire fence around the camp. A German-made freight car, one of 120,000 such rail cars that were used to transport Jews and others to ghettos and concentration camps during the Holocaust, is included in the exhibit and was placed outside the museum. An audio guide is available for visitors during their tours, and the exhibit information recommends spending two to three hours exploring the exhibit. (See Figure A.1)

Figure A.1 Students in front of concrete posts in the Auschwitz exhibit, December 26, 2019. Photograph by the author.

The Auschwitz exhibit is part of the work of Holocaust museums dedicated to teaching about the attempted genocide of the Jewish people, memorializing six million victims, and warning about the dangers of leaving hate unchecked. These spaces play a central role in educating millions of individuals about the Holocaust. However, visitors often arrive with little educational or psychological preparation for their encounter with difficult histories. Exhibit materials from *Auschwitz: Not Long Ago, Not Far Away* acknowledge as much and include the following statement:

> *Although the history of Auschwitz is challenging, we have developed this exhibition not only with profound respect for the victims, but also for our visitors. Care has been taken to ensure that there are no gratuitous depictions of violence. Every effort has been made to consider the emotional impact this story can have on our visitors, so that they can safely explore this history, seek to understand it better, and to make meaning for themselves.*[4]

Overview

I designed this study to dig deeper into the experiences of students visiting a Holocaust museum in order to understand how and why different students react differently. In particular, it looks at whether (and how) a student who experienced challenges during childhood (an "adverse childhood event") will cope differently when learning about this difficult and tragic history. My aim was to give Holocaust educators new insights into how to teach about the Holocaust and specifically create awareness for teachers about the emotional and psychological needs of students before, during, and after a visit to a Holocaust museum.

Traditionally, educators who teach about the Holocaust have focused on imparting knowledge and information about the Second World War and Holocaust history. Educational content centers around accounts of gruesome wars and genocide. Using photographs, video testimony, and object-based learning approaches, they try to impact the emotions and attitudes of their students while influencing their attitudes toward specific issues such as politics, antisemitism, and Jewish identity.[5] Holocaust educators often rely on storytelling techniques and (live or recorded) survivor testimony to create empathetic connections to the historical content and keep the memories of victims alive.[6] But instructional training and seminars offered to Holocaust educators often prioritize research, materials, and information about the history of the Holocaust, not pedagogical approaches for transmitting this difficult history. As a result, educators are forced to adapt existing knowledge about instructional models for teaching Holocaust history. Many museum docents are retired classroom educators and/or second-generation children of survivors who are passionate about the goal of teaching the Holocaust but have little experience or knowledge about the best methods for safely and effectively doing so.

What is doubly challenging is that while today's educators generally seek to provide a safe physical and emotional space for all learners, in the case of Holocaust education, triggering student reactions and emotions such as sadness, anger, and despair is considered an achievement. While awareness and training about trauma-informed education are on the rise, Holocaust educators continue to use images and testimonies about atrocities with little consideration of how and why some students may struggle or use negative coping styles during an encounter with such difficult knowledge.[7] At the same time, research shows that symptoms of PTSD can develop from vicarious exposure to trauma, such as hearing or reading about violence in the media or having a first-person connection to the victim of an attack.[8] Visitors to sites related to historical traumatization have been shown to exhibit PTSD, and a longitudinal study conducted at the Auschwitz Memorial Museum in Poland found that students who visited the site experienced STS.[9] It would seem obvious that in a field that measures success by its impact on a learner's sense of self and attitude toward others, leaders would want to know more about the specific means used to accomplish this.

My extensive research into studies about Holocaust museum visitors did not uncover any data sets related to visitors' emotional or psychological responses. While the USHMM conducted broad audience studies in 2004 and 2018, the studies investigated the knowledge and expectations visitors brought to the museum, learning outcomes gained from their visits, and the effectiveness of new storytelling techniques. The studies did not explore visitors' emotional responses or seek to identify traumatic stress symptoms that individuals might have experienced when visiting. It is intellectually interesting, though perhaps not surprising, that Holocaust museums have "played it safe" and not explored the psychological effects that their exhibitions have on visitors.

Study Design

I designed the study to focus on students in grades 10–12 who visited the Museum of Jewish Heritage in Manhattan and received a guided tour of the exhibition *Auschwitz: Not Long Ago, Not Far Away*. I designed the study to acquire a robust and varied sample from traditional public schools, charter schools, and private schools (including Jewish day schools) to represent students with varying levels of religious observance, ethnic/racial backgrounds, and socioeconomic status, and to have a population that included males, females, and non-binary students. The goal was to have a large sample size, which would allow for enough statistical power to find statistical significance in the analyses and allow for subgroup analyses (e.g., testing for gender differences and school type differences).

All schools that visited the Museum of Jewish Heritage beginning in January 2020 were offered the opportunity to participate in the study, and several accepted. Schools were instructed to email a Holocaust Museum Study Information and Parent Assent Form to all parents of children below the age of eighteen to obtain passive consent. This form informed them about the nature and specifics of the study and allowed them to opt out of their child's participation by sending an email before the visit. Schools were instructed to give the Holocaust Museum Study Information and Student Assent Form to all students aged 18 and older, which provided similar information to older students.

At the time of the visit, students experienced a guided tour led by a trained museum docent. At the conclusion of the tour, they were taken to a classroom where a member of the Museum of Jewish Heritage Education Department staff gave out the surveys. The survey included the following measures (described further below): the adapted Museum Experience Scale (MES), the adapted Adverse Childhood Experience Study (ACE), and the Coping Orientation to Problems Experienced Inventory (Brief COPE). The survey took approximately 10 minutes to complete.

Unfortunately, shortly after the study began, Covid-19 lockdowns occurred, and I had to prematurely terminate the study. As a result, the final sample contained only data from two schools. One of the schools was a Jewish day school, and the other was a specialized public school with a unique mission statement that differentiated it substantially from traditional public schools in terms of curricular methods and the type of students it recruited. One of the schools brought only tenth graders to the museum, and the other brought only twelfth graders. Both schools had only female students. The sample size was therefore very small (sixty-one students) and not representative of the intended demographics. As a result, the results of the study should be interpreted cautiously because of the restricted sample size and the lack of diverse representation.[10]

The Survey

Participants began by filling out basic demographic information, including their date of birth, grade, gender, the type of school they attended, if they were learning about the Holocaust in class, their religious orientation, if they were descendants of Holocaust survivors, and if they had ever met a Holocaust survivor or heard them speak about their experiences.[11]

The survey then shifted to ask the nineteen items from an adapted version of the MES using a 5-point Likert scale rating, with higher scores reflecting a better and more enriched museum experience.[12] This brief self-reporting scale comprises four factors for measuring visitors' experiences at museums and other cultural spaces:[13]

- *Engagement*: This five-item subscale refers to engagement with the exhibits (e.g., "The exhibition held my attention").
- *Learning/Knowledge*: This seven-item subscale refers to the knowledge gained from the exhibits and the preferred method of pedagogical instruction (e.g., "I learned new information about the Holocaust during my visit").
- *Meaningful Experience*: This three-item subscale refers to the quality of interaction with the exhibits and other visitors (e.g., "During my visit, I was able to reflect on the significance of the exhibits and their meaning").
- *Emotional Connection*: This *four*-item subscale refers to the emotional attachment to the context and contents of the exhibits (e.g., "The exhibition made me think about my past").

Next on the survey were questions adapted from the ACE survey and the Brief COPE.[14] Both were adapted for student use[15] and explored how students deal with stressful information when visiting a Holocaust museum (e.g., in the Brief COPE, students were asked questions about "the ways you may have been coping" with learning about the Holocaust). ACE measures all types of abuse, neglect, and other potentially traumatic experiences of people under eighteen.[16] The Brief COPE is a twenty-eight-item measure of the coping style used by individuals facing a variety of stressful situations across fourteen factors, four of which were the focus of this study:[17]

- *Behavioral Disengagement.* Whether a student has given up trying to process the Holocaust museum experience (e.g., "I have given up the attempt to cope with the pain and despair in the exhibit information").
- *Active Coping.* Whether a student is interested in taking action in response to the Holocaust museum experience (e.g., "I've been concentrating my efforts on what I can do because of what I've been learning").
- *Instrumental Support.* Whether students seek or receive advice on how to manage the feelings associated with the Holocaust museum experience (e.g., "I've been trying to get advice or help from other people about what to do with my feelings during this visit").
- *Religious Support.* Whether students use religion in processing the Holocaust museum experience (e.g., "I've been trying to find comfort in my religion or spiritual beliefs").[18]

Findings[19]

The students surveyed returned average scores of around four for the MES questions, indicating that they "agreed" that they were engaged with the exhibits, learned and gained knowledge from the exhibits, had a meaningful experience, and felt an emotional connection during the museum visit.[20] The range of average scores for the Brief COPE questions revealed lower averages (e.g., "haven't been doing this at all/a little bit") for behavioral disengagement and instrumental support, suggesting that on average, students did not tend to use these two coping strategies, and slightly higher averages (e.g., "been doing this a little bit/a medium amount") for active coping and religion, suggesting that these two coping strategies tended to be utilized more when students visited the museum.[21]

The nature of the questions asked on the survey allowed me to investigate several questions of interest to Holocaust educators. First and foremost among those was the question of whether students with greater exposure to adverse childhood events have more difficulty engaging, learning, finding meaning, or emotionally connecting during a visit to a Holocaust museum. There was limited support found for an affirmative answer to this question. One possibility for this finding is that the items included on the ACE survey are too varied, with only a few of the items related specifically to violence and events that worsen existing issues of traumatic stress when visiting a Holocaust museum. The secondary analysis I conducted on ACE questions exclusively related to violence suggests this is the case. Results calculated using a violence adversity measure indicate that experiencing violence is associated with less engagement and learning as well as a more negative overall immersive experience at the museum. These students may also have difficulty finding meaning and creating emotional connections within the exhibit.

PTSD influences the way an individual perceives the world, with the intensity and severity of the traumatic event influencing the impact and stress response a person will have.[22] A child who experiences violence (either directly or indirectly) by witnessing violent interactions in their home will often exhibit disruptive behaviors and psychological barriers in an educational environment.[23] Additionally, experiencing domestic violence or witnessing extreme violence (such as a school shooting) has been shown to have a severe impact on student achievement.[24] Educators should not be surprised when students who have previously experienced violence are triggered when learning about horrific massacres and harms perpetrated during the Holocaust. The strain of witnessing violent acts, especially the extensive graphic footage, images of atrocities, and survivor testimonies that are typically on exhibit in a Holocaust museum, may cause a neurobiological "fight or flight" response that prevents a student from engaging and learning during their visit.

In addition to these questions, students were asked directly on the survey if they had previously learned about the Holocaust in a scary or distressing way. Those who previously experienced fear or emotional distress scored significantly higher on all four subscales of the MES, indicating that they were immersed more deeply in the museum experience. It is possible that students who previously learned about the Holocaust in this way had a heightened awareness of the knowledge that would be on exhibit and were therefore more alert, aware of their surroundings, and open to the museum tour information. A previous traumatic educational experience may have prepared them to expect certain information, creating a situation where they were more sensitive to the Holocaust museum experience. This aligns with the literature that shows that traumatic experiences create a state of hypervigilance and shape how individuals view the world around them.[25] It is also possible that these students had greater empathic connectivity or dispositions of sensitivity and openness to experiences that allowed them to feel the emotions and connections of the exhibit more deeply than other students, in turn creating a situation where they learned more and were more deeply immersed in the museum experience. As has been noted, contemporary exhibitions use techniques that promote introspective reflection and empathetic connections between the viewer and the past.[26]

I next looked at whether adolescents have different levels of engagement, learning, finding meaning, and emotional connection in the Holocaust education process depending on their coping style with stressful materials. The students' answers revealed some links, though the strength of those connections was statistically limited. Overall, religious coping tended to be positively correlated with museum engagement, while behavioral disengagement, active coping, and instrumental support tended to be unrelated or negatively associated with museum engagement. The positive correlation regarding religious coping and a student's experience aligns with the literature that shows that faith-based coping is helpful in dealing with stressful situations and an effective method for dealing with trauma because it gives meaning to the situation and provides a sense of control.[27] Religious coping, ranging from praying for the dead or turning toward religious ideas and texts that provide consolation to viewing the event as a punishment from God or questioning where God was during the Holocaust, may improve emotional regulation, helping the individual develop a less negative view of the event or act as a buffer between the external force of the traumatic event and internal previously held beliefs.[28]

Krägeloh et al. note that most coping styles are classified as either problem-focused or emotion-focused, with the former addressing the root of the stressor and the latter aiming to change one's response to stress.[29] Religious coping is unique because it does not fall exclusively under either category. Individuals with higher levels of spirituality and religiosity tend to use religious coping in a problem-focused manner to address the issue directly, while individuals with lower levels of religiosity use it in an emotion-focused manner, often for distraction or avoidance of stress.

Museum knowledge was unexpectedly moderately negatively correlated with active coping and instrumental support. This is surprising because these forms of coping are generally associated with better stress management and lower stress levels—an emotional state conducive to increased learning and the absorption of knowledge.[30] Research also shows that active coping and the use of instrumental supports are beneficial for post-traumatic growth.[31] It is possible that the measures listed on the Brief COPE were too limited or that the time frame of the museum visit and the subsequent immediate completion of the surveys did not provide sufficient time for students to utilize these coping styles (or reflect upon how they may have relied on them during the tour).

Finally, I wanted to know whether there were significant differences in the museum experience for students who were descendants of a Holocaust survivor or had previously met a Holocaust survivor. Unsurprisingly, those who were a descendant of a Holocaust survivor found significantly more meaning during their visit to the museum compared to those who were not a descendant.[32] This aligns with the literature suggesting that the Holocaust is a lens through which victims and their descendants view identity, culture, religion, and political events.[33] In descendant families, there is a direct connection to the Holocaust, and many students attach a feeling of ownership to their family's Holocaust history, sometimes identifying from a perspective of victimhood.[34]

Research shows that the trauma experienced by a Holocaust survivor affects their descendants not just psychologically and culturally but also physiologically. Trauma is intergenerational because of physiological manifestations that alter the genetic sequencing in offspring.[35] Like Holocaust survivors, descendants have low levels of cortisol, a hormone that helps the body return to normal after experiencing stress.[36] Canetti et al. explain that epigenetic trauma is generally more subtle than direct trauma and rarely presents diagnosable PTSD; however, individuals who experience intergenerational trauma "may exhibit heightened individual and collective fear, feelings of vulnerability, inured national pride, and humiliation."[37]

Students who were a descendant of a Holocaust survivor were also marginally more engaged than those who were not, but interestingly didn't score significantly differently from non-descendants when asked about gaining knowledge, emotional connection, and overall immersive experience. That was not the case when comparing those who had met a Holocaust survivor to those who had not. Those who had were significantly more engaged, had a more meaningful experience, and had an overall more immersive experience at the museum; they also scored marginally higher than those who had not met a Holocaust survivor with respect to gaining more knowledge and having a stronger emotional connection to the exhibits. These findings highlight the power of survivor testimony and oral history in Holocaust education. Educators have long recognized the value of survivor testimony as a pedagogical approach because it encourages an emotional and personal connection to the material.[38] It provides a new perspective for listeners that is often surprising and challenges existing knowledge.[39] However, as time passes and the number of living survivors dwindles, educators are increasingly turning toward video testimony in place of the live survivor testimony experience.[40]

Conclusion

Museum educators are in a difficult position, where they meet visitors shortly before providing a tour or workshop and then have little (if any) follow-up after the visit. They are almost always unaware of violent childhood experiences previously experienced by students or other circumstances that may trigger traumatic stress reactions during a visit to a Holocaust museum. Without following up after the visit, museum educators do not know the psychological impact of their educational program and any long-term effects that students may experience because of viewing graphic images or learning difficult histories.

The possibilities of PTSD or other strong stress responses being triggered during a visit to a museum or memorial site dedicated to issues such as slavery, genocide, prisons, and so on are very real.[41] Every student should always feel physically and emotionally safe during a museum tour, and the study provides a framework for museum educators to understand the association between curatorial practices, education, and the emotional safety of visitors. My findings help explain how and why students may experience vicarious trauma or strong stress reactions during their visit to a Holocaust museum, and why a trauma-informed pedagogy ought to be used when teaching difficult histories in various settings.

Bilewicz and Wojcik recommend that intense preparations before visiting memorial sites with traumatic histories can help visitors prepare psychologically for their visit and reduce the detrimental psychological effects that may be experienced.[42] This recommendation applies to visitors at Holocaust museums to minimize the impact of an unprepared confrontation with difficult history and the vicarious trauma that can be experienced. At the same time, when teaching about the Holocaust, educators should look toward a trauma-informed lens not just as a pedagogical approach but also as a tool to help their students manage the psychological effects of learning about the Holocaust. As Wright and Ryan note, "Rather than devaluing the trauma response skills that children bring [. . .], we should honor these ways of responding as strengths in other parts of their lives."[43] Seemingly negative effects such as disengagement and hypervigilance can be potential conduits for increased learning opportunities.

Notes

1 Pearl Benisch, *To Vanquish the Dragon* (New York: Feldheim Publishers Ltd, 1991).

2 Auschwitz-Birkenau Memorial and Museum, "2 Million 320 Thousand Visitors at the Auschwitz Memorial in 2019," Auschwitz-Birkenau Memorial and Museum, https://www.auschwitz.org/en/museum/news/2-million-320-thousand-visitors-at-the-auschwitz-memorial-in-2019,1400.html (January 20, 2022).

3 Eve Young, "Most Comprehensive Auschwitz Exhibit in N. America to Open in Kansas City," *The Jerusalem Post*, September 16, 2020, https://www.jpost.com/diaspora/most-comprehensive-auschwitz-exhibit-in-n-america-to-open-in-kansas-city-642472.

4 Ronald Reagan Presidential Foundation & Institute, "Online Ticket Sales," *Ronald Reagan Presidential Foundation & Institute*, https://reagan.systemtickets.org/auschwitz/?sitePassword=9TalKgwa5JZcuXtXcF1FHTQM6VXTo&_gl=1*1n3lw4q*_ga*MjAxMzk1NDExNS4xNjY2NzA2ODM1*_ga_8LZKKVJJ5M*MTY2ODQ1NjQ0OC41LjEuMTY2ODQ1Njc4OC42MC4wLjA (January 2, 2024).

5 Nili Keren, "Teaching the Holocaust in Israel," *Internationale Schulbuchforschung* 22, no. 1 (2000): 95–108, http://www.jstor.org/stable/43057186; Leon Weissberg and Caren Schnur Neile, "Never Forget: March of the Living and Place-Based Holocaust Storytelling," *Storytelling, Self, Society* 11, no. 1 (2015): 121–36, https://digitalcommons.wayne.edu/storytelling/vol11/iss1/10.

6 Shoshana Felman, "Education and Crisis, or the Vicissitudes of Teaching," *American Imago* 48, no. 1 (1991): 13–73, http://www.jstor.org/stable/26304031; Alan S. Marcus et al., "Holocaust Education in Transition from Live to Virtual Survivor Testimony: Pedagogical and Ethical Dilemmas," *Holocaust Studies* 28, no. 3 (2021): 279–301, https://doi.org/10.1080/17504902.2021.1979176; Peter Novick, *The Holocaust in American Life* (New York: Houghton Mifflin, 2000); Weissberg and Neile, "Never Forget."

7 Tom Brunzell, Helen Stokes, and Lea Waters, "Trauma-Informed Flexible Learning: Classrooms That Strengthen Regulatory Abilities," *International Journal of Child, Youth and Family Studies* 7, no. 2 (2016): 218–39, https://doi.org/10.18357/ijcyfs72201615719; Salvatore Terrasi and Patricia Crain de Galarce, "Trauma and Learning in America's Classrooms," *The Phi Delta Kappan* 98, no. 6 (2017): 35–41, http://www.jstor.org/stable/26386969; Travis Wright and Sharon K. Ryan, "Toddlers Through Primary Grades: Too Scared to Learn: Teaching Young Children Who Have Experienced Trauma," *YC Young Children* 69, no. 5 (2014): 88–93, http://www.jstor.org/stable/ycyoungchildren.69.5.88.

8 Gil Zukerman and Liat Korn, "Post-Traumatic Stress and World Assumptions: The Effects of Religious Coping," *Journal of Religion and Health* 53, no. 6 (2013): 1676–90, https://doi.org/10.1007/s10943-013-9755-5.

9 Michał Bilewicz and Adrian Dominik Wojcik, "Visiting Auschwitz: Evidence of Secondary Traumatization among High School Students," *American Journal of Orthopsychiatry* 88, no. 3 (2018): 328–34, https://doi.org/10.1037/ort0000302.

10 Many students did not complete the entire survey, so the sample sizes in the analyses were smaller than sixty-one. Pairwise deletion was used to retain as much of the data as possible.

11 The responses collected in the study were self-reported by student visitors to Holocaust museums, and self-reporting measures are subjective by nature and can have inherent bias or accuracy concerns. Future researchers may wish to utilize measures that include behavioral observations of students during the tour, since watching what students do may be a way of getting a more objective and nuanced understanding of student engagement. A direct assessment that incorporates measures to test student knowledge before and after a visit to a Holocaust museum could also be used to objectively assess the knowledge gained during a visit.

12 Mohd Kamal Othman, Helen Petrie, and Christopher Power, "Engaging Visitors in Museums with Technology: Scales for the Measurement of Visitor and

Multimedia Guide Experience," in *Human-Computer Interaction—INTERACT 2011*, ed. Pedro Campos et al. (Berlin: Springer, 2011), 92–9, https://doi.org/10.1007/978-3-642-23768-3_8. It is worth noting that the MES scale is an adapted measure and is not intended for a museum exhibition that contains strong emotional content.

13 The four factors were derived through factor analysis, indicating that the four distinct subscales were correlated with one another. However, upon reviewing the individual items in each subscale, there appeared to be some conceptual overlap in content. Therefore, analyses were performed for the four subscales and then again using a scale total derived by averaging all the items on the subscales. The internal consistency for the scale total was .93, and the subscales ranged from .79 to .89, indicating that the total scale and subscales were internally consistent.

14 Charles S. Carver, "You Want to Measure Coping but Your Protocol's Too Long: Consider the Brief Cope," *International Journal of Behavioral Medicine* 4, no. 1 (1997): 92–100, https://doi.org/10.1207/s15327558ijbm0401_6.

15 K. Shawn, personal communication to author, January 2019. The original use of the Brief COPE was to measure coping and regulating cognitions in response to long-term stressors such as having an illness or caring for someone with an illness or dementia. The use of the Brief COPE for a stressful event that takes place during a shorter time frame, such as a one-time museum visit, may limit its efficacy. An alternative measure that directly assesses individual coping styles and reactions during short-term stressful life events could be considered in future research. Researchers could also use a longitudinal design to study long-term effects on visitors to better understand the effectiveness of Holocaust museum education.

16 Scores on the ACE were computed by totaling the number of items participants indicated they experienced, with higher scores reflecting more adverse experiences. This study modified the measure to provide a linguistically shorter survey for students while incorporating additional potentially traumatic major life events.

17 The four factors were internally consistent with Cronbach's alphas ranging from .71 to .84.

18 Importantly, the two measures on the Brief COPE about religious coping addressed positive religious coping and did not investigate possible negative religious coping. While positive religious coping is associated with better outcomes and includes behaviors such as seeking spiritual support and praying, negative religious coping manifests as discontent or doubt about religious beliefs and is associated with increased depression and anxiety (see

Gil Zukerman et al., "Avoidance Behavior Following Terror Event Exposure: Effects of Perceived Life Threat and Jewish Religious Coping," *Journal for the Scientific Study of Religion* 55, no. 3 (2016): 516–30, http://www.jstor.org/stable/26651594). Studies show that positive religious coping generally reduces stress, and sometimes a stressful situation can mobilize positive religious coping in students who normally would not have such a response. See Ziasma Haneef Khan, P. J. Watson, and Zhuo Chen, "Muslim Spirituality, Religious Coping, and Reactions to Terrorism among Pakistani University Students," *Journal of Religion and Health* 55, no. 6 (2016): 2086–98, https://doi.org/10.1007/s10943-016-0263-2.

19 All data were entered into SPSS statistical software and screened for unusual, out of range, or extreme scores. The data were also screened for univariate outliers and normality. No univariate outliers were identified. However, several of the variables were mildly skewed and/or kurtotic. Three of the four subscales on the Brief COPE showed evidence of non-normality. The instrumental support scale was mildly positively skewed. The behavioral disengagement scale was kurtotic and mildly positively skewed. The religion scale was mildly kurtotic. Logarithmic transformations were applied to reduce the skewness. However, only the behavioral disengagement subscale showed improvement. The primary hypotheses were then tested with the original and transformed behavioral disengagement scales, and the pattern of results was nearly identical. Therefore, the original variable was retained.

20 Detailed statistical analysis can be found at Julie J. Golding, Vicarious Trauma Experienced by Visitors to a Central Holocaust Museum (PhD diss., Yeshiva University, 2023), https://repository .yu .edu /items /2b5e4d06 -4b25 -46b7 -8a22 -d1fa3001e85c.

21 Detailed statistical analysis can be found at Golding, "Vicarious Trauma Experienced by Visitors." The MES scale has subscales that should be positively correlated with one another. The four subscales were strongly correlated, with the correlations ranging from .56 to .83. The four subscales also correlated strongly with the total museum experience score (rs range from .81 to .92). The four different coping styles measured by the Brief COPE were also highly positively correlated with one another. The exception was that religious coping was only mildly positively correlated with behavioral disengagement and instrumental support. Notably, the correlation between behavioral disengagement and instrumental support was very high ($r = .82$), suggesting that those who feel they can no longer cope with the experience also often turn to others to find ways to channel their emotions.

22 Wright and Ryan, "Toddlers Through Primary Grades." See also Jan Jeske and Mary Louise Klas, "Adverse Childhood Experiences: Implications for Family Law

Practice and the Family Court System," *Family Law Quarterly* 50, no. 1 (2016): 123–37, http://www.jstor.org/stable/44155200.

23 Michele Lloyd, "Domestic Violence and Education: Examining the Impact of Domestic Violence on Young Children, Children, and Young People and the Potential Role of Schools," *Frontiers in Psychology* 9 (2018): 1–11, https://doi.org/10.3389/fpsyg.2018.02094.

24 Louis-Philippe Beland and Dongwoo Kim, "The Effect of High School Shootings on Schools and Student Performance," *Educational Evaluation and Policy Analysis* 38, no. 1 (2016): 113–26, https://doi.org/10.3102/0162373715590683; Lian McGavock and Trevor Spratt, "Children Exposed to Domestic Violence: Using Adverse Childhood Experience Scores to Inform Service Response," *The British Journal of Social Work* 47, no. 4 (2016): 1128–46, https://doi.org/10.1093/bjsw/bcw073.

25 Bilewicz and Wojcik, "Visiting Auschwitz"; Wright and Ryan, "Toddlers Through Primary Grades."

26 Alan S. Marcus, Jeremy D. Stoddard, and Walter W. Woodward, *Teaching History with Museums: Strategies for K–12 Social Studies*, 2nd ed. (New York: Routledge, 2017), https://doi.org/10.4324/9781315194806; Andrea Witcomb, "Toward a Pedagogy of Feeling: Understanding How Museums Create a Space for Cross-cultural Encounters," in *The International Handbooks of Museum Studies*, ed. Andrea Witcomb and Kylie Message, 1st ed. (Chichester, Eng.: Wiley & Sons, 2015), 321–44.

27 Uzi Ben-Shalom and Yizhaq Benbenisty, "Coping Styles and Combat Motivation During Operations: An IDF Case Study," *Armed Forces & Society* 42, no. 4 (2016): 655–74, https://www.jstor.org/stable/48669898; Laura McIntire and Renae Duncan, "Associations among Religious Coping, Daily Hassles, and Resilience," *Archive for the Psychology of Religion* 35, no. 1 (2013): 101–17, https://doi.org/10.1163/15736121-12341252.

28 Zukerman and Korn, "Post-Traumatic Stress."

29 Christian U. Krägeloh et al., "How Religious Coping Is Used Relative to Other Coping Strategies Depends on the Individual's Level of Religiosity and Spirituality," *Journal of Religion and Health* 51, no. 4 (2010): 1137–51, https://doi.org/10.1007/s10943-010-9416-x.

30 Teresa Mayordomo-Rodríguez et al., "Coping Strategies as Predictors of Well-Being in Youth Adult," *Social Indicators Research* 122, no. 2 (2014): 479–89, https://doi.org/10.1007/s11205-014-0689-4.

31 Melanie Munroe et al., "Using Self-Compassion to Grow in the Face of Trauma: The Role of Positive Reframing and Problem-Focused Coping Strategies," *Psychological Trauma: Theory, Research, Practice, and Policy* 14, no. 1 (2022): 157–64, https://doi.org/10.1037/tra0001164.

32 Detailed statistical analysis can be found at Julie J. Golding, Vicarious Trauma Experienced by Visitors to a Central Holocaust Museum (PhD diss., Yeshiva University, 2023), https://repository .yu .edu /items /2b5e4d06 -4b25 -46b7 -8a22 -d1fa3001e85c.

33 Daphna Canetti et al., "Collective Trauma From the Lab to the Real World: The Effects of the Holocaust on Contemporary Israeli Political Cognitions," *Political Psychology* 39, no. 1 (2018): 3–21, http://www.jstor.org/stable/45094414; Janet Jacobs, "Traumatic Inheritance and the Demasculinization of God: Reimagining the Divine among Descendants of the Holocaust," *Journal of Feminist Studies in Religion* 31, no. 2 (2015): 65–82, https://doi.org/10.2979/jfemistudreli.31.2.65.

34 David H. Lindquist, "Complicating Issues in Holocaust Education," *The Journal of Social Studies Research* 34, no. 1 (2010): 77–93, https://eric.ed.gov/?id=EJ887319.

35 Rachel Yehuda, "Are Different Biological Mechanisms Involved in the Transmission of Maternal Versus Paternal Stress-Induced Vulnerability to Offspring?," *Biological Psychiatry* 70, no. 5 (2011): 402–3, https://doi.org/10.1016 /j.biopsych.2011.07.001.

36 Tori Rodriguez, "Descendants of Holocaust Survivors Have Altered Stress Hormones," *Scientific American Mind* 26, no. 2 (2015): 10, https://www.jstor.org/stable/24946475.

37 Canetti et al., "Collective Trauma," 4. See also Stanley Krippner and Deirdre Barrett, "Transgenerational Trauma: The Role of Epigenetics," *The Journal of Mind and Behavior* 40, no. 1 (2019): 53–62, https://www.jstor.org/stable/26740747.

38 Susanne Hillman, "Grim Expectations: Video Testimony in the College Classroom," *The History Teacher* 48, no. 2 (2015): 295–320, http://www.jstor .org/stable/43264406; Vera Schwarcz, "To Catch the Echo: Rethinking Acts of Witnessing to the Shoah," *History and Theory* 54, no. 3 (2015): 429–40, https://doi .org/10.1111/hith.10770.

39 Felman, "Education and Crisis."

40 Future research should consider the effects of video and holographic testimony on students, how viewing recorded testimony compares to witnessing live testimony, and when such testimony is most beneficial to be screened to students, as research shows that students are usually more critical and do not give the same attention and respect to recorded testimonies as live speakers. See Marcus et al., "Holocaust Education."

41 Dan Johnson and Rhiannon Pickin, "Suffering on Display: An Argument for Historical Nuance in British Prison Museums," *Crime, Histoire & Sociétés* 23, no. 1 (2019): 5–26, http://www.jstor.org/stable/45215848.

42 Bilewicz and Wojcik, "Visiting Auschwitz."

43 Wright and Ryan, "Toddlers Through Primary Grades," 90.

Bibliography

"75 Years since USS Intrepid's Darkest Day | Intrepid Museum." *Intrepidmuseum.org,* 2019. https://intrepidmuseum.org/75-years-uss-intrepids-darkest-day.

Aarons, Victoria, and Alan L. Berger. *Third-Generation Holocaust Representation: Trauma, History, and Memory*. Evanston, IL: Northwestern University Press, 2017. http://www.jstor.org/stable/j.ctt22727kb.

Amaral, Marina, and Dan Jones. *Colour of Time: A New History of the World 1850–1960*. Chicago: Head of Zeus Ltd., 2018.

American Psychological Association. "Trauma." January 23, 2022. https://www.apa.org/topics/trauma.

Anderson, Elizabeth M., Lisa V. Blitz, and Monique Saastamoinen. "Exploring a School-University Model for Professional Development with Classroom Staff: Teaching Trauma Informed Approaches." *School Community Journal* 25, no. 2 (2015): 113–34. https://files.eric.ed.gov/fulltext/EJ1085667.pdf.

Anderson, Mark M. "The Child Victim as Witness to the Holocaust: An American Story?" *Jewish Social Studies* 14, no. 1 (2007): 1–22. http://www.jstor.org/stable/40207081.

"A Night at the Garden." *A Night at the Garden,* 2017. https://anightatthegarden.com.

Anti-Defamation League. "Over 10,000 Antisemitic Incidents Recorded in the U.S. since Oct. 7, 2023, According to ADL Preliminary Data." October 6, 2024. https://www.adl.org/resources/press-release/over-10000-antisemitic-incidents-recorded-us-oct-7-2023-according-adl.

"Architecture." 2025. https://www.yadvashem.org/museum/holocaust-history-museum/architecture.html.

Arnold-de Simine, Silke. "The 'Moving' Image: Empathy and Projection in the International Slavery Museum, Liverpool." *Journal of Educational Media, Memory & Society* 4, no. 2 (2012): 23–40. http://www.jstor.org/stable/43049390.

"Artist Shames Tourists Taking Inappropriate Selfies at the Holocaust Memorial Site in Berlin (NSFW)." *Demilked,* April 10, 2019. https://www.demilked.com/holocaust-memorial-selfies-yolocaust-shahak-shapira/.

Assmann, Aleida, and Ines Detmers. "Introduction." In *Empathy and its Limits*, edited by Aleida Assmann and Ines Detmers, 1–17. New York: Palgrave Macmillan, 2016. https://doi.org/10.1057/9781137552372_1.

Associated Press Staff. "9/11 Memorial Museum Design to Lessen Emotional Impact." *CBC News*, May 21, 2014. https://www.cbc.ca/news/world/9-11-memorial-museum-design-to-lessen-emotional-impact-1.2649302.

Auschwitz-Birkenau Memorial and Museum. "2 Million 320 Thousand Visitors at the Auschwitz Memorial in 2019." Accessed January 20, 2022. https://www.auschwitz.org/en/museum/news/2-million-320-thousand-visitors-at-the-auschwitz-memorial-in-2019,1400.html.

Baker, Elise, Eric Stover, Rohini Haar, Andrea Lampros, and Alexa Koenig. "Safer Viewing: A Study of Secondary Trauma Mitigation Techniques in Open Source Investigations." *Health and Human Rights* 22, no. 1 (2020): 293–304. https://www.hhrjournal.org/2020/05/safer-viewing-a-study-of-secondary-trauma-mitigation-techniques-in-open-source-investigations/.

Balloffet, Pierre, François H. Courvoisier, and Joëlle Lagier. "From Museum to Amusement Park: The Opportunities and Risks of Edutainment." *International Journal of Arts Management* 16, no. 2 (2014): 4–18. http://www.jstor.org/stable/24587153.

Baum, Rachel N. "'What I Have Learned to Feel': The Pedagogical Emotions of Holocaust Education." *College Literature* 23, no. 3 (1996): 44–57. http://www.jstor.org/stable/25112273.

Beckman, Beth. 2017. "Under the Sea Times Square: A National Geographic Encounter." Little Kid Big City. October 6, 2017. https://littlekidbigcity.com/national-geographic-encounter-ocean-odyssey/.

Beland, Louis-Philippe, and Dongwoo Kim. "The Effect of High School Shootings on Schools and Student Performance." *Educational Evaluation and Policy Analysis* 38, no. 1 (2016): 113–26. https://doi.org/10.3102/0162373715590683.

"Bella Miller: Holocaust Survivor and Speaker." *NJ State Bar Foundation*. Accessed August 7, 2024. https://www.youtube.com/watch?v=7ybZNSycC3Q.

Benisch, Pearl. *To Vanquish the Dragon*. New York: Feldheim Publishers Ltd., 1991.

Bennett, Andrea Heather. "Exploring the Lived Experience of Vicarious Resilience Among Canadian Psychotherapists Treating Complex Trauma." PhD diss., University of British Columbia, 2025. https://doi.org/10.14288/1.0447327.

Ben-Shalom, Uzi, and Yizhaq Benbenisty. "Coping Styles and Combat Motivation During Operations: An IDF Case Study." *Armed Forces & Society* 42, no. 4 (2016): 655–74. https://www.jstor.org/stable/48669898.

Ben-Zur, Hasida, Sharon Gil, and Yinon Shamshins. "The Relationship Between Exposure to Terror Through the Media, Coping Strategies and Resources, and Distress and Secondary Traumatization." *International Journal of Stress Management* 19 (2012): 132–50.

Berardi, Anna, and Brenda M. Morton. "Maximizing Academic Success for Foster Care Students: A Trauma-Informed Approach." *Journal of At-Risk Issues* 20, no. 1 (2017): 10–16. https://files.eric.ed.gov/fulltext/EJ1148240.pdf.

Berenbaum, Michael. "America and the Holocaust: Reflections on Three Quarters of a Century and the Development of Holocaust Consciousness in American Society." *The American Jewish Year Book* 121 (2021): 79–126. https://www.jstor.org/stable/48771582.

Bernard-Donals, Michael. "Synecdochic Memory at the United States Holocaust Memorial Museum." *College English* 74, no. 5 (2012): 417–36. http://www.jstor.org/stable/23212923.

Bickman, Leonard, and Karl M. Hamner. "An Evaluation of the Yad Vashem Holocaust Museum." *Evaluation Review* 22, no. 4 (1998): 435–46. https://doi.org/10.1177/0193841x9802200401.

Bilewicz, Michał, and Adrian Dominik Wojcik. "Visiting Auschwitz: Evidence of Secondary Traumatization among High School Students." *American Journal of Orthopsychiatry* 88, no. 3 (2018): 328–34. https://doi.org/10.1037/ort0000302.

Bloomer, Martin, and Phil Hodkinson. "Learning Careers: Continuity and Change in Young People's Dispositions to Learning." *British Educational Research Journal* 26, no. 5 (2000): 583–97. http://www.jstor.org/stable/1501992.

Bogdaner, Paul. *Kasztner's Crime*. New York: Routledge, 2016.

Bolin, Annalisa. "On the Side of Light: Performing Morality at Rwanda's Genocide Memorials." *Journal of Conflict Archaeology* 7, no. 3 (2012): 199–207. https://www.jstor.org/stable/48601744.

Bornstein, Lilach Naishtat, and Eyal Naveh. "From Empathy to Critical Reflection: The Use of Testimonies in the Training of Holocaust Educators." *Journal of International Social Studies* 8, no. 1 (2017): 4–36. https://eric.ed.gov/?id=EJ1173482.

Böser, Ursula. "'A Film Unfinished': Yael Hersonski's Re-Representation of Archival Footage from the Warsaw Ghetto." *Film Criticism* 37, no. 2 (2012): 38–56. http://www.jstor.org/stable/24777861.

Boxer, Paul, and Elizabeth Sloan-Power. "Coping With Violence: A Comprehensive Framework and Implications for Understanding Resilience." *Trauma, Violence & Abuse* 14, no. 3 (2013): 209–21. https://www.jstor.org/stable/26638314.

Britzman, Deborah P. "Between Psychoanalysis and Pedagogy: Scenes of Rapprochement and Alienation." *Curriculum Inquiry* 43, no. 1 (2013): 95–117. http://www.jstor.org/stable/23524359.

Bruns, John. "Laughter in the Aisles: Affect and Power in Contemporary Theoretical and Cultural Discourse." *Studies in American Humor* 7 (2000): 5–23. http://www.jstor.org/stable/42573389.

Brunzell, Tom, Helen Stokes, and Lea Waters. "Trauma-Informed Flexible Learning: Classrooms That Strengthen Regulatory Abilities." *International Journal of Child, Youth and Family Studies* 7, no. 2 (2016): 218–39. https://doi.org/10.18357/ijcyfs72201615719.

"The Building." *National Museum of African American History and Culture*, n.d. https://nmaahc.si.edu/about/building.

Bundesamt für Verfassungsschutz. "Right-Wing Extremism." Accessed March 4, 2025. https://www.verfassungsschutz.de/EN/topics/right-wing-extremism/right-wing-extremism_node.html.

Buntman, Barbara. "Tourism and Tragedy: The Memorial at Belzec, Poland." *International Journal of Heritage Studies* 14, no. 5 (2008): 422–48. https://doi.org/10.1080/13527250802284867.

"But the Story Didn't End That Way." The International School for Holocaust Studies, Yad Vashem Information Systems, 2000, https://www.yadvashem.org/download/education/units/crystal.pdf.

Canetti, Daphna, Gilad Hirschberger, Carmit Rapaport, Julia Elad-Strenger, Tsachi Ein-Dor, Shifra Rosenzveig, Tom Pyszczynski, and Stevan E. Hobfoll. "Collective Trauma From the Lab to the Real World: The Effects of the Holocaust on Contemporary Israeli Political Cognitions." *Political Psychology* 39, no. 1 (2018): 3–21. http://www.jstor.org/stable/45094414.

Cantrell, Akiyo M. "The Management of Survivors' Guilt through the Construction of a Favorable Self in Hiroshima Survivor Narratives." *Discourse Studies* 19, no. 4 (2017): 377–401. https://www.jstor.org/stable/26377712.

Caruth, Cathy. "The Body's Testimony: Dramatic Witness in the Eichmann Trial." *Paragraph* 40, no. 3 (2017): 261. https://doi.org/10.3366/para.2017.0234.

Carver, Charles S. "You Want to Measure Coping but Your Protocol's Too Long: Consider the Brief Cope." *International Journal of Behavioral Medicine* 4, no. 1 (1997): 92–100. https://doi.org/10.1207/s15327558ijbm0401_6.

Casale, Carolyn, C. Adrainne Thomas, and Temika M. Simmons. "Developing Empathetic Learners." *Journal of Thought* 52, no. 3–4 (2018): 3–18. https://www.jstor.org/stable/90026734.

Cavanaugh, Brian. "Trauma-Informed Classrooms and Schools." *Beyond Behavior* 25, no. 2 (2016): 41–6. http://www.jstor.org/stable/26381827.

CBS News. "Museum In Brooklyn Shares Stories Of Children Who Survived The Holocaust." January 26, 2017. https://www.cbsnews.com/newyork/news/brooklyn-museum-holocaust-exhibit/.

Centers for Disease Control and Prevention. "About the CDC-Kaiser ACE Study." www.cdc.gov, April 6, 2021. https://www.cdc.gov/violenceprevention/aces/about.html.

Chakravarti, Sonali. "More than Cheap Sentimentality: Victim Testimony at the Nuremberg Trials, the Eichmann Trial, and the South African Truth and Reconciliation Commission." In *Sing the Rage: Listening to Anger after Mass Violence*, 24–56. Chicago: University of Chicago Press, 2014. https://doi.org/10.7208/chicago/9780226120041.003.0002.

Chancellor, Renate, and Shari Lee. "Storytelling, Oral History, and Building the Library Community." *Storytelling, Self, Society* 12, no. 1 (2016): 39–54. https://doi.org/10.13110/storselfsoci.12.1.0039.

Child and Adolescent Health Measurement Initiative (CAHMI). "2016 National Survey of Children's Health: Child and Family Health Measures and Subgroups." Data Resource Center for Child and Adolescent Health. Accessed January 15, 2022. www.childhealthdata.org.

Clarke, Suzan. "Holocaust Museum Adds New Exhibits." *The Journal News* (White Plains, NY), July 25, 2006.

Cohen, Erik H. "Educational Dark Tourism at an In Populo Site: The Holocaust Museum in Jerusalem." *Annals of Tourism Research* 38 (2011): 193–209.

Conference on Jewish Material Claims Against Germany. "New Survey by Claims Conference Finds Significant Lack of Holocaust Knowledge in the United States." Accessed January 15, 2022. https://www.claimscon.org/study/.

Coombs, Dawan, and Rachel Knecht Freeze. "Lives on Display: Examining Artifacts of Hope." *The English Journal* 108, no. 2 (2018): 20–30. https://www.jstor.org/stable/26610252.

"Courage to Act: Rescue in Denmark." Museum of Jewish Heritage — a Living Memorial to the Holocaust, n.d. https://mjhnyc.org/exhibitions/courage-to-act-rescue-in-denmark/.

Culbertson, Elaine A. "A Reflection on the Use of Iconic Holocaust Resources." In *Essentials of Holocaust Education: Fundamental Issues and Approaches*, edited by Samuel Totten and Stephen Feinberg, 131–46. New York: Routledge, 2016.

Davis, Colin. *Traces of War: Interpreting Ethics and Trauma in Twentieth-Century French Writing*. Liverpool: Liverpool University Press, 2018. https://doi.org/10.2307/j.ctt1ps33bb.

Dawson, Amanda, Sinéad O'Leary, and Noelle O'Connor. "Holocaust Tourism: Education or Exploitation?" *Tourism and Heritage Journal* 4 (2022): 37–52. https://doi.org/10.1344/THJ.2022.4.3.

Dean, Carolyn J. "Atrocity Photographs, Dignity, and Human Vulnerability." *Humanity: An International Journal of Human Rights, Humanitarianism, and Development* 6, no. 2 (2015): 239–64. https://doi.org/10.1353/hum.2015.0020.

Devilly, Grant J., Renee Wright, and Tracey Varker. "Vicarious Trauma, Secondary Traumatic Stress or Simply Burnout? Effect of Trauma Therapy on Mental Health Professionals." *Australian & New Zealand Journal of Psychiatry* 43 (2009): 373–85.

Donnelly, Mary Beth. "Educating Students about the Holocaust: A Survey of Teaching Practices." *Social Education* 70, no. 1 (2006): 51–4.

Dorfsman, Marcelo I., and Gabriel Horenczyk. "Educational Approaches and Contexts in the Development of a Heritage Museum." *Journal of Experiential Education* 41, no. 2 (2017): 170–86. https://doi.org/10.1177/1053825917740155.

Driscoll, Dana Lynn, and Jennifer Wells. "Beyond Knowledge and Skills: Writing Transfer and the Role of Student Dispositions." *Composition Forum* 26 (2012): 1–15. https://files.eric.ed.gov/fulltext/EJ985815.pdf.

Eckmann, Monique, Stevick Doyle, and Ambrosewicz Jolanta Jacobs. *Research in Teaching and Learning About the Holocaust: A Dialogue Beyond Borders*. Berlin: Metropol, 2017.

Edwards, Elizabeth, and Matthew Mead. "Absent Histories and Absent Images: Photographs, Museums and the Colonial Past." *Museum and Society* 11, no. 1 (2013): 19–38. https://citeseerx.ist.psu.edu/viewdoc/download?doi=10.1.1.967.3189&rep=rep1&type=pdf.

Ehrenreich, Robert M., and Jane Klinger. "War in Context: Let the Artifacts Speak." In *Does War Belong in Museums?: The Representation of Violence in Exhibitions*, edited by Wolfgang Muchitsch, 145–54. Wetzlar, Germany: Transcript Verlag, 2013. http://www.jstor.org/stable/j.ctv1wxr1z.14.

Ellison, Jeffrey Alan. "How They Teach the Holocaust in Jewish Day Schools." *Cogent Education* 4, no. 1 (2017): 1310010. https://doi.org/10.1080/2331186x.2017.1310010.

Endacott, Jason, and Sarah Brooks. "An Updated Theoretical and Practical Model for Promoting Historical Empathy." *Social Studies Research and Practice* 8, no. 1 (2013): 41–58. https://doi.org/10.1108/ssrp-01-2013-b0003.

Evces, Mark R. "What is Vicarious Trauma?" In *Vicarious Trauma and Disaster Mental Health: Understanding Risks and Promoting Resilience*, edited by Gertie Quitangon and Marc R. Evces, 9–23. New York: Routledge, 2015. https://doi.org/10.4324/9781315761343.

Facing History and Ourselves. "Mini Course: Teaching Holocaust and Human Behaviour (Canada)." Accessed January 2, 2024. https://www.facinghistory.org/learning-events/mini-course-teaching-holocaust-human-behaviour-canada.

Faiola, Anthony. "Berlin's Holocaust Memorial Is 'Not a Place for Fun Selfies.'" *The Washington Post*, January 28, 2017. https://www.washingtonpost.com/world/europe/berlins-holocaust-memorial-is-not-a-place-for-fun-selfies/2017/01/27/2e5b6324-e1ac-11e6-a419-eefe8eff0835_story.html.

Fallace, Thomas D. *The Emergence of Holocaust Education in American Schools*. New York: Palgrave Macmillan, 2014.

Farmaki, Anna, and Katerin Antoniou. "Politicising Dark Tourism Sites: Evidence from Cyprus." *Worldwide Hospitality and Tourism Themes* 9, no. 2 (2017): 175–86. https://doi.org/10.1108/WHATT-08-2016-0041.

Felman, Shoshana. "Education and Crisis, or the Vicissitudes of Teaching." *American Imago* 48, no. 1 (1991): 13–73. http://www.jstor.org/stable/26304031.

"Field Trips | Intrepid Museum." Intrepidmuseum.org, 2024. https://intrepidmuseum.org/plan-your-visit/group-visits/field-trips.

Figley, Charles R., and Marné Ludick. "Secondary Traumatization and Compassion Fatigue." *Handbook of Trauma Psychology* 1, no. 1 (2017): 573–93. https://doi.org/10.1037/0000019-029.

Fishman, David E. *The Book Smugglers: Partisans, Poets, and the Race to Save Jewish Treasures from the Nazis*. Lebanon, NH: University Press of New England, 2017.

Foster, Stuart, Andy Pearce, and Alice Pettigrew, eds. *Holocaust Education: Contemporary Challenges and Controversies*. London: UCL Press, 2020. https://doi.org/10.2307/j.ctv15d7zpf.

Frank, Anne. *The Diary of Anne Frank: The Critical Edition*. Edited by David Barnouw and Gerrold Van Der Stroom. Translated by Arnold J. Pomerans and B. M. Mooyaart. Doubleday, 1989.

Frankl, Viktor E. *Man's Search for Meaning: An Introduction to Logotherapy*. Boston: Beacon Press, 2006.

Friedman, James. "The Holocaust Didn't Happen in Black and White." *Shofar* 37, no. 1 (2019): 1–8. https://doi.org/10.5703/shofar.37.1.0001.

Friesem, Lia. "Holocaust Tweets as an Act of Resistance." *Israel Studies Review* 33, no. 2 (2018): 85–104. https://www.jstor.org/stable/48563790.

Galinsky, Ellen. "Words Matter: Moving from Trauma-Informed to Asset-Informed Care." *YC Young Children* 75, no. 3 (2020): 46–55. https://www.jstor.org/stable/26979164.

Garcia, Ben, Michael Murawski, and Ralph Cordova. "What We Do Best: Making the Case for the Museum Learning in Its Own Right." *The Journal of Museum Education* 37, no. 2 (2012): 47–55. http://www.jstor.org/stable/41705823.

Garrett, H. James. "Difficult Knowledge: Encounters with Social Trauma in Pedagogy." *Counterpoints* 506 (2017): 17–48. http://www.jstor.org/stable/45136321.

Gaudelli, William, Margaret Crocco, and Alexandra Hawkins. "Documentaries, Outtakes, and Digital Archives in Teaching Difficult Knowledge and the Vietnam War." *Education and Society* 30, no. 2 (2012): 5–25. https://doi.org/10.7459/es/30.2.02.

Gershenson, Olga. "Meta-Memory: About the Holocaust in New Israeli Video Art." *Jewish Film & New Media: An International Journal* 6, no. 1 (2018): 67–90. https://doi.org/10.13110/jewifilmnewmedi.6.1.0067.

Giordano, Francesca, Shannon Lipscomb, Petra Jefferies, Kyong-Ah Kwon, and Margherita Giammarchi. "Resilience Processes Among Ukrainian Youth Preparing to Build Resilience with Peers During the Ukraine-Russia War." *Frontiers in Psychology* 15 (February 20, 2024): 1331886. https://doi.org/10.3389/fpsyg.2024.1331886.

Golding, Julie. "Resilience in Holocaust Education: A Museum Based Approach." *Jewish Educational Leadership* 18, no. 2 (Spring 2020). https://www.lookstein.org/journal-article/spring-2020/resilience-in-holocaust-education/.

Golding, Julie J. *Vicarious Trauma Experienced by Visitors to a Central Holocaust Museum*. PhD diss., Yeshiva University, 2023. https://repository.yu.edu/items/2b5e4d06-4b25-46b7-8a22-d1fa3001e85c.

Golding, Rabbi Yosef C. *Faith Amid The Flames*. New York: ArtScroll Mesorah Publications, 2019. Also discussed in "Faith Amid The Flames." *The Lakewood Scoop*, July 18, 2019. https://thelakewoodscoop.com/news/faith-amid-the-flames-the-story-of-reb-yosef-friedenson-the-kiddush-hashem-he-witnessed-and-created%E2%80%8B%E2%80%8B-rabbi-yosef-c-golding/.

Gottschall, Jonathan. *The Storytelling Animal: How Stories Make Us Human*. Boston, MA: Mariner Books, 2013.

Gould, Rebecca Ruth. "The IHRA Definition of Antisemitism: Defining Antisemitism by Erasing Palestinians." *The Political Quarterly* 91, no. 4 (2020): 825–31. https://onlinelibrary.wiley.com/doi/pdfdirect/10.1111/1467-923X.12883.

Graves, Lisa. "Death & The Modern Visitor Experience." *Journal of Museum Ethnography* 30 (2017): 49–58. http://www.jstor.org/stable/44841226.

Gray, Michael. *Contemporary Debates in Holocaust Education*. Basingstoke, England: Palgrave Pivot, 2014.

Greenspan, Henry. "The Humanities of Contingency: Interviewing and Teaching beyond 'Testimony' with Holocaust Survivors." *The Oral History Review* 46, no. 2 (2019): 360–79. https://doi.org/10.1093/ohr/ohz008.

Greenspan, Henry, Sara R. Horowitz, Éva Kovács, Berel Lang, Dori Laub, Kenneth Waltzer, and Annette Wieviorka. "Engaging Survivors: Assessing 'Testimony' and 'Trauma' as Foundational Concepts." *Dapim: Studies on the Holocaust* 28, no. 3 (2014): 190–226. https://doi.org/10.1080/23256249.2014.951909.

Grindle, Nicholas, and Ben Thomas. "Curating Connections in the Art History Curriculum." In *Developing the Higher Education Curriculum: Research-based Education in Practice,* edited by Brent Carnell and Dilly Fung, 106–17. London: UCL Press, 2017. https://doi.org/10.2307/j.ctt1xhr542.13.

Grinstein-Cohen, O., A. Katz, and O. Sarid. "Religiosity: Its Impact on Coping Styles Among Women Undergoing Fertility Treatment." *Journal of Religion and Health* 56, no. 3 (2017): 1032–41. http://www.jstor.org/stable/26749277.

Gross, David C. "Holocaust Survival." *Aish.com*, 2002. Accessed January 2, 2025. http://www.aish.com/h/c/s/h/48956896.html.

Gross, Zehavit. "The Process of the Universalization of Holocaust Education: Problems and Challenges." *Contemporary Jewry* 38, no. 1 (2018): 5–20. http://www.jstor.org/stable/45209113.

Gubkin, Liora. "From Empathetic Understanding to Engaged Witnessing: Encountering Trauma in the Holocaust Classroom." *Teaching Theology and Religion* 18, no. 2 (2015): 103–20. https://doi.org/10.1111/teth.12273.

Gustems-Carnicer, Josep, and Caterina Calderón. "Coping Strategies and Psychological Well-Being among Teacher Education Students: Coping and Well-Being in Students." *European Journal of Psychology of Education* 28, no. 4 (2013): 1127–40. https://doi.org/10.1007/sl0212-012-0158-x.

Haas, Brandon J. "Bearing Witness: Teacher Perspectives on Developing Empathy through Holocaust Survivor Testimony." *The Social Studies* 111, no. 2 (2019): 86–103. doi:10.1080/00377996.2019.1693949.

Harel, Dorit. *Facts and Feelings: Dilemmas in Designing the Yad Vashem Holocaust History Museum*. Tel Aviv: Yad Vashem Publications, 2010, 54.

Harmeyer, Rachel. *Objects of Immortality: Hairwork and Mourning in Victorian Visual Culture.* Proceedings of the Art of Death and Dying Symposium. The University of Houston Libraries, 2018. http://hdl.handle.net/10657/3003.

Hendrickson, Lois. "Teaching with Artifacts and Special Collections." *Bulletin of the History of Medicine* 90, no. 1 (2016): 136–40. https://www.jstor.org/stable/26310794.

Hernández, Pilar, David Gangsei, and David Engstrom. "Vicarious Resilience: A New Concept in Work with Those Who Survive Trauma." *Family Process* 46, no. 2 (June 2007): 229–41. https://doi.org/10.1111/j.1545-5300.2007.00206.x.

Hillman, Susanne. "Grim Expectations: Video Testimony in the College Classroom." *The History Teacher* 48, no. 2 (2015): 295–320. http://www.jstor.org/stable/43264406.

"History of the Paperclip Project." *Whitwell Middle School*. Accessed June 20, 2024. https://www.whitwellmiddleschool.org/childrensholocaustmemorial/history.

Hoffman, Isabel. "Prayers in Majdanek." *Jewish Women's Archive*, October 16, 2019. https://jwa.org/blog/risingvoices/prayers-majdanek.

"Holocaust Instruction in NYS Public School Districts." *New York State Education Department*. Accessed July 2, 2024. https://www.nysed.gov/sites/default/files/programs/curriculum-instruction/holocaust-instruction-report-final-2022.pdf.

Holocaust Museum LA. "Student Tours." *Holocaust Museum LA*, 2020. https://www.holocaustmuseumla.org/student-tours.

"Holocaust Museum & Center for Tolerance and Education." Holocaust Museum & Center for Tolerance and Education, September 30, 2022. https://www.holocauststudies.org.

"Holocaust Survivor Demographic Reports." *Claims Conference*, January 23, 2024. https://www.claimscon.org/demographics/.

Huenink, Ellen, and Susan Porterfield. "Parent Support Programs and Coping Mechanisms in Nicu Parents." *Advances in Neonatal Care* 17, no. 2 (April 2017): E10–E18. https://doi.org/10.1097/anc.0000000000000359.

"Identity Card Project." United States Holocaust Memorial Museum. Accessed July 16, 2024. https://www.ushmm.org/m/pdfs/20121024-idcards.pdf.

Illinois Holocaust Museum & Education Center. "History." Accessed January 15, 2022. https://www.ilholocaustmuseum.org/about/history/.

Institute for Visual History and Education USC Shoah Foundation. "Dimensions in Testimony." Accessed January 5, 2022. https://sfi.usc.edu/dit.

Institute for Visual History and Education USC Shoah Foundation. "Institutions with Access to the Visual History Archive." Accessed January 5, 2022. https://sfi.usc.edu/vha/access.

International Holocaust Remembrance Alliance. "Recommendations for Teaching and Learning about the Holocaust." Accessed January 25, 2022. https://www.holocaustremembrance.com/sites/default/files/inline-files/IHRA-Recommendations-Teaching-and-Learning-about-Holocaust.pdf.

International March of the Living. About Page. Accessed January 25, 2022. https://www.motl.org/about/.

Intrepid Museum. 2019. "Support Intrepid: Spotlight on School Programs." YouTube, November 19, 2019. https://www.youtube.com/watch?v=eBn_po8iDcI.

"Introductory Panel – Flashes of Memory: Photography during the Holocaust." Yad Vashem, Jerusalem, June 30, 2024.

"Israeli Steals Auschwitz Items for Student Art Project." *BBC*, July 19, 2017. https://www.bbc.com/news/world-middle-east-40656748.

IWitness. "Teaching with Testimony." Accessed February 19, 2022. https://iwitness.usc.edu/home.

Jackson, Peter. "Peter Jackson Colourises World War One Footage." Interview by BBC Click, October 15, 2018. https://www.youtube.com/ watch?v=EYleactlMWo.

Jacobs, Janet. "Traumatic Inheritance and the Demasculinization of God: Reimagining the Divine among Descendants of the Holocaust." *Journal of Feminist Studies in Religion* 31, no. 2 (2015): 65–82. https://doi.org/10.2979/jfemistudreli.31.2.65.

Jenkins, C. S., and Daniel Nolan. "Disposition Impossible." *Noûs* 46, no. 4 (2012): 732–53. http://www.jstor.org/stable/41682694.

Jenkins, Sharon Rae, and Stephanie Baird. "Secondary Traumatic Stress and Vicarious Trauma: A Validational Study." *Journal of Traumatic Stress: Official Publication of The International Society for Traumatic Stress Studies* 15 (2002): 423–32.

Jenzer, Tiffany, Samuel N. Meisel, Jessica A. Blayney, Craig R. Colder, and Jennifer P. Read. "Reciprocal Processes in Trauma and Coping: Bidirectional Effects over a Four-Year Period." *Psychological Trauma: Theory, Research, Practice, and Policy* 12, no. 2 (2020): 207–18. https://doi.org/10.1037/tra0000500.

Jeske, Jan, and Mary Louise Klas. "Adverse Childhood Experiences: Implications for Family Law Practice and the Family Court System." *Family Law Quarterly* 50, no. 1 (2016): 123–37. http://www.jstor.org/stable/44155200.

Jikeli, Günther. "Anti-Semitism within the Extreme Right and Islamists' Circles." In *Being Jewish in 21st-Century Germany*, edited by Haim Fireberg and Olaf Glöckner, 1st ed., 188–207. De Gruyter, 2015.

Jinks, Rebecca. *Representing Genocide: The Holocaust as Paradigm?* London: Bloomsbury Academic, 2016.

Johnson, Dan, and Rhiannon Pickin. "Suffering on Display: An Argument for Historical Nuance in British Prison Museums." *Crime, Histoire & Sociétés* 23, no. 1 (2019): 5–26. http://www.jstor.org/stable/45215848.

Johnston, Tony. "The Geographies of Thanatourism." *Geography* 100, no. 1 (2015): 20–7. http://www.jstor.org/stable/43825410.

Jones, Jessimi. "Examining Why: Our Work with Teacher and Schools." *The Journal of Museum Education* 39, no. 2 (2014): 175–86. http://www.jstor.org/stable/43305024.

Jong, Steffi de. *The Witness as Object: Video Testimonies in Holocaust Museums*. New York: Berghahn Books, 2018. https://doi.org/10.2307/j.ctv3znzsd.

Juzwik, Mary M. "The Ethics of Teaching Disturbing Pasts: Reader Response, Historical Contextualization, and Rhetorical (Con)Textualization of Holocaust Texts in English." *English Education* 45, no. 3 (2013): 284–308. http://www.jstor.org/stable/23364870.

Kaplan, E. Ann. *Trauma Culture: The Politics of Terror and Loss in Media and Literature*. New Brunswick, NJ: Rutgers University Press, 2005.

Karayianni, Eleni. "Look before You Leap: Teaching about the Holocaust in Primary Schools." In *Holocaust Education: Contemporary Challenges and Controversies*, edited by Stuart Foster, Andy Pearce, and Alice Pettigrew, 95–113. London: UCL Press, 2020. https://doi.org/10.2307/j.ctv15d7zpf.11.

Karn, Alexander. "Toward a Philosophy of Holocaust Education: Teaching Values without Imposing Agendas." *The History Teacher* 45, no. 2 (2012): 221–40. http://www.jstor.org/stable/23265920.

Kasi, Pashtoon Murtaza, Haider Ali Naqvi, Abaseen Khan Afghan, Talha Khawar, Farooq Hasan Khan, Umber Zaheer Khan, Urooj Bakht Khuwaja, Jawad Kiani, and Hadi Mohammad Khan. "Coping Styles in Patients with Anxiety and Depression." *ISRN Psychiatry* (June 2012): 1–7. https://doi.org/10.5402/2012/128672.

Kassow, Samuel D. *Who Will Write Our History?: Rediscovering a Hidden Archive from the Warsaw Ghetto*. Bloomington: Indiana University Press, 2007.

Kataoka, Sheryl H., Pamela Vona, Alejandra Acuña, Lisa Jaycox, Pia Escudero, Claudia Rojas, Erica Ramirez, Audra Langley, and Bradley D. Stein. "Applying a Trauma Informed School Systems Approach: Examples from School Community-Academic Partnerships." *Ethnicity & Disease* 28 (2018): 417–26. https://www.jstor.org/stable/48667763.

Kello, Katrin. "Sensitive and Controversial Issues in the Classroom: Teaching History in a Divided Society." *Teachers and Teaching* 22, no. 1 (2015): 35–53. https://doi.org/10.1080/13540602.2015.1023027.

Keren, Nili. "Teaching the Holocaust in Israel." *Internationale Schulbuchforschung* 22, no. 1 (2000): 95–108. http://www.jstor.org/stable/43057186.

Keynan, Irit. "The Memory of the Holocaust and Israel's Attitude Toward War Trauma, 1948–1973: The Collective vs. the Individual." *Israel Studies* 23, no. 2 (2018): 95–117. https://doi.org/10.2979/israelstudies.23.2.05.

Khan, Ziasma Haneef, P. J. Watson, and Zhuo Chen. "Muslim Spirituality, Religious Coping, and Reactions to Terrorism among Pakistani University Students." *Journal of Religion and Health* 55, no. 6 (2016): 2086–98. https://doi.org/10.1007/s10943-016-0263-2.

King, Lisa. "Rhetorics in a Museum Space: Connecting Exhibit Spaces, Contexts, and Audiences." *JAC* 33, no. 3/4 (2013): 671–88. http://www.jstor.org/stable/43854572.

Koffler, Jacob. "2 Teenagers Arrested for Theft of Auschwitz Artifacts." *TIME*, June 23, 2015. https://time.com/3931830/teenagers-arrested-auschwitz-artifacts/.

Kolk, Bessel van der. *The Body Keeps the Score: Brain, Mind, and Body in the Healing of Trauma*. London: Penguin Books, 2015.

Krägeloh, Christian U., Penny Pei Chai, Daniel Shepherd, and Rex Billington. "How Religious Coping Is Used Relative to Other Coping Strategies Depends on the Individual's Level of Religiosity and Spirituality." *Journal of Religion and Health* 51, no. 4 (2010): 1137–51. https://doi.org/10.1007/s10943-010-9416-x.

Kratz, Corinne A. "Where Did You Cry? Crafting Categories, Narratives, and Affect through Exhibit Design." *Kronos* 44 (2018): 229–52. https://www.jstor.org/stable/26610867.

Kredlow, Alexandra M., Richard J. Fenster, Erika S. Laurent, Ewgeni Jakubovski, David A. Pisner, Matthew J. Friedman, Ann M. Rasmusson, Danielle S. Bassett, and Kerry

J. Ressler. "Prefrontal Cortex, Amygdala, and Threat Processing: Implications for PTSD." *Neuropsychopharmacology* 47 (2022): 247–59. https://doi.org/10.1038/s41386-021-01155-7.

Krieg, Lisa Jenny. "'Who Wants to Be Sad Over and Over Again?' Emotion Ideologies in Contemporary German Education about the Holocaust." *Journal of Educational Media, Memory & Society* 7, no. 2 (2015): 110–28. http://www.jstor.org/stable/44319958.

Krippner, Stanley, and Deirdre Barrett. "Transgenerational Trauma: The Role of Epigenetics." *The Journal of Mind and Behavior* 40, no. 1 (2019): 53–62. https://www.jstor.org/stable/26740747.

Krondorfer, Björn. "Unsettling Empathy: Intercultural Dialogue in the Aftermath of Historical and Cultural Trauma." In *Breaking Intergenerational Cycles of Repetition: A Global Dialogue on Historical Trauma and Memory,* 1st ed., edited by Pumla Gobodo-Madikizela, 90–112. Berlin: Barbara Budrich, 2016. https://doi.org/10.2307/j.ctvdf03jc.11.

Laguardia, Francesca, Venezia Michalsen, and Holly Rider-Milkovich. "Trigger Warnings: From Panic to Data." *Journal of Legal Education* 66, no. 4 (2017): 882–903. https://www.jstor.org/stable/26453524.

Langer, Lawrence. *Admitting the Holocaust: Collected Essays.* Oxford: Oxford University Press, 1996.

Langer, Lawrence. "The Dilemma of Choice in the Death Camps," *Centerpoint: A Journal of Interdisciplinary Studies* 4, no. 1 (1980): 53–9.

Lawless, Kate. "Memory, Trauma, and the Matter of Historical Violence: The Controversial Case of Four Photographs from Auschwitz." *American Imago* 71, no. 4 (2014): 391–415. https://www.jstor.org/stable/26305100.

Lenga, Ruth-Anne. "Seeing Things Differently: The Use of Atrocity Images in Teaching about the Holocaust." In *Holocaust Education: Contemporary Challenges and Controversies*, edited by Stuart Foster, Andy Pearce, and Alice Pettigrew, 195–220. London: UCL Press, 2020. https://doi.org/10.2307/j.ctv15d7zpf.16.

Leung, Tiffany, Fred Schmidt, and Christopher Mushquash. "A Personal History of Trauma and Experience of Secondary Traumatic Stress, Vicarious Trauma, and Burnout in Mental Health Workers: A Systematic Literature Review." *Psychological Trauma: Theory, Research, Practice, and Policy* 15, no. Suppl 2 (2023). https://doi.org/10.1037/tra0001277.

Lindquist, David H. "Complicating Issues in Holocaust Education." *The Journal of Social Studies Research* 34, no. 1 (2010): 77–93. https://eric.ed.gov/?id=EJ887319.

Linfield, Susie. "When Genocide Is Caught on Film." February 21, 2021. https://www.nytimes.com/2021/02/16/books/review/the-ravine-holocaust-photo-wendy-lower.html.

Lipstadt, Deborah E. *The Eichmann Trial*. New York: Schocken Books, 2011.

Liss, Andrea. *Trespassing Through Shadows: Memory, Photography, and the Holocaust*. Minneapolis: University of Minnesota Press, 1998. 22–3.

Lloyd, Michele. "Domestic Violence and Education: Examining the Impact of Domestic Violence on Young Children, Children, and Young People and the Potential Role of Schools." *Frontiers in Psychology* 9 (2018): 1–11. https://doi.org/10.3389/fpsyg.2018.02094.

Los Angeles Holocaust Museum. "2019 Annual Report." Accessed January 23, 2022. https://www.holocaustmuseumla.org/financials.

Lowe, Hilary Iris. "Dwelling in Possibility: Revisiting Narrative in the Historic House Museum." *The Public Historian* 37, no. 2 (2015): 42–60. https://doi.org/10.1525/tph.2015.37.2.42.

Lower, Wendy. *The Ravine: A Family, a Photograph, a Holocaust Massacre Revealed*. New York: Mariner Books, 2021.

Magid, Shaul. "The Holocaust and Jewish Identity in America: Memory, the Unique, and the Universal." *Jewish Social Studies* 18, no. 2 (2012): 100–35. https://doi.org/10.2979/jewisocistud.18.2.100.

Malka, Tali, Ilanit Hasson-Ohayon, Gil Goldzweig, and David Roe. "Coping Style Is Associated with Parental Distress Beyond Having a Mental Illness: A Study among Mothers with and without Mental Illness." *Psychiatric Rehabilitation Journal* 43, no. 2 (2020): 170–3. https://doi.org/10.1037/prj0000381.

Maloney, Carolyn B. "Maloney's Never Again Education Act Signed into Law." *Press Release*, May 29, 2020. https://maloney.house.gov/media-center/press-releases/maloney-s-never-again-education-act-signed-into-law.

Magano, José, José António Fraiz-Brea, and Ângela Leite. "Dark Tourism, the Holocaust, and Well-Being: A Systematic Review." *Heliyon* 9, no. 1 (2023). https://doi.org/10.1016/j.heliyon.2023.e13064.

Magano, José, José A. Fraiz-Brea, and Ângela Leite. "Dark Tourists: Profile, Practices, Motivations and Wellbeing." *International Journal of Environmental Research and Public Health* 19, no. 19 (2022): 12100. https://doi.org/10.3390/ijerph191912100.

Marcus, Alan S., Rotem Maor, Ian M. McGregor, Gary Mills, Simone Schweber, Jeremy Stoddard, and David Hicks. "Holocaust Education in Transition from Live to Virtual Survivor Testimony: Pedagogical and Ethical Dilemmas." *Holocaust Studies* 28, no. 3 (2021): 279–301. https://doi.org/10.1080/17504902.2021.1979176.

Marcus, Alan S., Jeremy D. Stoddard, and Walter W. Woodward. *Teaching History with Museums: Strategies for K–12 Social Studies*, 2nd ed. New York: Routledge, 2017. https://doi.org/10.4324/9781315194806.

Mayordomo-Rodríguez, Teresa, Juan Carlos Meléndez-Moral, Paz Viguer-Segui, and Alicia Sales-Galán. "Coping Strategies as Predictors of Well-Being in Youth Adult." *Social Indicators Research* 122, no. 2 (2014): 479–89. https://doi.org/10.1007/s11205-014-0689-4.

McGavock, Lian, and Trevor Spratt. "Children Exposed to Domestic Violence: Using Adverse Childhood Experience Scores to Inform Service Response." *The British Journal of Social Work* 47, no. 4 (2016): 1128–46. https://doi.org/10.1093/bjsw/bcw073.

McIntire, Laura, and Renae Duncan. "Associations among Religious Coping, Daily Hassles, and Resilience." *Archive for the Psychology of Religion* 35, no. 1 (2013): 101–17. https://doi.org/10.1163/15736121-12341252.

McLaughlin, Katie A., and Margaret A. Sheridan. "Beyond Cumulative Risk: A Dimensional Approach to Childhood Adversity." *Current Directions in Psychological Science* 25, no. 4 (2016): 239–45. http://www.jstor.org/stable/44318964.

Menyhért, Anna. "Digital Trauma Processing in Social Media Groups: Transgenerational Holocaust Trauma on Facebook." *The Hungarian Historical Review* 6, no. 2 (2017): 355–76. http://www.jstor.org/stable/26374322.

Merwe, Amelia van der, and Xanthe Hunt. "Secondary Trauma Among Trauma Researchers: Lessons from the Field." *Psychological Trauma: Theory, Research, Practice, and Policy* 11, no. 1 (2019): 10–18. https://doi.org/10.1037/tra0000414.

Meseth, Wolfgang, and Matthias Proske. "Mind the Gap: Holocaust Education in Germany, Between Pedagogical Intentions and Classroom Interactions." In *As the Witnesses Fall Silent: 21st Century Holocaust Education in Curriculum, Policy and Practice*, edited by Zehavit Gross and E. Dolye Stevick, 159–82. Berlin: Springer International Publishing, 2015. https://doi.org/10.1007/978-3-319-15419-0_10.

Michelson, David. "Personality and the Varieties of Fictional Experience." *Journal of Aesthetic Education* 48, no. 2 (2014): 64–85. https://doi.org/10.5406/jaesteduc.48.2.0064.

Michman, Dan. "Historiography on the Holocaust in Poland: An Outsider's View of Its Place within Recent General Developments in Holocaust Historiography." In *New Directions in the History of the Jews in the Polish Lands*, edited by Antony Polonsky, Hanna Węgrzynek, and Andrzej Żbikowski, 386–401. Boston: Academic Studies Press, 2018. https://doi.org/10.2307/j.ctv7xbrh4.38.

Miller, Mara. "Terrible Knowledge and Tertiary Trauma, Part I: Japanese Nuclear Trauma and Resistance to the Atomic Bomb in the Classroom." *The Clearing House* 86, no. 5 (2013): 157–63. http://www.jstor.org/stable/43999342.

Missouri's Early Care & Education Connections. "Trauma-Informed Care | Early Connections." Earlyconnections.mo.gov, 2022. https://earlyconnections.mo.gov/professionals/trauma-informed-care.

Muir, Simo. "Rumkowski's Scapegoat? The Case of Łódź Ghetto Functionary Maks Szczęśliwy at a Rabbinic/Honor Court in Helsinki, 1949–1953." *Holocaust and Genocide Studies* 35, no. 2 (2021): 185–210. https://doi.org/10.1093/hgs/dcab035.

Munroe, Melanie, Mohamed Al-Refae, Helen W. Chan, and Michel Ferrari. "Using Self-Compassion to Grow in the Face of Trauma: The Role of Positive Reframing and Problem-Focused Coping Strategies." *Psychological Trauma: Theory, Research, Practice, and Policy* 14, no. 1 (2022): 157–64. https://doi.org/10.1037/tra0001164.

Museum of Jewish Heritage – A Living Memorial to the Holocaust. "Mission." Accessed January 3, 2022. https://www.mjhnyc.org/mission/.

National Storytelling Network. "What is Storytelling?" Accessed January 3, 2022. https://storynet.org/what-is- storytelling/.

National Child Traumatic Stress Network. *Taking Care of Yourself.* Accessed February 20, 2025. https://www.nctsn.org/resources/taking-care-of-yourself.

National Child Traumatic Stress Network. "Trauma Informed Care." Accessed January 13, 2022. https://www.nctsn.org.

National Study of Secondary Teaching Practices in Holocaust Education. Arlington, VA: SRI International, 2004. Accessed January 13, 2022. www.policyweb.sri.com/cep/publications/SRI_Natl-Study_TeachingPractices.pdf.

Never Again Education Act of 2020. H.R. 943, 116th Cong. https://www.congress.gov/bill/116th-congress/house-bill/943/text.

New England Holocaust Memorial. "Design of the Memorial." *New England Holocaust Memorial | A Beacon of Memory and Hope*, 2013. Accessed March 11, 2013. https://www.nehm.org/the-memorial/design-of-the-memorial/.

New York Times. "Laughter at Film Brings Spielberg Visit." *The New York Times,* April 13, 1994. https://www.nytimes.com/1994/04/13/us/laughter-at-film-brings-spielberg-visit.html.

Ng, Jenna. "Holograms/Holographic Projections: Ghosts Amongst the Living; Ghosts of the Living." In *The Post-Screen Through Virtual Reality, Holograms and Light Projections: Where Screen Boundaries Lie*, edited by Jenna Ng, 155–88. Amsterdam: Amsterdam University Press, 2021. https://doi.org/10.2307/j.ctv23985t6.8.

Norris, Linda, Danny Cohen, and Stacey Mann. "When Histories Horrify: Supporting Visitors' Responses through Responsible Interpretation." *History News* 67, no. 4 (2012): 16–20. https://www.jstor.org/stable/26453343.

"Nova Exhibition." Nova Exhibition, 2023. https://www.novaexhibition.com.

Novick, Peter. *The Holocaust in American Life.* New York: Houghton Mifflin, 2000.

Nuttman-Shwartz, Orit. "Shared Resilience in a Traumatic Reality: A New Concept for Trauma Workers Exposed Personally and Professionally to Collective Disaster."

Trauma, Violence & Abuse 16, no. 4 (2015): 466–75. https://www.jstor.org/stable/26638374.

Obrist, Hans Ulrich. *Ways of Curating*. London: Penguin Books, 2015.

Ofer, Dalia. "Studying the Holocaust in Israel." *Israel Studies* 23, no. 3 (2018): 96–105. http://www.jstor.org/stable/10.2979/israelstudies.23.3.13.

Ofer, Dalia. "We Israelis Remember, But How?: The Memory of the Holocaust and the Israeli Experience." *Israel Studies* 18, no. 2 (2013): 70–85. https://doi.org/10.2979/israelstudies.18.2.70.

Oklahoma Department of Mental Health and Substance Abuse Services. *Vicarious Trauma*. Accessed January 9, 2024. https://oklahoma.gov/content/dam/ok/en/odmhsas/documents/a0004/vicarioustrauma-transcript.pdf.

Oliver, Sophie. "The AESTH- Ethics of Empathy: Bakhtin and the Return to Self as Ethical Act." In *Empathy and its Limits*, edited by Aleida Assmann and Ines Detmers, 166–86. New York: Palgrave Macmillan, 2016. https://doi.org/10.1057/9781137552372_10.

"On Trial." *Time*, July 11, 1955. https://web.archive.org/web/20081217113419/http://www.time.com/time/magazine/article/0,9171,807322-3,00.html.

Othman, Mohd Kamal, Helen Petrie, and Christopher Power. "Engaging Visitors in Museums with Technology: Scales for the Measurement of Visitor and Multimedia Guide Experience." In *Human-Computer Interaction – INTERACT 2011*, edited by Pedro Campos, Nicholas Graham, Joaquim Jorge, Nuno Nunes, Philippe Palanque and Marco Winckler, 92–9. Berlin: Springer, 2011. https://doi.org/10.1007/978-3-642-23768-3_8.

"Out of Chaos: Hidden Children Remember the Holocaust." Illinois Holocaust Museum & Education Center. Accessed August 23, 2024. https://www.ilholocaustmuseum.org/wp-content/uploads/2022/11/IHM_TRAVELexhibit_CHILDREN-111422.pdf.

Pawlowicz, Rachel, and Walter E. Grunden. "Teaching Atrocities: The Holocaust and Unit 731 in the Secondary School Curriculum." *The History Teacher* 48, no. 2 (2015): 271–94. http://www.jstor.org/stable/43264405.

Pearce, Andy. "Challenges, Issues and Controversies: The Shapes of 'Holocaust Education' in the Early Twenty-First Century." In *Holocaust Education: Contemporary Challenges and Controversies*, edited by Andy Pearce, Stuart Foster, and Alice Pettigrew, 1–27. London: UCL Press, 2020. https://doi.org/10.2307/j.ctv15d7zpf.7.

Pearce, Andy, and Arthur Chapman. "Holocaust Education 25 Years on: Challenges, Issues, Opportunities." *Holocaust Studies* 23, no. 3 (2017): 223–30. https://doi.org/10.1080/17504902.2017.1296082.

Peng, Ann Chunyan, Laura T. Riolli, John Schaubroeck, and Everett S. Spain. "A Moderated Mediation Test of Personality, Coping, and Health among Deployed Soldiers." *Journal of Organizational Behavior* 33, no. 4 (2011): 512–30. https://doi.org/10.1002/job.766.

Pinchevski, Amit. *Transmitted Wounds: Media and the Mediation of Trauma*. Oxford: Oxford University Press, 2019. https://doi.org/10.1093/oso/9780190625580.001.0001.

Pinnock, S. K. "Atrocity and Ambiguity: Recent Developments in Christian Holocaust Responses." *Journal of the American Academy of Religion* 75, no. 3 (2007): 499–523. https://doi.org/10.1093/jaarel/lfm038.

Piotrowska, Marea Ferenc, Kamila Radecka-Mikulicz, and Justyna Majewska. "Curatorial and Educational Challenges in Creating the Holocaust Gallery." In *New Directions in the History of the Jews in the Polish Lands*, edited by Antony Polonsky, Hanna Węgrzynek, and Andrzej Żbikowski, 29–39. Boston: Academic Studies Press, 2018. https://doi.org/10.2307/j.ctv7xbrh4.10.

Plessow, Oliver. "Agents of Transnationalization in the Field of Holocaust Education." In *Entangled Memories: Remembering the Holocaust in a Global Age*, edited by Marius Henderson and Julia Lange, 315–52. Hamburg: Universitat Hamburg, 2017.

Plessow, Oliver. "Agents of Transnational Memory? Holocaust Museums in Australia and Germany." *Memory Studies* 13, no. 6 (2020): 1232–45.

President's Commission on the Holocaust. "Report to the President." Accessed February 19, 2022. https://www.ushmm.org/m/pdfs/20050707-presidents-commission-holocaust.pdf.

Preston, Andrew. "An Authentic Voice: Perspectives on the Value of Listening to Survivors of Genocide." *Teaching History* 153 (2013): 62–9. http://www.jstor.org/stable/43260632.

Price, Rebecca, and Mark Shores. "Dark Tourism: A Guide to Resources." *Reference & User Services Quarterly* 57, no. 2 (2017): 97–101. https://www.jstor.org/stable/90017127.

Pulh, Mathilde, and Rémi Mencarelli. "Web 2.0: Is the Museum–Visitor Relationship Being Redefined?" *International Journal of Arts Management* 18, no. 1 (2015): 43–51. http://www.jstor.org/stable/24587086.

Rankin, Beth A. "Secondary Traumatic Stress: One Teacher's Experience." *The Phi Delta Kappan* 102, no. 4 (2020): 58–9. https://www.jstor.org/stable/26977217.

Ray, Beverly, and Martha Hocutt. "Learning From and Teaching About Disaster: The Case of the April 2011 Tornado Outbreak." *American Secondary Education* 44, no. 2 (2016): 66–84. http://www.jstor.org/stable/45147975.

Reich, Walter. "Unwelcome Narratives: Listening to Suppressed Themes in American Holocaust Testimonies." *Poetics Today* 27, no. 2 (2006): 463–72. https://doi.org/10.1215/03335372-2005-014.

"Remember the Children: Daniel's Story." United States Holocaust Memorial Museum. Accessed August 23, 2024. https://www.ushmm.org/information/exhibitions/museum-exhibitions/remember-the-children-daniels-story.

"Resilience: Children, Families, and Communities During the Holocaust." Exhibition. Holocaust Museum & Center for Tolerance and Education. Curated by Abigail E. Miller, Isabella Costa, and Julie Golding. 2018.

Rodriguez, Tori. "Descendants of Holocaust Survivors Have Altered Stress Hormones." *Scientific American Mind* 26, no. 2 (2015): 10. https://www.jstor.org/stable/24946475.

Ronald Reagan Presidential Foundation & Institute. "Online Ticket Sales." Accessed January 2, 2024. https://reagan.systemtickets.org/auschwitz/?sitePassword=9TalKgwa5JZcuXtXcF1FHTQM6VXTo&_gl=1*1n3lw4q*_ga*MjAxMzk1NDExNS4xNjY2NzA2ODM1*_ga_8LZKKVJJ5M*MTY2ODQ1NjQ0OC41LjEuMTY2ODQ1Njc4OC42MC4wLjA.

Rosen, Alan, ed. *Literature of the Holocaust*. Cambridge: Cambridge University Press, 2013. https://doi.org/https://doi.org/10.1017/CBO9781139022125.

Rosen, Jonathan. "The Misguided Holocaust Museum." *New York Times*, April 18, 1993. https://www.nytimes.com/1993/04/18/opinion/the-misguided-holocaust-museum.html.

Rubin, Hannah. "A People and its Parchments." August 24, 2022. https://www.tabletmag.com/sections/community/articles/people-parchments-exhibit-scrolls.

"Rumkowski in Auschwitz." *Commentary*, December 1979. https://www.commentary.org/articles/reader-letters/rumkowski-in-auschwitz/.

Rumsey, Amanda D., and Amy Milsom. "Supporting School Engagement and High School Completion Through Trauma-Informed School Counseling." *Professional School Counseling* 22, no. 1 (2018): 1–10. https://www.jstor.org/stable/26784475.

Ryan, Patrick, and Donna Schatt. "Can You Describe the Experience?" *Storytelling, Self, Society* 10, no. 2 (2014): 131–55. https://doi.org/10.13110/storselfsoci.10.2.0131.

Saakvitne, Karen W., and Laurie Anne Pearlman. *Transforming the Pain: A Workbook on Vicarious Traumatization*. New York: W.W. Norton & Company, 1996.

Sa'ar, Gideon (@gidonsaar). "Hamas has Committed Crimes Against Humanity Against Civilian Hostages. This Hamas-Nazi Evil Must be Eradicated!" X (formerly Twitter), February 11, 2025. https://x.com/gidonsaar/status/1888194414964781493.

Sacks, Vanessa, and David Murphey. "The Prevalence of Adverse Childhood Experiences, Nationally, by State, and by Race or Ethnicity." *Child Trends*. Last modified February 12, 2018. www.childtrends.org/publications/prevalence-adverse-childhood-experiencesnationally-state-race-ethnicity.

Salmons, Paul. "Universal Meaning or Historical Understanding? The Holocaust in History and History in the Curriculum." *Teaching History* 141 (2010): 57–63. http://www.jstor.org/stable/43260782.

Savenije, Geerte M., and Pieter de Bruijn. "Historical Empathy in a Museum: Uniting Contextualisation and Emotional Engagement." *International Journal of Heritage Studies* 23, no. 9 (2017): 832–45. https://doi.org/10.1080/13527258.2017.1339108.

Schiavo, Laura. "What to Do with Heritage: The Museum of Jewish Ceremonial Objects, 1931–43." In *Radical Roots: Public History and a Tradition of Social Justice Activism*, edited by Denise D. Meringolo, 395–426. Amherst, MA: Amherst College Press, 2021. http://www.jstor.org/stable/10.3998/mpub.12366495.18.

Schreiber, James B., Andrew J. Pekarik, Nadine Hanemann, Zahava Doering, and Ah-Jin Lee. "Understanding Visitor Engagement and Behaviors." *The Journal of Educational Research* 106, no. 6 (2013): 462–8. http://www.jstor.org/stable/43824302.

Schwarcz, Vera. "To Catch the Echo: Rethinking Acts of Witnessing to the Shoah." *History and Theory* 54, no. 3 (2015): 429–40. https://doi.org/10.1111/hith.10770.

"Seven Poems, Seven Paintings." 2025. https://www.yadvashem.org/education/educational-materials/lesson-plans/poems-paintings.html.

Shahak, Shapira. "YOLOCAUST - the Aftermath." Yolocaust.de, 2014. https://yolocaust.de.

Sharp, Sarah Rose. "The Disturbing Force of Early Color Photos of Nazi Camps." *Hyperallergic*, October 26, 2017. https://hyperallergic.com/407605/james-friedman-holocaust-angela-meleca-gallery/.

Shenker, Noah. "ThroughJeske the Lens of the Shoah: The Holocaust as a Paradigm for Documenting Genocide Testimonies." *History & Memory* 28, no. 1 (2016): 141–75. https://doi.org/10.2979/histmemo.28.1.141.

"Stitching History From the Holocaust." Jewish Museum Milwaukee. Accessed June 24, 2024. https://jewishmuseummilwaukee.org/exhibit/stitching-history-from-the-holocaust/.

"Stitching History From the Holocaust – Rental Information." Jewish Museum Milwaukee. Accessed June 24, 2024. https://jewishmuseummilwaukee.org/wp-content/uploads/2022/01/Stitching-History-From-the-Holocaust-Rental-Information.pdf.

Singer, Sarri. *Written Testimony Before the House Committee on Oversight and Government Reform*. February 2, 2016. Accessed January 22, 2024. https://oversight.house.gov/wp-content/uploads/2016/02/2016-2-2-Written-Testimoney-for-Sarri-Singer1.pdf.

Smith, Laurajane. "Affect and Registers of Engagement: Navigating Emotional Responses to Dissonant Heritages." In *Representing Enslavement and Abolition in Museums: Ambiguous Engagements,* 1st ed., edited by Laurajane Smith, Geoff Cubitt, Kalliopi Fouseki, and Ross Wilson, 264–307. New York: Routledge, 2011. https://doi.org/10.4324/9780203808252.

Smith, Samuel A., and Kenneth E Foote. "Museum/Space/Discourse: Analyzing Discourse in Three Dimensions in Denver's History Colorado Center." *Cultural Geographies* 24, no. 1 (2017): 131–48. https://www.jstor.org/stable/26168796.

"Social Studies." New York State Education Department, n.d. https://www.nysed.gov/standards-instruction/social-studies.

Sodaro, Amy. "The United States Holocaust Memorial Museum: The Creation of a 'Living Memorial.'" In *Exhibiting Atrocity: Memorial Museums and the Politics of Past Violence*, edited by Amy Sadaro, 30–57. New Brunswick, NJ: Rutgers University Press, 2018. https://doi.org/10.2307/j.ctt1v2xskk.6.

Sorene, Paul. "A Night at the Garden: Incredible Footage of the American Nazi Rally in New York – February 20, 1939." *Flashbak*, October 19, 2017. https://flashbak.com/night-garden-incredible-footage-american-nazi-rally-new-york-february-20-1939-388675/.

Spector, Karen. "God on the Gallows: Reading the Holocaust through Narratives of Redemption." *Research in the Teaching of English* 42, no. 1 (2007): 7–55. http://www.jstor.org/stable/40171747.

Spolar, Christine. "The Kids Who Laughed Till It Hurt." *The Washington Post*, March 10, 1994. https://www.washingtonpost.com/archive/lifestyle/1994/03/10/the-kids-who-laughed-till-it-hurt/61462b5b-4c73-46f3-97e7-5e01e4c7f138/.

Stoddard, Jeremy D., Alan S. Marcus, and David Hicks. *Teaching Difficult History Through Film*. New York: Routledge, 2017. https://doi.org/10.4324/9781315640877.

Strength to Strength. "Connect. Share. Heal." Accessed January 27, 2025. https://www.stosglobal.org.

"Study Examines Higher Suicide Rates among First Responders." U.S. Fire Administration, June 16, 2023. https://www.usfa.fema.gov/blog/study-examines-higher-suicide-rates-among-first-responders/.

Sutzkever, Abraham. "Grains of Wheat." In *Geveb,* translated by James Adam Redfield, January 2025. Accessed March 05, 2025. https://ingeveb.org/texts-and-translations/grains.

Tarc, Aparna Mishra. "'I Just Have to Tell You': Pedagogical Encounters into the Emotional Terrain of Learning." *Pedagogy, Culture and Society* 21, no. 3 (2013): 383–402. https://doi.org/10.1080/14681366.2012.759132.

Teicholz, Tom. "Denmark's Safe Harbor Is a Children's Exhibit at NY's Museum of Jewish Heritage." *Forbes*, October 27, 2023. https://www.forbes.com/sites/tomteicholz/2023/10/27/denmarks-safe-harbor-is-a-childrens-exhibit-at-nys-museum-of-jewish-heritage/.

Temiz, Nida. "An Instructional Planning and Implementation of a Museum Tour Addressing Multiple Intelligences for First Graders." *Participatory Educational Research* 8, no. 3 (2021): 24–43. https://doi.org/10.17275/per.21.52.8.3.

Terrasi, Salvatore, and Patricia Crain de Galarce. "Trauma and Learning in America's Classrooms." *The Phi Delta Kappan* 98, no. 6 (2017): 35–41. http://www.jstor.org/stable/26386969.

Terreri, Cydney J., and David S. Glenwick. "The Relationship of Religious and General Coping to Psychological Adjustment and Distress in Urban Adolescents." *Journal of Religion and Health* 52, no. 4 (2011): 1188–202. https://doi.org/10.1007/s10943-011-9555-8.

Timothy, Dallen J., and Stephen W. Boyd. "Heritage Tourism in the 21st Century: Valued Traditions and New Perspectives." *Journal of Heritage Tourism* 1, no. 1 (2006): 1–16. https://doi.org/10.1080/17438730608668462.

Trainer, Laureen, Marley Steele-Inama, and Amber Christopher. "Uncovering Visitor Identity: A Citywide Utilization of the Falk Visitor-Identity Model." *The Journal of Museum Education* 37, no. 1 (2012): 101–14. http://www.jstor.org/stable/41705813.

Trofanenko, Brenda. "Affective Emotions: The Pedagogical Challenges of Knowing War." *Review of Education, Pedagogy, and Cultural Studies* 36, no. 1 (2014): 22–39. https://doi.org/10.1080/10714413.2014.866820.

Tröndle, Martin. "Space, Movement and Attention: Affordances of the Museum Environment." *International Journal of Arts Management* 17, no. 1 (2014): 4–17. http://www.jstor.org/stable/24587224.

United Hatzalah. "Psychotrauma Trailblazers | Masters of Emergency." YouTube, September 24, 2024. https://www.youtube.com/watch?v=Ip7AixA3TBw&list=PLY8odRz2guQxayKUnnqKKjfBZIj4SXqRw&index=9.

U.S. Department of State. Deployment Stress Management Program. "What is Resilience?" Accessed March 10, 2025. https://2009-2017.state.gov/m/med/dsmp/c44950.htm.

U.S. Department of Veterans Affairs. "Understanding PTSD." Accessed February 1, 2022. https://www.ptsd.va.gov.

United States Holocaust Memorial Museum. "Museum Press Kit; Facts and Figures." Accessed February 15, 2022. https://www.ushmm.org/information/press/press-kits/united-states-holocaust-memorial-museum-press-kit/.

United States Holocaust Memorial Museum. "Where Holocaust Education is Required in the US." Accessed February 15, 2022. https://www.ushmm.org/teach/fundamentals/ where-holocaust-education-is-required-in-the-us.

van der Kolk, B. A. *The Body Keeps the Score: Brain, Mind, and Body in the Healing f Trauma.* Viking, 2014.

"Van Gogh Philadelphia, PA Exhibit: The Immersive Experience." Vangoghexpo.com, 2021. https://vangoghexpo.com/philadelphia/?utm_source=landing&utm_medium=landing_vangoghexperience_nyc&utm_campaign=96017_nyc&cp_landing=cta_hero&cp_landing_term=cta_hero&cp_landing_source=vangoghexpo.

Vitale, Monica, and Rebecca Clothey. "Holocaust Education in Germany: Ensuring Relevance and Meaning in an Increasingly Diverse Community." *FIRE: Forum for International Research in Education* 5, no. 1 (2019): 44–62. https://doi.org/10.32865/fire201951139.

Volková, Bronislava. *Forms of Exile in Jewish Literature and Thought: Twentieth-century Central Europe and Migration to America*. Boston: Academic Studies Press, 2021. https://doi.org/10.2307/j.ctv2175r23.15.

Wagaman, M. Alex, Jennifer M. Geiger, Clara Shockley, and Elizabeth A. Segal. "The Role of Empathy in Burnout, Compassion Satisfaction, and Secondary Traumatic Stress among Social Workers." *Social Work* 60, no. 3 (2015): 201–9. http://www.jstor.org/stable/24881483.

Wallace, Amy. "A High-Tech Walk Down the Corridors of Bigotry: Museum: L.A.'s Wiesenthal Center Adopts Provocative Strategy to Document and Teach Lessons from Holocaust." January 30, 1993. https://www.latimes.com/archives/la-xpm-1993-01-30-mn-1892-story.html.

Wang, Xiaotao, Liu Liu, Binli Chen, Wing Hong Chui, and Xiying Wang. "The Mediating Effect of Self-Control on the Relationship between Exposure to Violence and Fighting among Chinese Secondary School Students." *Journal of School Violence* 21, no. 1 (2021): 34–47. https://doi.org/10.1080/15388220.2021.1985325.

Watkins, Liz. "The Politics of Nostalgia: Colorization, Spectatorship and the Archive." *Comparative Cinema* 9, no. 17 (2021): 123–45. https://doi.org/10.31009/cc.2021.v9.i17.07.

Webber, Jonathan. "Jewish Tourism to Poland: The Opportunities for New Museum Narratives to Recontextualize Jewish Histories." In *New Directions in the History of the Jews in the Polish Lands*, edited by Antony Polonsky, Hanna Węgrzynek, and

Andrzej Żbikowski, 139–49. Boston: Academic Studies Press, 2018. https://doi.org/10.2307/j.ctv7xbrh4.21.

Weinberg, Michael, Sharon Gil, and Ora Gilbar. "Forgiveness, Coping, and Terrorism: Do Tendency to Forgive and Coping Strategies Associate with the Level of Posttraumatic Symptoms of Injured Victims of Terror Attacks?" *Journal of Clinical Psychology* 70, no. 7 (2013): 693–703. https://doi.org/10.1002/jclp.22056.

Weissberg, Leon, and Caren Schnur Neile. "Never Forget: March of the Living and Place-Based Holocaust Storytelling." *Storytelling, Self, Society* 11, no. 1 (2015): 121–36. https://doi.org/10.13110/storselfsoci.11.1.0121.

"Why Do We Love Black and White Photography?" Headshot London, February 9, 2015. https://www.headshotlondon.co.uk/blog/why-do-we-love-black-and-white-photography/.

"Why Six Million Voices." *Six Million Voices*, 2024. Accessed February 14, 2024. https://sixmillionvoices.org/about-us/.

Wiesel, Elie. "A Prayer for the Days of Awe." *New York Times*, October 2, 1997.

Wiesel, Elie. "Report to the President." President's Commission on the Holocaust, September 27, 1979, https://www.ushmm.org/m/pdfs/20050707-presidents-commission-holocaust.pdf.

Wiesel, Elie, and Marion Wiesel. *Night*. Penguin Classics, 2004.

Wieseltier, Leon. "After Memory." *The New Republic*, May 3, 1993, 16–26. https://static1.squarespace.com/static/55955834e4b00f5f813573d5/t/56be5c4d356fb031229f4f0d/1455316046428/After+Memory.pdf.

Witcomb, Andrea. "Toward a Pedagogy of Feeling: Understanding How Museums Create a Space for Cross-cultural Encounters." In *The International Handbooks of Museum Studies,* 1st ed., edited by Andrea Witcomb and Kylie Message, 321–44. Chichester, England: Wiley & Sons, 2015.

Wright, Robert R., Cynthia D. Mohr, Robert R. Sinclair, and Liu-Qin Yang. "Sometimes Less Is More: Directed Coping with Interpersonal Stressors at Work." *Journal of Organizational Behavior* 36, no. 6 (2015): 786–805. https://doi.org/10.1002/job.2002.

Wright, Travis, and Sharon K. Ryan. "Toddlers Through Primary Grades: Too Scared to Learn: Teaching Young Children Who Have Experienced Trauma." *YC Young Children* 69, no. 5 (2014): 88–93. http://www.jstor.org/stable/ycyoungchildren.69.5.88.

Yad Vashem. "A Workshop with Psychotherapist Moshe Sternberg and Three Holocaust Survivors." *Learning to Make a Difference: Teaching the Shoah, Antisemitism, and Contemporary Israel.* Jewish Educators Seminar, Yad Vashem, Israel, December 31, 2007.

Yad Vashem Information Systems, 2000. https://www.yadvashem.org/download/education/units/crystal.pdf.

Yad Vashem, The World Holocaust Remembrance Center. "What is Yad Vashem." Accessed February 9, 2022. https://www.yadvashem.org/about/yad-vashem.html.

Yale Fortunoff Video Archive for Holocaust Testimonies. "About the Fortunoff Archive." Accessed February 9, 2022. https://fortunoff.library.yale.edu/about-us/our-story/.

Yehuda, Rachel. "Are Different Biological Mechanisms Involved in the Transmission of Maternal Versus Paternal Stress-Induced Vulnerability to Offspring?" *Biological Psychiatry* 70, no. 5 (2011): 402–3. https://doi.org/10.1016/j.biopsych.2011.07.001.

Yehuda, Rachel, and Amy Lehrner. "Intergenerational Transmission of Trauma Effects: Putative Role of Epigenetic Mechanisms." *World Psychiatry* 17 (2018): 243–57.

"Yesodeinu – Building the Future on the Foundation of the Past." Yesodeinu.org, 2021. https://yesodeinu.org.

Yilmaz, Kaya. "Historical Empathy and Its Implications for Classroom Practices in Schools." *The History Teacher* 40, no. 3 (2007): 331–7. http://www.jstor.org/stable/30036827.

Young, Eve. "Most Comprehensive Auschwitz Exhibit in N. America to Open in Kansas City." *The Jerusalem Post*, September 16, 2020. https://www.jpost.com/diaspora/most-comprehensive-auschwitz-exhibit-in-n-america-to-open-in-kansas-city-642472.

Zalewska, Maria. "Holography, Historical Indexicality and the Holocaust." *Technologies of Knowing* 36, no. 1 (2016): 25–32. https://cinema.usc.edu/spectator/36.1/3_Zalewska.pdf.

Zeck, William. "William 'Bill' Zeck Describes the Role of the Nuremberg Trials in Establishing a Historical Record." United States Holocaust Memorial Museum. Accessed August 22, 2024. https://encyclopedia.ushmm.org/content/en/oral-history/william-bill-zeck-describes-the-role-of-the-nuremberg-trials-in-establishing-a-historical-record.

Zembylas, Michalinos. "'Pedagogy of Discomfort' and Its Ethical Implications: The Tensions of Ethical Violence in Social Justice Education." *Ethics and Education* 10, no. 2 (2015): 163–74. https://doi.org/10.1080/17449642.2015.1039274.

Zembylas, Michalinos. "Teacher Resistance to Engage with 'Alternative' Perspectives of Difficult Histories: The Limits and Prospects of Affective Disruption." *Discourse: Studies in the Cultural Politics of Education* 38, no. 5 (2016): 659–75. https://doi.org/10.1080/01596306.2015.1132680.

Zembylas, Michalinos. "Theorizing 'Difficult Knowledge' in the Aftermath of the 'Affective Turn': Implications for Curriculum and Pedagogy in Handling Traumatic Representations." *Curriculum Inquiry* 44, no. 3 (2014): 390–412. http://www.jstor.org/stable/43941648.

Zembylas, Michalinos, Loizos Loukaides, and Petroula Antoniou. "Teachers' Understandings of Empathy in Teaching about the Holocaust in Cyprus: The Emotional Risks of Identification and the Disruptive Potential of 'Empathic Unsettlement.'" *Teaching and Teacher Education* 89 (2020): 103007. https://doi.org/10.1016/j.tate.2019.103007.

Zembylas, Michalinos, and Claire McGlynn. "Discomforting Pedagogies: Emotional Tensions, Ethical Dilemmas and Transformative Possibilities." *British Educational Research Journal* 38, no. 1 (2012): 41–59. http://www.jstor.org/stable/23211443.

Zerubavel, Yael. *Time Maps: Collective Memory and the Social Shape of the Past.* Chicago: University of Chicago Press, 2003.

Zukerman, Gil, and Liat Korn. "Post-Traumatic Stress and World Assumptions: The Effects of Religious Coping." *Journal of Religion and Health* 53, no. 6 (2013): 1676–90. https://doi.org/10.1007/s10943-013-9755-5.

Zukerman, Gil, Liat Korn, Ephraim Shapiro, and Leah Fostick. "Avoidance Behavior Following Terror Event Exposure: Effects of Perceived Life Threat and Jewish Religious Coping." *Journal for the Scientific Study of Religion* 55, no. 3 (2016): 516–30. http://www.jstor.org/stable/26651594.

Index

About the Author

Julie J. Golding is a Holocaust educator and museum professional, serving as Assistant Professor and Deputy Chair of the master's in Holocaust, Genocide & Tolerance Education at Touro University. She is also a curator at the Holocaust Museum & Center for Tolerance and Education. A Wexner Graduate Fellow and Davidson Scholar, she earned her PhD from Yeshiva University and was honored with the New York State Board of Regents Louis E. Yavner Citizen Award for excellence in Holocaust education.